THE PLEA OF INNOCENCE

The Plea of Innocence

Restoring Truth to the American Justice System

Tim Bakken

NEW YORK UNIVERSITY PRESS
New York

NEW YORK UNIVERSITY PRESS
New York
www.nyupress.org

References to Internet websites (URLs) were accurate at the time of writing. Neither the author nor New York University Press is responsible for URLs that may have expired or changed since the manuscript was prepared.

Please contact the Library of Congress for Cataloging-in-Publication data.
ISBN: 9781479817122 (hardback)
ISBN: 9781479817146 (library ebook)
ISBN: 9781479817139 (consumer ebook)

New York University Press books are printed on acid-free paper, and their binding materials are chosen for strength and durability. We strive to use environmentally responsible suppliers and materials to the greatest extent possible in publishing our books.

Manufactured in the United States of America

10 9 8 7 6 5 4 3 2 1

Also available as an ebook

CONTENTS

Introduction

The Importance of Facts

A nineteen-year-old man beginning a life sentence for murder once told me when I worked in a legal assistance program that he was innocent and we should appeal to the U.S. Supreme Court to obtain his release. I don't know whether he was innocent, but the reality is that almost none of the two million or so people in prison, as well as the millions who have been convicted of crimes in the United States, will ever be exonerated. Almost none of them will ever have a case heard by the Supreme Court.

The teenager, who would have been a high school student if not an inmate, had been convicted in Washington, D.C., and transported on a bus by marshals nine hundred miles away from his home to one of the relatively few federal prisons in the United States, in a rural town in a midwestern state. He had been found guilty by a jury, but, as we will see, a trial in the adversarial system is not designed to separate the innocent from the guilty. We know that juries convict a significant number of innocent people. The adversarial system, while providing procedures and processes, does not have a meaningful mechanism to permit innocent people to discover exonerating facts, present them at trial, and escape conviction once they have been charged with a crime. Emotionally and practically, the imprisoned teenager was alone, with no ability to find exonerating facts, and likely to remain in prison until well into middle age, possibly longer, or for life if not paroled.

The adversarial legal system is no system at all. *Adversarial system* is a term we've come to use to encapsulate all the ad hoc investigative procedures and rules of evidence for trials that have been collected in the common law countries over the past three hundred years, beginning in the late 1600s and early 1700s. Then, judges in England first allowed defense lawyers to participate regularly in criminal trials as a way to

1

confront unreliable witnesses and limit death penalties for such crimes as "deer stealing" and "wrecking a fishpond."

The system that developed is not cohesive, like a structure built from the ground up based on architectural plans. It's a creaky cottage made of synthetic products, the purpose of one patch to repair leaks in the others, renovations of the day piled atop renovations from earlier generations, some of them necessary, but others inspired by ideological, political, financial, and professional self-interests of lawyers, the gatekeepers, who revere and elevate procedures over a search for truth. It is true that, in the absence of a plan, rules can arise from social practices and behavior. But the result will be more disorganized and haphazard than if a structure is planned and includes methods through which to reform it over the upcoming years. Where there is no scheme or plan, reformists are likely to misinterpret the reasons for the previous ad hoc changes and misconstrue how to coordinate old and new rules and procedures.

With its unrelenting combat ethos, the adversarial system, despite platitudes to the contrary, is devoid of a formal search for truth. Each year, law enforcement officers in the United States make more than ten million arrests.[1] Each year, the U.S. Supreme Court accepts for briefing and decision only twenty to thirty criminal cases, or fewer, fourteen in the 2021–2022 term, and almost all of those concern interpretations of federal statutes or the application of constitutional provisions to criminal cases.[2] To date, the Court has never held that it may reject a jury's guilty verdict of a person who is "actually innocent."

While almost all the participants within this system hope that only guilty people will be convicted, there is no one who must not rest until the truth is found, where truth is defined as a correct determination of whether a person committed a crime. With the defense institution privatized, accused people are responsible for finding the facts that can exonerate them. Yes, the poor are represented by public defenders—and, in fact, almost no one who is charged with a crime has enough money to pay for a complete defense—but they're representing a private person. Defendants, like the teenager from Washington, not a public official, bear the entire burden of not only looking for exonerating facts but also proving their innocence.

Several years after speaking with the teenage prison inmate, I was working as an assistant district attorney in Brooklyn. In a courtroom, a defense attorney, about a month after a jury found his client guilty of robbery and moments before sentencing, told me that the client admitted to committing some robberies, but said that he did not commit this one. If true, this meant that the only eyewitness in the case had identified the wrong person.

Poor and unable to post bond, the client/defendant had been held in jail prior to the trial and could not participate fully in his defense. Because of a prior criminal record, he could not risk testifying and the jurors' discovering his past crimes and believing that they indicated he committed this robbery. The only defense witness, his mother, produced an alibi that the jury apparently disbelieved. To date, there is no legal procedure or method in the adversarial system that would help this defendant find additional facts or permit him to tell his story to the jury without increasing the likelihood of conviction.

Indeed, most innocent people are unable to find or access the facts and evidence that could exonerate them. To rectify this problem, this book describes a fundamental reform to the three-hundred-year-old adversarial system: a formal plea of innocence and a requirement that truth be a goal in every case. In essence, the government should be responsible for searching for exonerating facts rather than being satisfied with due process. While it is improbable that all the facts in any case will ever be known, the essential conceptual point is that the acquisition of facts will almost always benefit an innocent person who has been accused of a crime.

Errors and Innocent-Person Convictions

Despite the hubbub and publicity surrounding litigation that has led to the release of innocent people from prison, the adversarial system has not accounted adequately for the one condition from which almost all innocent-person convictions originate: human error. Error lies within all the participants in the legal system, and because it is less observable and egregious than intentional misconduct, by investigators and witnesses, for example, it is difficult to detect and correct. Much of the error is inherent in the human condition and cannot be corrected. As a result, we should recognize that such error will recur and find a way to limit the number of discretionary decisions the participants in the system are required to make. The only way to do this is to collect additional facts.

That is, researchers have identified some of the most common errors that contribute to innocent-person convictions, but they are the same errors that have existed over generations. There are "at least eight major sources of wrongful convictions: (1) mistaken eyewitness identification; (2) false incriminating statements or confessions; (3) tunnel vision; (4) perjured informant testimony; (5) forensic error; (6) police error; (7) prosecutorial error; and (8) inadequate defense representation. . . . The most recent comprehensive compilation of exonerations in the United States confirms that the majority of cases involved at least one, but often several, of the above factors."[3] If we've known of the errors for nearly one hundred years, as we have, why have they not been fixed? Another question might provide an answer. Can human error be eliminated?

Researchers have found several additional factors that supercharge the likelihood of a conviction: young defendants, defendants with criminal histories, jurisdictions that have the death penalty, and jurisdictions with "punitiveness." They've also identified subsets of the factors that contribute to wrongful convictions, including prosecutors' withholding of exculpatory evidence, non-eyewitnesses' lying, and family members' testifying on behalf of the defendant.[4] Without this valuable research, who would have known that a mother who testifies on behalf of her son probably increases the likelihood that he will be convicted?

After someone has been formally charged, the researchers (Jon B. Gould, Julia Carrano, Richard A. Leo, and Katie Hail-Jares), in their 2014 study, found that certain factors presumed to lead to erroneous convictions *do not* increase the likelihood of conviction. The factors include the victim's demographics, the defendant's race and education level, and intentional misidentification; that is, lying *eyewitnesses* are apparently revealed prior to a conviction. "Among defendant characteristics, the defendant's age and any prior criminal history influence case outcome. Older defendants are less likely to be erroneously convicted, and defendants with prior criminal histories are more likely to face an erroneous conviction. Other defendant characteristics, such as race and high school graduation, have no impact in distinguishing between an erroneous conviction and near miss."[5]

Professor Gould and his colleagues reported, "At the same time, perhaps one of the most important findings from this project is which variables do *not* explain the different outcomes between erroneous convictions and near misses. Indeed, a number of variables that are often discussed by scholars as possible 'causes' of erroneous convictions were not correlated with case outcome in the bivariate analysis. . . . Among these are official error and misconduct . . . jailhouse informants, false incriminating statements/confessions, and various eyewitness misidentification variables." These results do not mean that "these variables are unrelated to either erroneous convictions or near misses. . . . But, once a factually innocent defendant enters the criminal justice system, the findings here indicate that conviction will not statistically turn on differences in those factors."[6]

In a remarkable turn, this research indicates that scholars and practitioners in the legal system have been careening down one track for generations when they should have been running research and litigating cases on several additional tracks. Based on two statistical methods (bivariate analysis and logistic regression), the researchers identified ten particular factors that distinguish erroneous convictions from near-miss convictions—"the age and criminal history of the defendant, punitiveness of the state, Brady violations [prosecutors not disclosing exculpatory evidence], forensic error, weak defense, weak prosecution case, family defense witness, non-intentional misidentification, and lying by a non-eyewitness." These factors "help explain why an innocent defendant's case, after indictment, is either dismissed or leads to an erroneous conviction."[7]

Perhaps most significant and disturbing is the study's findings that repairing current procedures in the adversarial system—virtually the only method lawyers and judges have used to try to improve the system—may not sufficiently protect innocent people. The factors that actually lead to erroneous convictions, according to Gould and the researchers, "include several of the traditional legal sources of erroneous convictions as well as sociological (*but not procedural*) variables, suggesting that the difference in case outcome for an innocent defendant is the result of a relatively complex and diverse process."[8]

The Science Surrounding Mental Errors

If the legal system had focused less on procedures and more on the efficacy of adversarial investigation and the perceptual abilities of witnesses, we would have learned long ago that a large amount of human error in the legal system cannot be avoided. Much sooner, we could have reduced or mitigated the adverse consequences of the error by emphasizing the importance of finding additional facts.

Professor Daniel Kahneman, who received the Nobel Prize in Economic Sciences in 2002, described what seems to be the futility of trying to correct mistaken perceptions. "The question that is most often asked about cognitive illusions is whether they can be overcome. The message of these examples [in his book, *Thinking, Fast and Slow*] is not encouraging . . . [because] errors of intuitive thought are often difficult to prevent. . . . Even when cues to likely errors are available, errors can be prevented only by enhanced monitoring and effortful activity. . . . As a way to live your life, however, continuous vigilance is not necessarily good, and it is certainly impractical. Constantly questioning our own thinking would be impossibly tedious. . . . The best we can do is a compromise: learn to recognize situations in which mistakes are likely and try harder to avoid significant mistakes when the stakes are high."[9]

Professor Gould and his colleagues, in describing the investigation process in the adversarial system, illustrate what Professor Kahneman's research shows: the implacability of human error. "Tunnel vision is defined as the social, organizational, and psychological tendencies" that impel investigators in the adversarial system to suspect only one person or overvalue one piece of evidence, such as not collecting forensic evidence because the suspect has confessed. "As more resources—money, time, and emotions—are placed into a narrative involving a suspect, criminal justice professionals are less willing or able to process negative feedback that refutes their conclusions."[10] This can be attributed "to a police and prosecutorial culture in which questioning and independent thinking are not valued, procedures are not designed to probe already-gathered evidence, and little or no concern is given to learning from past errors."[11]

In what appears to have been a misplaced focus, the actors in the adversarial legal system, from beginning to end, police officers to Supreme Court justices, have expended almost all their resources and energy on repairing and adding procedures, when the origin of innocent-person convictions is human error. While not enamored with Professor Kahneman's dual structure (reason and intuition as separate entities), cognitive scientists Hugo Mercier and Dan Sperber, in their 2017 book *The Enigma of Reason*, seem to arrive at the same conclusion: human error cannot be appreciably reduced, especially when variables are numerous. In referring to the psychology of reasoning, they recognize two approaches, "mental logic" and "mental models." Both approaches "assume that humans have mechanisms capable of producing genuine logical inferences."[12]

Mercier and Sperber's perspective, however, does not lead to optimism that reasoning will produce correct decisions, because reason is often absent from decision making: "Both approaches recognize that all except the simplest reasoning tasks can trip people and cause them to come to unwarranted conclusions. As they become more complex, reasoning tasks rapidly become forbiddingly difficult and performance collapses." For mental logicians, complexity lies within "the number of steps that must be taken and rules that must be followed." For mental modelers, complexity lies within "the number of models that should be constructed and integrated to arrive at a certain conclusion."[13] Complexity in the adversarial system, whether within the procedures that have accumulated over centuries (many of which in the United States require extensive pretrial hearings) or a relatively large number of variables present in investigations, may increase, not decrease, the likelihood of human error.

Rather than finding solace almost solely within procedures, the adversarial legal system should have focused on producing knowledge and discovering facts. The research of Gould and his colleagues indicates that the innocence movement does not recognize sufficiently the influence of sociological variables on erroneous convictions and that its traditional focus on eyewitness identifications, confessions, and misconduct by various actors, while relevant, is off target. As Professor Kahneman's research shows, human error is pervasive, and much of it cannot be corrected. Similarly, Mercier and Sperber admonish us to "remember: a logical demonstration can never be stronger than its weakest part."[14] Legal procedures are optimal only when all the people implementing them make no errors.

As it turns out, the architecture of innocent-person convictions is very different from the popular perception of the problem. In general, innocent-person convictions result primarily from unintentional human error. The convictions do not generally occur because of intentional misconduct by investigators, prosecutors, jurors, or judges. Research does not indicate that racial discrimination or animus, which is a component of intentional misconduct, has a significant effect in causing the convictions, even if only for practical reasons. For 2018, the U.S. Bureau of Justice Statistics, based on reports by victims, found that "the offender was of the same race or ethnicity as the victim in 70% of violent incidents involving black victims, 62% of those involving white victims, 45% of those involving Hispanic victims, and 24% of those involving Asian victims."[15] Black victims of violent crime report their offenders to be Black (70 percent) and less frequently white (10.6 percent) and Hispanic (7.9 percent).[16] Thus, even "cross-racial" identification (a witness of one race identifying someone of another race), which can be a suspect procedure, applies in a relatively small number of cases, and only those in which the offender and complainant do not know each other, an even smaller subset.

The plea of innocence provides a method through which to collect facts and thus mitigate the consequences of human error. To help ensure that guilty people cannot use the plea to avoid conviction, innocence pleas must be accompanied by defense lawyers' affirmations that they believe their clients are innocent. Then, client/defendants will have to agree to an interview with prosecutors or investigators and assert the existence of exonerating facts. Prosecution offices will be required to undertake or supervise a reasonably diligent search for the exonerating facts identified by the defendants.[17]

If, after the search, the prosecution does not move to dismiss charges or the defendant does not plead guilty to reduced charges, the case will go to trial. The burden of persuasion will be higher than beyond reasonable doubt to compensate for the disadvantages defendants will experience from their disclosures to investigators and prosecutors. In the event of bad-faith conduct by the prosecution or defense, the aggrieved party may ask the judge to instruct the jury to draw adverse inferences against the party that acted in bad faith.

There will be cases in which no one can find facts that will exonerate an innocent defendant. This should not be the end of an inquiry into someone's plausible claim of innocence. By pleading innocent and consenting to an interview, and engaging in other behaviors that indicate innocence, defendants should have the right, as provided in new instructions to juries, to argue that their behaviors may be manifestations of innocence. Ideally, social scientists should conduct research into what behaviors or expressions, specifically, indicate innocence; behaviors and expressions without a scientific basis should not be admitted. Until the results of the research are available, judges should allow into evidence the behaviors of defendants on the same basis they allow the behaviors of complainants and witnesses.

This reform of the adversarial system is designed to correct inalterable human error. Professor Kahneman asked, "What can be done about biases? How can we improve judgments and decisions, both our own and those of the institutions that we serve and that serve us? The short answer is that little can be achieved without a considerable investment of effort. . . . Except for some effects that I attribute mostly to age, my intuitive thinking is just as prone to overconfidence, extreme predictions, and the planning fallacy ['plans and forecasts that are unrealistically close to best-case scenarios'] as it was before I made a study of these issues."[18] As we will see, the enormous time and resources spent on procedural justice over the past three hundred years have been misplaced. A more effective way to lessen the consequences of inevitable human error is to find the exonerating facts that every innocent person knows to exist.

PART I

Why Innocent People Are Convicted

1

Human Error

The adversarial system has not developed a method to process separately cases in which an accused person asserts a plausible claim of innocence. On the surface, the reason why is that we do not know who is guilty or innocent, and thus all suspects and defendants, regardless of their apparent level of culpability, should be lumped together and receive the same treatment. While this seems fair, it is not. Defendants who have plausible claims of innocence, especially if they are willing to tell their stories to investigators, should have a greater opportunity to be acquitted compared with all the other defendants who appear to be more guilty and are unwilling to tell their stories.

With the legal system providing the same protections to every accused person, the primary beneficiaries are guilty people. Probably at least 75 percent of the people who are arrested actually committed some crime. As Professor Michael Risinger recognized, people who make strong claims of innocence should receive additional scrutiny. He wrote that "claims of actual innocence in fact . . . possess a moral purchase far superior to other moral claims that animate the legal process."[1] He proposed "special trial rules for such claims, aimed at curbing adversary excess, and . . . review of convictions in such cases by a new standard of review, borrowed in part from British jurisprudence, the 'unsafe verdict' standard" (giving judges authority to overturn jury verdicts).[2]

As Professor Risinger noted, defendants who have plausible claims of innocence have no special way to notify prosecutors, judges, or jurors of the possibility of exonerating facts and thereby decrease the risk they will be convicted. But in the same courtroom, defendants who probably committed a crime obtain acquittals by using the protections designed to ensure that innocent people are not convicted. Minutes after hearing a jury's not-guilty verdict in a murder case, for example, I was in the hallway of a Brooklyn courthouse when two of the jurors approached me to offer an unsolicited review of the evidence.[3] The jurors congratulated me on my presentation of the prosecution case, a lesson in civics they said, and were satisfied with their verdict. They commented on the credibility of the only eyewitness at the trial, a teenager who testified that he saw the acquitted defendant kill the victim.

"Great kid," said one of the jurors.

"Very believable," said the second juror. "I'm sure he was very scared."

About the defendant, the first juror said, "I'm sure he was guilty. I just wanted to see more evidence." The second juror nodded in agreement.

It is an ironic condition, indeed, when jurors are convinced of the guilt of the defendant but content in reaching a not-guilty verdict that does not reflect the truth. This is, of course, one component of the adversarial legal system, requiring proof beyond a reasonable doubt. The only reason for this approach is to protect innocent people who have been accused, but they have no special method to decrease the likelihood of conviction. Thus, guilty people, who are far more numerous, receive the lion's share of the benefits of the rules and procedures that are designed to protect those who are innocent.

Indeed, nothing in the adversarial system is easy for people who know they are innocent. Absent an early guilty plea, all defendants plead not guilty and are personally responsible for initiating some kind of defense and carrying it through a trial and appeals.[4] A study by the U.S. Bureau of Justice Statistics found that about 66 percent of arrestees are convicted and another 9 percent receive "diversion and deferred adjudication," which do not result in conviction.[5] If prosecutors believe that at least 75 percent of defendants are guilty (and there are surely additional guilty people amid the 25 percent of the cases that are dismissed), they will look skeptically at an innocent person in the same way they look with disbelief at the multitude of guilty people who claim falsely to be innocent. In this system, where even defense lawyers, with good reason, believe their clients are guilty, an innocent person is alone.

One of the most comprehensive studies (discussed in detail in chapter 5) on innocent-person convictions found that at least 4 percent of the people who are convicted and sentenced to death in the United States are actually innocent. Because death-penalty cases receive more resources and attention, the rate of error in other cases might be higher. Nonetheless, a 4 percent innocent-person conviction rate would translate to about 57,000 innocent people imprisoned at all times in the United

States. One study from 2015, by the U.S. Census Bureau, concluded that 8 percent of the adults in America have been convicted of a felony.[6] With an adult population of more than 255 million in 2019, according to the Census Bureau, that translates into more than 20.4 million Americans with a felony conviction.[7]

A 4 percent error rate would mean that about 816,000 innocent people (greater than the individual populations of four states, North Dakota, Alaska, Vermont, and Wyoming, as well as the District of Columbia) currently suffer the disabling effects of a felony conviction. An advocacy group, the Death Penalty Information Center, found that, as of 2021, of the 1,534 people executed in the United States since 1976, 20 of them had "cases with strong evidence of innocence."[8]

The Elusiveness of Knowledge

Adversarial processes are competitive and harsh, including investigations, trials, and appeals, and each year millions of people are vacuumed into the jaws of the system. Every legal system will produce some incorrect judgments, and innocent people will, unfortunately, suffer, but this truism doesn't tell us how many innocent-person convictions a society should accept. For guidance, some look to the Blackstone ratio, that it's better to free ten guilty people to ensure that one innocent person will go free, as conceived by the English jurist William Blackstone (1723–1783).[9] Assuming we could estimate the number of innocent-person convictions and guilty-person acquittals, a very difficult measurement to make, society would benefit if we debated and decided what is an acceptable ratio of guilty-person acquittals to innocent-person convictions. We could then determine how much to change the adversarial system or how much of it to leave intact. Any ratio of guilty-person acquittals to innocent-person convictions, however, is based in social policy, not logic or science, and trying to find it will not offer any immediate practical assistance to innocent people.

Some might argue that it is superfluous to consider whether the outcomes of cases are correct because the purpose of the adversarial system is only to ensure due process. "In the adversarial tradition it is assumed that justice is done if the parties are treated equally in presenting their (side of the) case. . . . Because fair-play is the proximate goal, the [adversarial] tradition occasionally appears willing to compromise its search for the truth in order to uphold the rules of fair-play," Professor Hans Crombag wrote.[10]

Perhaps this reasoning was once modestly sensible because we had no way of determining, with certainty, who was innocent or guilty. Therefore, truth was too high a bar to set for a legal standard.[11] To many in the legal profession and society, this uncertainty was reassuring because generally no one could prove definitively that adversarial legal procedures were not adequate to the task of freeing innocent people. One federal judge, Learned Hand, in 1923, in denying a defense motion to dismiss indictments, wrote, "Our dangers do not lie in too little tenderness to the accused. Our procedure has been always haunted by the ghost of the innocent man convicted. It is an unreal dream."[12] Judge Hand and almost everyone else exalted the adversarial system because they could not see the magnitude of error within it. Scientific advances and DNA testing, however, revealed the error that has existed since the beginning of law.

Over the past thirty years, the innocence movement (consisting largely of professors and defense lawyers), relying on DNA testing (deoxyribonucleic), has focused on litigating cases in which innocent people have been convicted and on improving traditional procedures. But, generally, it has not focused on reforming or even questioning the moorings of the adversarial system.[13] One innocence project (programs run through law schools) reported, through early 2022, 375 exonerations through postconviction DNA testing.[14] However, because all jurisdictions now provide DNA testing prior to trial, the number of exonerations from *postconviction* testing will continue to dwindle and soon become negligible. There will be little untested evidence, such as a bloody shirt collected from a crime scene prior to DNA technology; almost all new evidence will be DNA tested prior to trial. The traditional case-by-case litigation approach of the innocence movement will continue, which is important. But this approach can save only relatively few innocent people, most of whom are placed in jeopardy and convicted because of human perceptual error, which often cannot be observed or tested in the way we can find and test the blood from a shirt.

Criminal cases, especially investigations, are saturated with human error and subjectivity, which science and legal procedures have been unable to correct. To illustrate, consider the facts in the following exercise. The purpose of the exercise will be discussed after you complete it. For now, this is your instruction: "Below are several problems that vary in difficulty. Try to answer as many as you can."[15]

(1) A bat and ball cost $1.10 in total. The bat costs $1.00 more than the ball. How much does the ball cost? _____ cents

(2) If it takes 5 machines 5 minutes to make 5 widgets, how long would it take 100 machines to make 100 widgets? _____ minutes

(3) In a lake, there is a patch of lily pads. Every day, the patch doubles in size. If it takes 48 days for the patch to cover the entire lake, how long would it take for the patch to cover half the lake? _____ days[16]

This is the Cognitive Reflection Test (CRT), created by Shane Frederick, now a professor at Yale University. Like a witness, juror, or judge watching an event or listening to testimony, one's first response or answer to the questions on the CRT, *intuition* perhaps, often will be incorrect. Professor Frederick administered the test to undergraduate college students and reported the results in 2005.

In 2006, three legal researchers, in their effort to determine how trial judges view facts and cases, gave the CRT to 295 judges at a conference in Florida and received responses from 252 of them, almost half of all the trial judges in Florida. The researchers, two law professors and a federal magistrate, noted the correct answers and described why they were correct, as follows:

> Consider the first question. For many people, the answer that immediately jumps to mind is ten cents. Though intuitive, this answer is wrong. . . . If the ball costs ten cents and the bat costs one dollar more, the bat must cost $1.10. Adding those two figures together, the total cost of the bat and ball would be $1.20, not $1.10. Therefore, the correct answer is five cents—the ball costs five cents, the bat costs $1.05, and together they cost $1.10. For the second question, the answer that immediately jumps to mind is 100 minutes. Though intuitive, this answer is also wrong. If five machines make five widgets in five minutes, then each machine makes one widget in that five-minute time period. Thus, it would take only five minutes for 100 machines to produce 100 widgets, just as 200 machines

would make 200 widgets during that same period. The third question immediately invites an answer of twenty-four days, which is wrong. The correct answer—obvious upon reflection—is forty-seven days. If the patch of lily pads doubles each day and covers the entire lake on the forty-eighth day, it must cover half the lake the day before.[17]

After reading the explanation, most people will understand the faulty reasoning that led to their incorrect answers. It's not that they were incapable of finding the answers. Rather, they didn't look carefully enough.

The mean number of correct answers of the Florida judges was 1.23 (below 50 percent). Students at nine colleges also took the test. Like the mean number correct of the judges, the mean number correct of the students within six colleges was also below 50 percent (Harvard, 1.43; Michigan–Ann Arbor, 1.18; Bowling Green, 0.87; Michigan–Dearborn, 0.83; Michigan State, 0.79; and Toledo, 0.57). Only students at Carnegie Mellon (1.51), Princeton (1.63), and MIT (2.18) were above 50 percent in the mean number of correct answers.[18]

Professor Frederick noted, "Men scored significantly higher than women on the CRT" (1.47 mean correct for men and 1.03 correct for women). He found, "Women's mistakes tend to be of the intuitive variety, whereas men make a wider variety of errors. . . . Thus, the data suggest that men are more likely to reflect on their answers and less inclined to go with their intuitive responses."[19] Probably most witnesses have only a few moments to view criminal acts and very little time to reflect on what they are seeing, hearing, or otherwise perceiving. The same can be said of jurors and judges who are exposed to witnesses at trials. They hear or see from witnesses only secondhand reports of what happened months or years ago.

Professor Daniel Kahneman has spent much of his career researching the errors people make when relying on their intuition and emotion, their first, less-deliberative impressions. They miss or relegate to irrelevancy the most obvious, simple—but most important—facts. In one experiment, he and a colleague asked subjects whether "Steve [is] more likely to be a librarian or a farmer." Steve is described as "very shy and withdrawn" and a "meek and tidy soul," with "a need for order or structure, and a passion for detail." In answering, people do not consider that "there are more than 20 male farmers for each male librarian in the

United States," and, therefore, it's more likely that Steve will be a farmer. "Because there are so many more farmers, it is almost certain that more 'meek and tidy' souls will be found on tractors than at library information desks."[20]

Professors Frederick and Kahneman seem to ascribe a unique character to intuition and possibly give too much credit to it as a method of investigation. Cognitive scientists Hugo Mercier and Dan Sperber question the idea, of Kahneman and others, of a "whole dual process approach." The duel process approach "has at its core the assumption that intuitive inference and reasoning are achieved through two quite distinct types of mechanisms. We disagree." They believe that "*reasoning is not an alternative to intuitive inference; reasoning is a use of intuitive inferences about reasons.*"[21] Intuition is not a special telescope that savvy investigators use to espy the truth when their usual senses and regular searches do not produce relevant or dispositive facts. Intuition is hasty reasoning with few facts (because available facts are missed) and leads to a greater number of errors than deliberate consideration of facts. Deliberate consideration produces a more accurate analysis of available facts and, through curiosity, the discovery of additional facts. Intuition is not a hopeful avenue for innocent people.

In regard to Steve, librarian or farmer, we should think first to investigate the actual number of male farmers and male librarians. The high error rate of Florida judges and college students on the Cognitive Reflection Test (correct answers less than 50 percent of the time) pertains to similarly obvious facts in plain view. On the CRT, many people would arrive at two or three correct answers if they had deliberated longer. At the scene of a crime, witnesses view events and jump to conclusions but misperceive what occurred. Witnesses and investigators, too quickly, try to make sense of what they've perceived and create a cohesive story about what happened.

Judges and jurors, who are prone to the same kinds of mental errors, make inferences about what they saw or heard from the witnesses and then reach back in time to try to decide whether defendants' actions, back then, make them guilty or not guilty now. These kinds of human extrapolations, and many resulting errors, have significant implications for society, where the legal system is the final decision maker of most serious disputes. Juries, which are one-off decision makers, and judges, who receive more deference than almost anyone, are, by design, to ensure their independence, relatively impervious to scientific influence (except that which self-interested lawyers urge upon them). Shrouding people's judgment is what Professor Kahneman described as "a puzzling limitation of our mind: our excessive confidence in what we believe we know, and our apparent inability to acknowledge the full extent of our ignorance and the uncertainty of the world we live in."[22]

Commenting on the dismal performance of the students and judges on the Cognitive Reflection Test—presumably some of the brightest and most educated people in society—the legal researchers concluded that the "intuitive approach might work well in some cases, but it can lead to erroneous and unjust outcomes in others. The justice system should take what steps it can to increase the likelihood that judges will decide cases in a predominately deliberative, rather than a predominately intuitive, way."[23] This is a far too modest proposal. No matter how attuned we become to our biases (mistakes) and intuition (decisions based on relatively few facts), judges, witnesses, jurors, defense lawyers, investigators, and prosecutors will forever rotate through the adversarial system and bring with them all the errors that are ingrained in the human condition.

The False Promise of Trials and Science

There is an allure to believing that scientific methods and trials are sufficient work-arounds through which to mitigate error. But dispositive forensic testing is rare because of a lack of testable evidence; most cases depend on eyewitness testimony for resolution. Investigations, not trials, are the most important parts of cases, and they are conducted in relative secrecy by police and prosecutors, without the presence of a suspect, defense lawyer, or magistrate. Throughout adversarial history, observers believed that juries would provide a final barrier to government overreaching and innocent-person convictions. But guilty pleas today produce at least 97 percent of all convictions, and some of the few jury trials that do occur have taken on the authoritarian characteristics of investigations: anonymous juries.

While juries can be traced to Rome, Greece, Egypt, and Scandinavia (Vikings), their influence in cases has been supplanted by lawyers' control of the legal process. Prior to the entry of lawyers, jurors participated from the beginning to the end of cases, when English jurors "knew the parties or the facts."[24] Jurors were selected publicly so that defendants and the community could identify them. The colonists, and their Constitution, imported this jury model to America to act as "a bulwark against oppression," a method to protect those who were unpopular.[25] Beginning with a case in New York City in 1977, however, when a federal judge ordered that jurors be anonymous to prevent the defendants from bribing or threatening them, anonymous juries have sprung up in many states and almost every federal jurisdiction.[26]

The practical and constitutional argument against anonymous juries is that they lead jurors to believe the defendant is dangerous and guilty, thus upending the presumption of innocence. Some defendants are dangerous and guilty, and they will, in fact, bribe, threaten, assault, or kill jurors, witnesses, or anyone, if they can get away with it. Where there is reason to believe defendants will engage in this type of behavior, anonymous juries are a last resort.

However, the rationale for control over the judicial process can seamlessly lead to a diminution of jurors' independence and their scrutiny of cases, which can produce unobservable error. In one of the most highly publicized recent cases, for example, in expanding the rationale for anonymous juries, the trial judge in Minnesota's 2021 prosecution of a former police officer, Derek Chauvin, charged with murder in the death of George Floyd, ordered an anonymous jury for reasons having nothing to do with the defendant. There was no evidence that either Mr. Chauvin or anyone on his behalf would influence the jurors or witnesses. Rather, the judge feared that the jurors, if identified, could be influenced or threatened by members of the community.

In ordering the anonymous jury, the judge cited protests, media coverage, and threats against the defendants and their defense lawyers (other police officers were scheduled to be tried after Chauvin). "Although most of the hundred or so participants remained peaceful throughout, at the conclusion of the hearing, some protesters physically and verbally harassed the Defendants and their attorneys as they departed the Family Justice Center," the judge wrote in his order. "One protester damaged one Defense Counsel's truck by ramming it with a bicycle . . . [and] the defense attorneys have expressed concern for their personal safety and the safety of their clients. The Court finds those concerns credible."[27] In what might signal a turn in U.S. history, the Minnesota judge was trying to protect the defendant and jurors from members of the community, while in the past juries were designed to protect the defendant and community from the government.

The judge referred to "motions" for anonymity, presumably referring to the defense, as well as the prosecution. But psychological theories suggest that anonymity leads to "reduced responsibility." As a result, researchers hypothesized, correctly it appears, that anonymous juries will produce more convictions than nonanonymous juries.[28] In a study using college students as juror-subjects, two psychology professors concluded, "As predicted, anonymous juries had a higher conviction rate (37%) than did nonanonymous juries (22%) when all jury verdicts were analyzed . . . [and] the effect of anonymity was greatest when the evidence of guilt was relatively strong."[29] (Chauvin was recorded on video kneeling on the neck of the victim for over nine minutes, and the jury found him guilty of murder.)

Also, where the evidence is strong, the experimental juries were more punitive in their sentencing.[30] Under Minnesota's sentencing guidelines, Chauvin was due a 12.5-year sentence. But the judge, Peter Cahill, citing Chauvin's "abuse of a position of trust and authority and also the particular cruelty," sentenced Chauvin to 22.5 years in prison. Following the trial, the judge continued to refuse to allow the release of the names of the jurors and the questionnaires they completed prior to the trial.[31] After media organizations protested, he released the jurors' names six months later, despite a request by prosecutors to keep them secret.[32]

* * *

In the Chauvin case, social science might have been useful to the defense in arguing that the jury should *not* be anonymous. Science can, indeed, be useful in mitigating human error, but, from the point of view of the legal system, this depends on the type of science at issue in a case. Expert testimony has long been used in litigation, especially when *physical* sciences can help determine what happened, such as chemistry and biology when drugs and blood are recovered from a crime scene and engineering when a bridge or building collapses. Psychology and sociology are less useful because findings from their studies are more difficult to apply to individual cases. That is, cognitive tests (questions and answers) are used to try to discern whether a defendant is faking an insanity defense, for example, but it is more difficult to see the defendant's brain processes than it is to see whether engineers used defective steel or concrete in the construction of a bridge.

The most common error in criminal cases probably arises from witnesses' misperception, a process in their brains that is very difficult to see and can rarely be discerned from any scientific test. Through social science studies, it is possible, however, to reach general conclusions about perceptual error, such as that most people have more difficulty identifying someone of a different skin color than someone of their own skin color. However, with few exceptions, courts do not allow general scientific conclusions into cases because the conclusions cannot be shown to apply to a specific witness or defendant. For instance, the defense is not allowed to introduce into evidence a reliable study showing that most people over fifty years of age have impaired vision, despite several witnesses in the case being over fifty.

A 1987 Supreme Court case, *McCleskey v. Kemp*, employed this reasoning and limited the use of general scientific conclusions in federal courts' review of criminal convictions.[33] Though our focus is on actually innocent people, the *McCleskey* case, concerning a presumably guilty defendant, shows the importance of collecting additional facts on every matter, including those that affect sentencing. The case illustrates courts' reluctance to incorporate scientific findings into cases and helps emphasize the point that the most effective way to mitigate error is to find facts.

The defendant, Warren McCleskey, did not claim that he was innocent of the murder for which he had been convicted and sentenced to death. Instead, he argued that he should be allowed to introduce a new fact into his case—the inference, from social science research unrelated to his case, that the death-penalty process in Georgia is racially biased and that, therefore, the jury's death sentence in his case was likely influenced by racial bias. The Supreme Court described the facts surrounding the killing for which he had been convicted and sentenced:

> [The conviction of] McCleskey, a black man . . . arose out of the robbery
> of a furniture store and the killing of a white police officer during the
> course of the robbery. The evidence at trial indicated that McCleskey and

three accomplices planned and carried out the robbery. All four were armed. . . . During the course of the robbery, a police officer, answering a silent alarm, entered the store through the front door. As he was walking down the center aisle of the store, two shots were fired. Both struck the officer. One hit him in the face and killed him. Several weeks later, McCleskey was arrested in connection with an unrelated offense. He confessed that he had participated in the furniture store robbery, but denied that he had shot the police officer. . . . The State also introduced the testimony of two witnesses who had heard McCleskey admit to the shooting.[34]

On appeal, the defense argued that Mr. McCleskey should not be executed because at least one study showed that Georgia's legal system discriminated against killers of white victims.

According to the Court, "One of his [McCleskey's] models concludes that, even after taking account of 39 nonracial variables, defendants charged with killing white victims were 4.3 times as likely to receive a death sentence as defendants charged with killing blacks. According to this model, black defendants were 1.1 times as likely to receive a death sentence as other defendants. Thus, the Baldus study indicates that black defendants, such as McCleskey, who kill white victims have the greatest likelihood of receiving the death penalty."[35]

But McCleskey could not show that he experienced purposeful racial discrimination from the jury, prosecutor, police, or judge in his case. "Accordingly, we hold that the Baldus study is clearly insufficient to support an inference that any of the decisionmakers in McCleskey's case acted with discriminatory purpose," the Court decided.[36] (Georgia executed McCleskey in 1991.)

McCleskey illustrates that neither science nor modified adversarial procedures will likely diminish significantly the number of innocent-person convictions. *General* scientific conclusions (from past studies) will rarely be allowed into trials because courts consider them to be irrelevant, in that they do not concern any of the people connected to the actual case on trial. (A new exception in a few states concerns cases involving identifications, discussed in chapter 6.) In most cases, *specific* scientific conclusions, such as DNA testing that confirms the blood on the defendant's shirt is from the victim, are rarely available because of a lack of testable evidence. This means that virtually all cases are resolved through the statements and testimony of witnesses who, like all people, are prone to intuitive, but incorrect, observations. Given these conditions, every innocent person accused of a crime, more than anything, needs to find exonerating facts to counter human error.

Following a conviction, such discoveries do not occur frequently in the current adversarial system. The National Registry of Exonerations is a public-interest project run by three universities, and it collects and disseminates data and conducts studies on innocent-person convictions and exonerations. For the years 1989 to 2021, the registry counted only 2,809 exonerations in the United States, an average of 85 per year.[37]

Even this might overestimate the number of factually innocent people who are exonerated because the registry's definition of exoneration is broad. It includes not only factually innocent people, as declared by a governmental official or agency, but also defendants who might be innocent.[38] These are convicted people who, later, receive a full pardon; are acquitted at trial after their original conviction is overturned; or, for some reason, have their cases dismissed following a conviction.[39] During the time that the registry counted exonerations, over thirty-three years, there were more than 423 million arrests in the United States.[40] This large number seems to indicate there are many more innocent-person convictions than have been discovered.

2

Devaluation of Freedom

One reason a new method through which to discover exonerating facts has not evolved in the adversarial system is that many people do not recognize problems in the systems in which they live or work or, if they do, the consequences of the remedies they implement. In colonial India, the British paid bounties for dead cobras to try to stop the spread of deadly snakes in Delhi. After people bred cobras for income, the British stopped paying bounties, but the breeders released their snakes into the streets.

In colonial Vietnam, the French paid bounties for dead rats in Hanoi, with the proof of a dead rat the production of a rat tail. When rats without tails appeared, the French realized that people were catching rats, slicing off their tails, and releasing them to breed more rats. New freeways around U.S. cities reduce traffic congestion, but they lead to an increase in traffic and the number of miles driven when commuters use the new roads to build homes farther away from the cities in which they work (at least prior to the pandemic).

These kinds of approaches might be beneficial temporarily, but they do not offer a long-term solution to the disease produced by additional snakes and rats and pollution from automobile driving. British, French, and American officials did not anticipate the broad scope of human behavior, though they tried to use incentives to eliminate what they could see (snakes, rats, and traffic jams). They could not legislate or provide rewards to counter human behavior they did not observe or anticipate.

The consequences of legal errors are more difficult to observe. Researchers in the physical sciences can run controlled experiments in which half the subjects receive an experimental vaccine and half receive a placebo. If 95 percent of the subjects who received the vaccine do not contract a disease, and everyone without the vaccine contracts the disease, then it is clear the vaccine is effective. In contrast, following trials in criminal cases, guilty people who have been acquitted will never tell us they committed the crime. Innocent people who have been convicted will continue to protest their innocence, but almost no one will believe them because the evidence pointed to their guilt. The correctness of verdicts is far less clear than the effectiveness of vaccines.

Perhaps because of our relative inability to identify incorrect verdicts, at least absent DNA testing, we have not seen the need to change the adversarial system. Judges, juries, defense lawyers, and prosecutors perform the same functions and resort to the same tactics they employed in the early 1700s. In their 1957 book *Not Guilty*, Jerome Frank, a federal appellate judge, and Barbara Frank, his daughter, described how the legal profession and public view the courtroom as a coliseum and the trial as a game. They quote a reporter describing a murder case: "'Neither Neary [prosecutor] nor Lebowitz [defense attorney] was missing a trick in this courtroom battle. Each was at his brilliant best, and Judge Courtney, knowledgeable, completely fair, supervised the legal duel the way a really great boxing referee handless a championship fight.'" The reporter wrote of "'the excitement' of 'watching two champions in action.'"[1]

This kind of argumentation between lawyers, rather than an independent collection of facts, remains the primary method of defense of criminal cases. Once an innocent person has been charged, the defense lawyer's argumentation—the attempts to exclude unfavorable evidence, cross-examination of witnesses, and pleas to judges and juries—is almost the only safeguard against an erroneous conviction. But this argumentation, unlike the Greek ideal, is an artificial dialectic because the goal of the parties is to win cases, not to reveal the truth (except lawyers who work for the government). "In a dialectic, the presumed objective of both sides is to find the truth through logical argumentation. Conversely, the objective in an adversarial trial is victory," wrote Franklin Strier, in 1996, and now a judge in Arizona.[2] The "substantial truth-seeking deficiencies of current trial procedure represent a failure of the essential purpose of the trial," according to Judge Strier.[3]

The deficiencies extend to the courts. A 1996 federal statute, the Antiterrorism and Effective Death Penalty Act, passed with bipartisan approval and signed by President Bill Clinton, prohibits federal courts from hearing a convicted prisoner's factual claim unless "the facts underlying the claim would be sufficient to establish by clear and convincing evidence that but for constitutional error, no reasonable factfinder would have found the applicant guilty of the underlying offense."[4] Few defendants, usually imprisoned, have the wherewithal to acquire any new facts, and if they did they have almost no ability to show that "no reasonable" juror would have found them guilty given the new facts, a standard so high it is almost impossible to attain.

Writing in a law review article, one federal appeals court judge found that the Supreme Court, in six terms (2007–2013), ruled against prisoners in twenty-six of twenty-eight habeas corpus cases (93 percent).[5] Another federal appeals court judge, recognizing the restrictions on reviewing state convictions, in a 2015 article wrote, "We now regularly have to stand by in impotent silence, even though it may appear to us that an innocent person has been convicted."[6]

The Constitution is the only authority that could override the statute's restrictions on prisoners' habeas corpus petitions, but the Court has never concluded that it protects an *actually innocent* person from conviction or execution. In a 2009 case, *In re Davis*, Justice Antonin Scalia, joined by Justice Clarence Thomas, dissented from the Court's decision to grant a hearing to a prison inmate who had been sentenced to death but claimed years later that newly discovered evidence could exonerate him. (Seven of nine eyewitnesses changed their stories, and new witnesses named someone else as the perpetrator.) The Constitution promises due process and fair procedures, but not correct verdicts, according to Justice Scalia.

"This Court," he wrote (and the same holds true today), "has *never* held that the Constitution forbids the execution of a convicted defendant who has had a full and fair trial but is later able to convince a habeas court that he is 'actually' innocent. Quite to the contrary, we have repeatedly left that question unresolved, while expressing considerable doubt that any claim based on alleged 'actual innocence' is constitutionally cognizable."[7] After the Supreme Court intervened in *Davis*, a lower federal court held a hearing but did not upset the state conviction.

In other words, if federal judges believe that a convicted person is innocent, the judges may not have the authority—because the Constitution doesn't provide it—to overturn a conviction, even a death sentence, if government agents did not violate the procedures mandated by the Constitution. That's because the Constitution sometimes protects people from the errors and misdeeds of police officers, prosecutors, and judges, but the Court has not decided whether the Constitution prohibits mistaken verdicts by juries. The inmate, Troy Davis, was executed by Georgia in 2011.

Reasonable Injustice

Letting stand the conviction of an innocent person is unfair, but from the perspective of a utilitarian society the conviction is unreasonable only when its costs are too high. Even if we can estimate the number of convicted people who are innocent, it is very difficult to know whether the number is too high, too low, or acceptable because we do not know, and probably never will know, the number of guilty people who are acquitted. Few of them, if any, will ever say after acquittal that "I did it." This inhibits a cost-benefit analysis into whether the adversarial system should be reformed.

There is, nonetheless, one inarguable conceptual approach to satisfy a utilitarian society: create a method that will likely exonerate only innocent people. But, after three centuries of adversarial practice, aren't we already aware of every possible method of exoneration? After being exonerated and released from prison in 2013, Ryan Ferguson, who had served ten years for murder in Missouri, said that "to get arrested and charged for a crime you didn't commit is incredibly easy, and you lose your life very fast. But to get out of prison, it takes an army."[8] As Mr. Ferguson knew, the practical problem that leads to incorrect verdicts is that innocent people cannot access or present at their trials the exonerating facts and evidence that will convince juries to acquit them.

In the American adversarial system, the only allies of most innocent people are overworked, under-resourced public defenders. These lawyers' efforts are often futile because they do not have the resources to search effectively for exonerating evidence. In some cases, facts that may indicate innocence may not be discovered, if ever, until years or decades after a conviction, such as where new DNA testing permits more accurate analysis of old evidence. But, by then, incarceration in America's archaic and brutal prisons will have destroyed the lives of innocent people and their families (as well as the lives of guilty people and their families), and all the while the person who actually committed the crime will remain free.

Along with an absence of facts, innocent-person convictions occur because of witnesses' mistaken perceptions. While overwhelmed with more than ten million arrests each year, the U.S. adversarial system has come to accept, perhaps first from necessity but now as a matter of principled decision making, that due process is a replacement for seeking the truth.[9] One of the most eloquent expressions about how this approach plays out in real cases was offered by David Ranta, who was convicted of a 1990 murder. Mr. Ranta served twenty-three years in prison (including in jail prior to trial) before being exonerated in 2013.[10]

The killing of the victim in the case, a rabbi, stirred emotions and demands for a quick arrest. The rabbi's death occurred in the Williamsburg neighborhood of Brooklyn, where a jewel courier was headed to Kennedy Airport to take fifty pounds of gems to Central America for cutting. Accosted and trying to save the jewels, the courier backed his car into the robber and sped away safely. Frightened, the robber shot and killed the rabbi, who was nearby, and he commandeered the rabbi's car and escaped. The police conducted a frenzied investigation and found Ranta, who resembled the killer, white, tall, and lean, with blond hair and a big nose, according to testimony at Ranta's 1991 trial.

Two informants who made deals with the prosecution and had violent criminal histories testified (as did the woman companion of one of them) that they and Ranta planned the robbery and that Ranta killed the rabbi. A thirteen-year-old boy who witnessed the carjacking identified Ranta in a lineup and at trial. The lead Brooklyn detective, despite not producing notes or reports, testified that Ranta made spontaneous, incriminating statements.

The diamond courier, who had the best view of the robber/killer, testified he was "100 percent" certain that Ranta was not the robber. Nonetheless, the jury found Ranta guilty of murder, and despite questioning the evidence and police detectives' conduct the trial judge sentenced Ranta to life in prison, with parole possible after serving over thirty-seven years.[11]

Four years after the conviction, in a proceeding before the same judge, Francis X. Egitto, a woman testified that her husband, Joseph Astin, a Ranta look-alike, confessed to her that he killed the rabbi. Astin was a longtime criminal and armed robber. He died two months after the rabbi's killing when he crashed his car during a police chase. Despite again expressing reservations about Ranta's guilt, Judge Egitto refused to set aside the conviction.

After twenty-three years, the case against Ranta finally disintegrated. The thirteen-year-old boy who had identified Ranta at trial was now a man in his mid-thirties. He came forward to say the case had disturbed him all his life. He said that when he viewed the lineup, with Ranta in it, a police officer, whom he could not recall, told him to identify the man with the big nose (Ranta), which he did. Then, the woman companion admitted she had made up her story about Ranta to help her informant-boyfriend. The boyfriend admitted that he and the other informant fabricated their stories to obtain leniency on their separate criminal cases and claimed they and detectives framed Ranta.[12]

The Brooklyn District Attorney's Office reviewed over seventy cases, including fifty murders, in which the detective in Ranta's case had been the lead detective.[13] Though consenting to the release of several inmates who appeared to be innocent, the district attorney could not find any case where the available evidence showed that the detective engaged in misconduct.[14]

But that conclusion is probably more sobering than if the detective had been caught framing innocent people. This shows how convictions of innocent people occur when government agents are working in good faith, albeit perhaps not competently.

At his sentencing hearing, on June 9, 1991, better than any lawyer or philosopher, Ranta, a man without formal higher education, a drug addict and petty criminal, described to Judge Egitto the reasons why he believed he was falsely convicted:

> I'm stating today that I'm not the man that shot the rabbi. All your witnesses you put up against me were from Detectives Scarcella and Camille who I find two very corrupt cops. They put a hooker, a junkie, they put somebody who had raped, Dametrik [informant], who told them where the gun was. They put him away with a deal. They put Allan Bloom [informant], who faced 109 years away with a deal, they had Sherry, a known junkie who's on programs, welfare and then you take my credible witness,

the Diamond carry [*sic*] [diamond courier] who looked at me face-to-face supposedly I'm the shooter right, but he said it wasn't me. He said it wasn't me. . . . Now you people do what you got to do because I feel this is all a total frame setup, whatever you want to call it, but it's not going to stick. We are going to meet again. And when I come down on my appeal I hope to God he brings out the truth because a lot of people are going to be ashamed of themselves. I will take this and I will feel remorse, I will feel bad because of the rabbi, but I didn't do it and I'm not going to feel any worse than that.[15]

Two days after he was released from prison, in 2013, Ranta suffered a severe heart attack.[16] A year later, New York City agreed to pay him $6.4 million to compensate him for his twenty-three years in prison.[17]

David Ranta was fortunate in that the witnesses who testified against him changed their stories, albeit over two decades later. In a 1984 Supreme Court case, Justice William Brennan, in a dissenting opinion, described the short shrift with which courts usually view witnesses who later disavow their trial testimony. "Recantation testimony is properly viewed with great suspicion. It upsets society's interest in the finality of convictions, is very often unreliable and given for suspect motives, and most often serves merely to impeach cumulative evidence rather than to undermine confidence in the accuracy of the conviction. For these reasons, a witness' recantation of trial testimony typically will justify a new trial only where the reviewing judge after analyzing the recantation is satisfied that it is true and that it will 'render probable a different verdict.'"[18] Even if lying or mistaken witnesses are revealed at some time in the future, by then the innocent person has suffered incalculable damage.

In July 2020, the Brooklyn District Attorney's Office (Kings County) released a report on twenty-five cases in which innocent people had been convicted.[19] Collectively, they had served 426 years in prison before exoneration, an average of over 17 years each. In 2022, the Innocence Project, at Cardozo School of Law, reported the exoneration of 375 people through DNA testing and that the average time the innocent people served in prison before exoneration was 14 years, "including 21 who served time on death row."[20]

The Other Side of the Coin

Before jumping on a bandwagon for defendants and to ensure that our focus is on the discovery of truth, we should be reminded that reforms have to be designed to prevent guilty people from escaping responsibility. One way to achieve this is to recognize, from the perspective of victims, that the discovery of facts is as important to them as it is to innocent defendants. With most of the people arrested having committed some crime, overall the people who suffer most are the victims, not the people arrested, assuming they receive just treatment.

On a bright, late morning on New Year's Day over thirty-four years ago, I was walking from my apartment building down Flatbush Avenue in Brooklyn when one of the two police officers in a parked patrol car rolled down his passenger-side window to smile at me. "Hey, Counselor," he said.

From a small town in rural Wisconsin and relatively new to New York City, I felt the unexpected warmth of running into someone who likes you, though this cop made everyone feel that way. "Officer Herman, Jeff, great to see you again," I said. Herman was on duty and I was headed to a party to watch the college football bowl games. He stuck his hand out the window, and we shook and briefly discussed the minor criminal case that had brought us together.

In my first job after law school, I was an assistant district attorney in Brooklyn, and Herman was the first witness I called to testify at one of my first trials, an attempted assault case decided by a judge. A mother was renting her basement apartment to her son, and when she went to tell him to vacate because he wouldn't pay the rent he encouraged his leashed dog to bite her. Backing away, the mother was scared but unhurt, disbelieving what a son can become. Officer Herman arrested the son and at the trial testified to the presence of the dog and gave the judge a summary of the events on the day of the arrest.

Possibly concluding the son didn't want to hurt his mother, but more likely finding that a criminal conviction would harm the family, the judge found the son not guilty of attempted assault and added a new charge, disorderly conduct, and found him guilty of that. The judge might not have acted altogether legally, but the outcome was reasonable and fair, one that was more likely than any other to benefit the family and society. Providing the mother with an *order of protection*, the judge knew the son would not appeal and the order would serve as a shield or dagger, depending on how the mother wanted to use it, one of the many creative, informal methods used by everyone drawn into the criminal legal system.

That New Year's Day was the last time Officer Herman and I saw each other. Herman continued with the NYPD, working in plain clothes, a step up from the patrol car, and I moved on to handling other cases in the District Attorney's Office. Sometime after the trial, in May 1989, an assistant district attorney I knew was standing up one day representing the state of New York in arraignments, the courtroom where an arrested person first sees a judge. At arraignments, the prosecutor recommends whether accused people (*defendants* once in court) should be released or held in jail because they are unlikely to return voluntarily for the next scheduled court appearance or are likely to harm witnesses, often the unstated reason to hold someone who has not yet been found guilty.

Especially in those grim days of relentless violence, when the number of murders in New York City neared or exceeded 2,000 every year (down to 485 in 2021), the arraignment courtroom was a chaotic place.[21] Except for a meal break, which might begin at nine o'clock if working a night shift, prosecutors stand for six or seven hours and have only seconds, sometimes a minute, to distill for the judge the most important information in the disorganized paper files used decades ago. In this small amount of time, no prosecutor can assimilate all the facts in a file. The prosecutor must rely on the previous prosecutor on the case, who initially spoke to the arresting officer and prepared the file, to highlight the key points that should be relayed to the judge.

In one case, a police officer heard a suspect, arrested for harassing and kidnapping a woman companion, say that he would kill a police officer if he were released. Through miscommunication, the suspect's statement was not conveyed to the judge presiding over arraignments. The arraignments prosecutor recommended bail of $250 when the amount should have been $1,500 under the district attorney's internal guidelines. Unaware of the threat, the judge released the defendant on his own recognizance, that is, without requiring him to pay any money or guarantee any property, which, if he had money or property, he would forfeit to the state if he did not show up for his next court date.

A few weeks later, on May 30, 1989, the defendant was back at the place of the woman he had allegedly kidnapped, threatening and trying to convince her to drop the charges. Officer Herman and his partner responded and approached the man. With his illegal handgun, the man shot the woman in the back, and then he opened fire on Herman. He hit Herman twice, once in the leg. Herman was wearing a bullet-resistant vest, but the gunman's other bullet pierced and passed through Herman's arm from the side and slammed into his chest, between the front and back flaps of the vest.

Mortally wounded, Herman tried desperately to live. Strong and young, twenty-five when he died, but smart and aware and surely knowing his predicament, he lost a lung and then fought a raging infection. Four days after being shot, he died in the hospital. Two days later, with the police closing in on him, the gunman killed himself with a bullet to his head.

The focus of this book is on how to free innocent people, but the primary method through which to do that—find the facts that exist—ensures also that guilty people will not go free. Knowledge of the gunman's prior threat to kill a police officer might have convinced the prosecutor to ask for higher bail. Aware of the threat, the judge might have set bail instead of releasing the gunman. Usually in life, the collection of all the facts will ensure that most events result in relatively acceptable outcomes. Prosecutors will have enough facts to decide not to charge someone with a crime, but, if they do, erroneously, jurors will have enough facts to enable them to find an innocent person not guilty.

In this tragedy, the most important fact was available (the killer's threat), but it was not communicated to the judge, the decision maker. Officer Herman's death would have been averted if the gunman had not been released. This leads to another problem. At this early stage of any criminal case, a judge cannot know who is innocent or guilty and who, if released, will try to harm a witness or police officer. Poor people often cannot afford to pay any amount of money to gain their release prior to trial.

If a judge sets almost any amount of money bail before a defendant can be released, an innocent person will be jailed and have little or no opportunity to help defend against the charges, such as walking the streets in a search for witnesses. It is, therefore, critical that the government be willing to search for exonerating facts identified by plausibly innocent people even after being satisfied it has enough evidence to charge someone with a crime. As we will see next, however, law enforcement agents do not have any obligation to help defendants conduct their own search.

3

Defense of Falsity

The adversarial system, especially in the United States, vows that its purpose is to search for truth, even as its lawyers take all possible measures legally to conceal evidence. When beneficial to their clients, lawyers try to lead juries and judges into believing that something the lawyers know to be false is true, and the other way around. John Langbein, an emeritus professor of law at Yale, outlines the "incentives to distort or suppress the truth": the withholding of factual information that will benefit the other side; concealment of witnesses; coaching witnesses; and abusive cross-examination of witnesses, especially when the lawyer conducting the cross-examination knows the witness is telling the truth.[1]

These practices have become norms in the legal system, despite the Supreme Court's extolling the virtues of searching for truth. In 1986, in *Nix v. Whiteside*, the Court agreed that lawyers should not "either advocate or passively tolerate a client's giving false testimony." In *Nix*, the Court wrote about its aspiration for America's legal system. "This, of course, is consistent with the governance of the trial conduct in what we have long called a 'search for truth.'"[2]

Despite the Court's optimism, in actual cases, no one searches for truth. Through its decisions, the Court has injected perpetual falsity into criminal litigation, such as through the exclusionary rule.[3] The rationale for the falsity is the belief that legal or social policies should override the truth to achieve a greater goal. One can agree or disagree with the policies, but the Court and legal system find it very difficult to acknowledge that the quest for falsity by the parties in litigation is an animating and dominant practice, an everyday norm, in American law. The Court and the profession would better serve society if they explained what they believe to be the virtues of allowing lawyers to urge juries and judges to reach verdicts and decisions on evidence that the lawyers know to be false.

To begin, the Court and lawyers might acknowledge that the projection of falsity, as well as lying and misrepresentation by the police, is a Court-approved practice in investigations and litigation. In *Alford v. North Carolina*, in 1970, the Court upheld a guilty plea and conviction of murder where the defendant claimed to be innocent but said he was pleading guilty in return for the prosecution's promise not to seek his execution. "An individual accused of crime may voluntarily, knowingly, and understandingly consent to the imposition of a prison sentence even if he is unwilling or unable to admit his participation in the acts constituting the crime," the Court concluded.[4] Whether an *Alford* plea is a good social or legal policy, the Court did not seem to appreciate that a defendant's presumably false plea to murder as a way to avoid execution is not conceivably, at least given how normal people look at life, a *voluntary* choice. This kind of coercion is not a method through which to find truth.

Even in a death-penalty case, a deal is a deal, according to the Court. In one sense, the Court was practical and merciful, in that the defendant (who later contested his guilty plea) could have been executed if not given the right to plead guilty while claiming innocence. This illustrates how the fear induced by severe punishment in any context and the death penalty in criminal cases foster dishonesty, silence, and a truth-averting ethos and culture. As we will see, English juries and judges in the early 1700s, like courts today, actively introduced falsity into their decisions. The English impetus, as sometimes in America today, was the death penalty. Juries and judges would reduce the actual value of goods stolen, for example, so that they would not have to find the thieves guilty of felonies, which carried an almost automatic sentence of death.

America's sentences are far more severe than those in any other Western country, and thus the likelihood of false guilty pleas is significantly greater. Just ahead of the United States in the number executions administered from 2013 to 2019 are China, Iran, Saudi Arabia, Iraq, and Egypt, and just behind the United States are Pakistan, Somalia, South Sudan, and Yemen.[5] In addition to the death penalty, the United States sentences 69.9 percent of its convicted persons to prison, while Canada, England and Wales, Finland, and Germany, respectively, send only 33.8, 9.2, 7.2, and 7.5 percent of their convicted people to prison, opting instead for controls on freedom, fines, and community service, according to the Justice Policy Institute. "The average sentence length for all sentences in the U.S. (sixty-three months) is higher than that in Australia

(36 months) and Germany (between one and two years). Differences in sentencing for drug offenses, in particular, likely contribute to this disparity in average sentences. People convicted of drug offenses in the U.S. receive an average sentence of five years compared to just thirty-two months in England and Wales."[6]

The National Registry of Exonerations conducts research on known and presumed exonerations that have occurred since 1989. Through November 2015, the registry reported 1,702 exonerations, 261 of which arose from defendants who had pleaded guilty.[7] In other words, 15 percent of the people who were exonerated had pleaded guilty despite being innocent. According to Professor Hans Crombag, "plea bargaining is a device for systematically sacrificing the truth to expediency."[8]

As the juries and judges in England found over three hundred years ago, the death penalty is a powerful method through which to introduce falsity into a legal system. The National Registry reported: "Almost three-quarters of homicide exonerees who pled guilty were convicted of murder (44/61). It appears that the great majority did so to avoid the risk of execution. All but 2 were prosecuted in death penalty states, and 70% had falsely confessed (31/44). . . . They all avoided the death penalty, but the sentences they did receiver were stiff: 14 were sentenced to life without parole, [and] the rest got sentences that averaged 22 years."[9] In July 2021, the registry reported 2,810 exonerations. The total number of years exonerated innocent people spent in prison were 25,177 (about 9 years per exoneree).[10] Similarly, in 2017, the Innocence Project reported, "In nearly 11% of the nation's 349 DNA exoneration cases, innocent people entered guilty pleas."[11]

Defense Lawyers' Practical Considerations

Professor Robert P. Mosteller, a former public defender, describes how defense lawyers' self-interests can lead to guilty pleas by their clients. "Public defenders receive the same salary whether they try a case or their client enters a plea of guilty, and with a guilty plea, their leisure time should increase. Assuming that at least short run handling of one's case load is all that is required to receive full pay, public defenders have an incentive to have their clients enter guilty pleas even if the client's interest is to go to trial."[12]

Another perspective is that public defenders do not have the time or resources to take every case to trial. They may even make utilitarian decisions in urging innocent people to plead guilty. One criminal defense lawyer, Professor Abbe Smith, of Georgetown University Law School, described the rationale: "On the other hand, there are considerable systemic pressures on defendants to plead guilty. This is especially problematic for those who may be innocent but cannot afford bail. Most defenders [lawyers] will admit, albeit uneasily, that they have talked factually innocent people into pleading guilty. The guilty and those who value the swift disposition of cases above all else tend to be the beneficiaries of plea bargaining."[13]

District attorneys and county and state prosecutors, most of whom are elected locally, have their own interests and may be reluctant to relinquish convictions obtained by their offices. For instance, upon the postconviction discovery of evidence that indicates innocence (but not with certainty), they may offer plea agreements if incarcerated defendants agree to drop their appeals.[14] On one case, based on a 1997 burglary, "Sherman Townsend spent 10 years in prison for burglary, before another man came forward and took responsibility for the crime. . . . Townsend had a hearing before a judge [in 2007]. . . . The other man, David Jones, testified on the stand that he committed the crime. He drew a map of the crime scene, and described that night in detail. . . . But the judge never ruled on whether Townsend deserved a new trial. Because before she could [rule], Hennepin County [Minnesota] Attorney Mike Freeman offered Townsend a deal. He could drop his appeal, and walk free. But he'd keep the conviction on his record," according to a television station in Minneapolis.[15]

Without money for bail, Mr. Townsend was incarcerated prior to his trial. At the trial, he did not testify because he had prior burglary convictions, which, if he testified, the prosecution could probably ask him about on cross-examination. The judge, nonetheless, allowed the prosecution to introduce one of the burglary convictions into evidence, presumably to show Townsend's motive or intent in regard to the current charged burglary.[16] The victims of the burglary, who had been assaulted (not sexually) in their bed, could not identify the offender. The only witness who connected Townsend to the burglary was David Jones, thirty-two, who, like Townsend, matched the general physical description of the perpetrator, except that Townsend, at age forty-seven, was older than the victims' estimate of their assailant ("20s or 30s").

Mr. Jones, who later confessed to committing the burglary, was the prosecution's main witness at the 1997 trial. He testified that he saw Townsend leaving the scene of the crime. At the 2007 hearing, Jones, who by then had been convicted of criminal sexual conduct and was incarcerated in the same prison as Townsend, testified that he intended to sexually assault women who lived in the apartment building where the burglary occurred. But Jones also testified that, while in prison, he had a "'crisis of conscience.'" He said that he identified Townsend to deflect suspicion of himself.

After Townsend pleaded guilty and was released, Freeman, the county attorney, said, "We believe Mr. Townsend did it. We no longer have the evidence to prove that beyond a reasonable doubt."

Of his time in prison, Townsend said that he missed "the beach, spending time with family, spending time with my grandchildren, I wanted to do everything I was doing in normal life. The TV doesn't help because you're watching everybody else do everything."[17]

Without additional evidence, such as a credible witness who can attest whether it was Townsend or Jones who exited the apartment building, many prosecutors would be unconvinced of Townsend's innocence. Knowing of his prior burglaries in the same area, prosecutors would think, as was apparently considered in this case, that Jones confessed ten years later because he was influenced or coerced by Townsend while they were in the same prison. Jones could have reasoned that he had nothing to lose by confessing because he was serving a long prison term on his own case; the prosecution would not want to spend additional time on his misdeeds if his prison term was sufficient.

From the defense perspective, even if he were innocent, Townsend's guilty plea to one additional burglary would have little effect on his future because he was already experiencing the disabling social consequences of prior criminal convictions. (Prior to trial, prosecutors offered Townsend a four-year sentence if he pleaded guilty.)[18] Any guilty plea now would probably eliminate any opportunity to be compensated by the state for serving time in prison, assuming he could prove his innocence in a civil proceeding. (In 2013, the Minnesota Board of Pardons denied Townsend's request for a pardon.)[19] However, because the hearing judge had not yet decided whether to vacate Townsend's conviction, the possibility of immediate release after serving ten years (his sentence was twenty years' imprisonment, with parole possible after thirteen), especially if he had committed the burglary, might outweigh possible financial compensation. Moreover, the judge might have found that Jones was not credible and allowed Townsend's conviction to stand. Even if Townsend appealed, appellate courts would be unlikely to second-guess the judge's factual finding on credibility. Then, Townsend, whose only way out of prison was Jones's testimony—inherently unreliable, according to Justice William Brennan's view (from chapter 2) of witnesses who recant—would be left to serve the remainder of his twenty-year sentence.

These are the kinds of considerations that have to be weighed when the truth is not obvious or cannot be found. A plea of innocence would have permitted Townsend, who was in jail prior to his trial, to require the state to try to find a credible witness to verify whether it was Townsend or Jones who left the scene of the crime. If Townsend had committed the burglary, however, he would not plead innocent because the last person he'd want to see at his trial is a relevant and credible witness.

Professor Keith Findley, who cofounded the innocence project at the University of Wisconsin Law School, noticed how prosecution offices, after evidence indicated that a convicted person was innocent, would offer the person (then a prison inmate) an opportunity to plead guilty with the promise of a sentence of *time served*, which, effectively, means immediate release. "One of the things that innocence advocates have noticed over the years is that not always, but sometimes, prosecutors, when confronted with very powerful evidence of innocence, go to great lengths to try to preserve the convictions. Including making plea offers that are essentially so good that it's hard to turn them down, even for an innocent individual," Findley said.[20]

Through a survey of innocence projects throughout the United States, Findley found that in 272 cases in which evidence indicated innocence prosecutors offered plea deals in 64 (23.5 percent). "Remember," said Findley, referring to inmates who have been offered a plea deal and time served (immediate release), "as a category, this is a group of people who already put their faith in the trial process and lost once. So why would they have any faith that they would fare any better the second time, right? So you can see why these kinds of very generous plea offers, even for stone cold individuals, are going to be really, really tempting. It's going to take only the bravest, the most risk-tolerant individuals who are going to be willing to test the system a second time after having tried it and lost once already."[21]

* * *

Even the two most prominent rules designed to protect innocent people countenance falsity, under the rationale that they protect innocent people. Dating to classical Roman law, the presumption of innocence, for example, is "the idea that doubt should be resolved in favor of a criminal defendant."[22] In a 1985 case, *Coffin v. U.S.*, the Supreme Court found that the "principle that there is a presumption of innocence in favor of the accused is the undoubted law, axiomatic and elementary, and its enforcement lies at the foundation of the administration of our criminal law."[23]

Similarly, the beyond-reasonable-doubt standard, the highest burden of persuasion (above clear and convincing evidence and a preponderance of evidence) is not premised on a search for truth. The standard arose in the mid-1700s, possibly as late as 1770 in Massachusetts in the Boston Massacre trials and in Ireland in 1798 in treason trials.[24] It was not until 1970 that the Supreme Court held the Constitution requires the prosecution to prove guilt beyond a reasonable doubt in all state criminal trials.[25]

"The rise of the adversary criminal trial may have affected the development of the beyond-reasonable-doubt standard of proof in a different way, by disposing the judges [in England] to feel the need to further safeguard against the failure of adversary procedure," according to Professor Langbein.[26] Judges in England were less concerned that innocent people would be convicted than that they would be executed. Langbein, in studying trial records from the Old Bailey (*Sessions Papers*), found that the beyond-reasonable-doubt standard evolved in felony cases. In summary offenses, with lighter sentences and no "adversary jury trial," there was movement away from the beyond-reasonable-doubt standard.[27] The high beyond-reasonable-doubt standard developed because the adversary system was infirm; the standard helped to prevent both innocent and guilty people from suffering execution. It was not designed to help find the truth.

In the Absence of Facts

In the three hundred years since the beginning of the adversarial system, courts have introduced or permitted rules of falsity in an effort to overcome deficient fact-finding. A year prior to its decision in *Alford*, the Supreme Court, in 1969, did not object to police lying to a suspect in an effort to obtain a confession and conviction. In *Frazier v. Cupp*, the police told the suspect, falsely, that his alleged accomplice had confessed. The suspect then confessed to participating in the killing of the victim; he was convicted of second-degree murder.

The Court affirmed the conviction and opened the door wider for the police to lie to suspects and witnesses, a practice that is now a regular part of criminal investigations in America. The Court concluded, "The questioning was of short duration, and petitioner was a mature individual of normal intelligence. The fact that the police misrepresented the statements that Rawls [the accomplice] had made is, while relevant, insufficient in our view to make this otherwise voluntary confession inadmissible. These cases must be decided by viewing the 'totality of the circumstances' . . . and on the facts of this case we can find no error in the admission of petitioner's confession."[28]

In 1986, in *Moran v. Burbine*, the Court extended the misrepresentation that is allowed, this time by the police to a lawyer. In *Moran*, a lawyer called a police station and told the person who answered that she represented the suspect the police were holding (and interrogating). The lawyer was told the suspect would not be questioned further until the next day. Less than an hour later, detectives began a series of interviews during which the suspect admitted to a murder. Finding no right to a lawyer because an investigation is not an "accusation" (and the suspect did not know that his sister had retained the lawyer on his behalf), the Court permitted the deception of the lawyer and upheld the murder conviction of the suspect.[29]

In 1993, the Court, in *Herrera v. Collins*, indicated that it might be obligated to accept convictions of innocent people. In *Herrera*, the Court had to decide whether evidence of actual innocence is a sufficient basis on which to grant a hearing to an inmate who contested his conviction via federal habeas corpus, after Texas courts had upheld his death sentence.[30] If the defendant were granted a hearing in federal court, he could introduce evidence (new facts) to show that he did not commit the crimes and ask the federal court to order a second trial in the state court in which he had been convicted.

Lionel Herrera had been convicted in Texas of murdering two police officers and sentenced to death. Years after his convictions, his brother was murdered. Two witnesses then came forward, the brother's lawyer and the brother's former cellmate. They swore in affidavits that, at some time before the brother died, he admitted to them he had killed the police officers. The defense lawyer's affidavit described a drug-sale conspiracy involving Herrera and his brother, his father, and the Hidalgo County Sheriff. The brother shot the two police officers and, years later, was killed by a fellow conspirator, according to the lawyer.[31]

Texas's criminal procedures did not allow Herrera, or any defendant, to introduce new evidence, including the affidavits, except within thirty days after conviction. A formal conviction occurs upon sentencing and, in most states, comes only days or weeks, possibly a month or two at most, after the jury's guilty verdict. With a trial and sentence only weeks in the past, there is no one to look for or even think about new evidence. The best efforts of the defense have been expended recently at trial. Most new evidence, if any, is discovered years or decades later, only after lying or mistaken witnesses have been revealed or, over time, have had pangs of remorse and a change of heart. In Herrera's case, the affidavits from his brother's lawyer and cellmate were produced nearly nine years after Herrera's conviction.

Herrera's legal claim was that the execution of an innocent person would violate the Constitution's Eighth Amendment prohibition on cruel and unusual punishment. But, in a five-to-four majority opinion, authored by Chief Justice William Rehnquist, the Court concluded that habeas corpus provides federal courts with the legal jurisdiction to hear a case only if the convicted person claims that a government agent, such as a police officer, violated the Constitution. The Court concluded that because Herrera was basing his claim of innocence on the discovery of new facts, the affidavits, rather than on police or prosecution error or misconduct, for example, Herrera was not entitled to present the affidavits to a federal court. He was not entitled to a hearing, regardless of whether he was plausibly innocent, a determination, of course, that could not be made without a hearing. Justice Rehnquist wrote that Herrera's only alternative was to ask for clemency from the Texas governor, Ann Richards. The governor rejected clemency, and Texas executed Herrera four months after the Court's decision.

Just prior to his execution, Herrera made a final statement: "I am innocent, innocent, innocent. Make no mistake about this; I owe society nothing. Continue the struggle for human rights, helping those who are innocent. . . . I am an innocent man, and something very wrong is taking place tonight. May God bless you all. I am ready."[32]

Herrera's legal claim is what the Supreme Court characterizes as a "freestanding" claim, an assertion that the Constitution bars the conviction of a person who is actually innocent. Providing a slight opening, the Court, in 2013, found that convicted people may assert, in rare instances, actual innocence to overcome a statute or rule that prevents them from arguing that a constitutional right was violated during the trial. In the case, *McQuiggin v. Perkins*, a statute-of-limitations provision in the Antiterrorism and Effective Death Penalty Act barred the inmate/petitioner from receiving a hearing because he was late in claiming that he received ineffective assistance of counsel at his trial. The Court decided that, if evidence of actual innocence is strong enough, a federal court may overlook the inmate's procedural failure to raise a claim (such as taking too long). If the court finds a constitutional violation, such as ineffective assistance of counsel, it will order a new trial in the state court where the defendant was convicted.

Writing for the Supreme Court, Justice Ruth Bader Ginsburg emphasized that the bar (a "miscarriage of justice") is extremely high. "We caution, however, that tenable actual-innocence gateway pleas are rare: '[A] petitioner does not meet the threshold requirement unless he persuades the district court that, in light of the new evidence, no juror, acting reasonably, would have voted to find him guilty beyond a reasonable doubt.'"[33] The Court remanded the case, but doubted that the inmate's asserted facts (affidavits) would be sufficient to establish actual innocence.[34] Just over four months later, a federal district court dismissed the inmate's claims.[35]

Citing *Herrera*, Justice Ginsburg continued to recognize that a plausible claim of actual innocence, even if proven, may not be a constitutional basis on which to reverse a conviction. "We have not resolved whether a prisoner may be entitled to habeas relief based on a freestanding claim of actual innocence."[36]

* * *

It can be difficult to understand how a legal system could permit the conviction or execution of a person who is plausibly innocent, unless one finds that the adversarial system was infirm from the beginning or that along the way it developed truth-averting characteristics. As part of the "process that led to the creation of the modern democratic states,"[37] the adversarial system arose in the eighteenth and nineteenth centuries[38] to rectify previous failures to develop a method through which to search for truth.[39] Though the Supreme Court attributes its decisions, like *Herrera*, to its interpretation of the Constitution, the Court's approach to constitutional decision making seems to be influenced by its view that due process is all that a legal system can promise.

Members of society have learned to believe that due process is a proxy or socially acceptable substitute for truth-seeking. "When the adversary system allowed the lawyers to gain control over gathering and adducing the evidence, responsibility for the conduct of the proofs passed to persons who became professionally skilled at techniques of defeating the truth," Professor Langbein concluded.[40] Contrary to the aspirations of democratic states, secrecy became an important value within the adversarial system, from government investigations to lawyers' litigation of cases. The oldest and most prominent confidential communication in the professions,[41] the attorney-client privilege,[42] evolved and continues even after a client's death.[43]

Contained in ethical rules, this privilege permits lawyers not to reveal communications in some of the most extreme circumstances.[44] For instance, even if lawyers believe their clients will kill someone, the American Bar Association's ethics rules—its *Model Rules of Professional Conduct* is an exemplar for every state—do not require lawyers to inform the soon-to-be-deceased victims. A "lawyer may reveal information relating to the representation of a client to the extent the lawyer reasonably believes necessary . . . to prevent reasonably certain death or substantial bodily harm," the applicable rule provides.[45] Obviously, the word *may* indicates the lawyer is free not to alert the police or the potential homicide victim even when the lawyer is "reasonably certain" the lawyer can save the victim's life.[46]

Loyalty over Truth

This rule applies to all lawyer-client interactions. Probably more sobering, the rule shows that the legal system places a higher value on loyalty than on truth, including in civil cases in which the client is a corporation with nothing to lose except money. Some of the unnecessary deaths detailed below could probably have been prevented had the corporation's lawyers revealed the danger of a defective ignition part that General Motors installed in its automobiles. The events indicate that the lawyers' justification for remaining silent is outweighed by requiring them to speak up when doing so could save lives. We should ask why, then, secrecy and silence prevail in the adversarial legal system.

In 2014, after General Motors emerged from its 2009 bankruptcy, investigators discovered that GM had not revealed, for over a decade, an ignition defect in some of its cars. Causing cars to shut down and drivers to lose control at high speeds, the defect led to thirteen deaths, GM conceded, and up to three hundred deaths according to an independent analysis. One reason GM recorded fewer deaths was that it counted only the dead people who had been sitting in the front seats in front-end crashes.[47] In 2015, the administrator for a victims' compensation fund approved fifty-one death claims and one hundred twenty-eight claims for serious injuries.[48]

Emails among employees at Delphi, the company that supplied the defective ignition switch to GM, appeared to show that employees knew the switch was defective. A Delphi employee wrote that the switch "was never able to cut it." The employee continued, "I want it to be known that at the start of the [ignition switch] program I insisted that the product be tested at 265 application current levels [a higher standard], not 2A. Everyone [at Delphi] agreed to 2A [the lower standard] without a whimper."[49] But the ignition switch could not apparently meet even the lower standard.

When the families of dead drivers brought lawsuits, part of GM's legal strategy was to argue that it could not be held liable for the deaths arising from the defective cars it sold prior to its bankruptcy declaration.[50] In 2004, prior to the 2009 bankruptcy, GM had rejected an insurance claim on behalf of the first victim, who died when her Saturn Ion car inexplicably crashed into a tree, without her airbag deploying. At the bottom of page 103 of a 315-page report on the defect, which GM had commissioned, the woman's name was blacked out. GM refused to say whether it had informed the families of the other victims that their deaths were caused by the defective ignition switches.[51]

GM remained silent in a peripheral case involving the ignition and allowed a different kind of harm to occur. In Texas, in 2007, a woman pleaded guilty to negligent homicide because she believed she was responsible for killing her boyfriend, a passenger in her GM Saturn Ion. When the car crashed into a tree and killed the man, she had a trace amount of Xanax in her body. Prior to the woman's guilty plea, a GM investigation found that the Ion's ignition defect was probably the cause of the crash. But, in a "death inquiry," GM reported to the National Highway Traffic Safety Administration "that it had not assessed the cause of the crash when, in fact, it had: A G.M. engineer had ruled just a month earlier that power to the vehicle had most likely shut off" (from the defective ignition switch), according to the New York Times.[52]

Four months later, the woman pleaded guilty to a felony and, after that, paid $10,000 in fines and restitution and served five years of probation. When GM's actions were aired nationally at a congressional hearing, its chief executive, Mary Barra, and its top lawyer, Michael Millikin, refused to support a pardon for the woman.

Two of the deaths from the GM cars occurred in 2006, in Wisconsin, where two teenagers were killed when their car swerved off the road and crashed into a tree without the airbags deploying. A police investigator found evidence of a possible defect. "The car's ignition switch had powered off seconds before the accident, and G.M. had received reports of similar incidents, pointing to a possible defect," reported the Times.[53]

A legal ethics professor, Ellen C. Yaroshefsky, concluded that the lawyers for an outside law firm hired by GM could have revealed the defect to GM management or law enforcement officials, but they were not required to reveal it.[54] General Motors, with headquarters in Detroit, fired six of its corporate attorneys, presumably for not reporting the ignition defect to GM executives. But, in 2016, after a legal ethics complaint filed by a father whose daughter had been killed in a defective-ignition collision with a tractor trailer, the Michigan Attorney Grievance Commission declined to open an ethics investigation of the lawyers. "Michigan does not require corporate lawyers to reveal client confidences to warn consumers at risk of death or bodily harm," reported the *ABA Journal*, in citing a legal ethics expert, Professor Stephen Gillers.[55]

"The basic allegation was that certain GM inside counsel violated their professional obligations by failing to make a public disclosure of the ignition switch issues of which they were purportedly aware. . . . Likely critical to this determination [that the lawyers acted within the ethics rules that applied to them] was the fact that Michigan professional rules do not require counsel to disclose confidential information necessary to warn consumers at risk of death or bodily harm," concluded two lawyers not involved in the ethics allegations.[56]

* * *

Under legal ethics rules, criminal defense lawyers enjoy even broader latitude than those in civil practice. In the litigation of cases, according to ABA Model Rule 3.1, lawyers must have a good-faith belief in the truth of an assertion they make. "A lawyer shall not bring or defend a proceeding, or assert or controvert an issue therein, unless there is a basis in law and fact for doing so that is not frivolous, which includes a good faith argument for an extension, modification or reversal of existing law."

But, a different section of the rule provides that the "the lawyer for the defendant in a criminal proceeding . . . that could result in incarceration [which is almost every criminal case] . . . may nevertheless so defend the proceeding as to require that every element of the case be established."[57]

The ABA's *Defense Function*, a guide for criminal defense lawyers, provides further that a lawyer's "belief or knowledge that the witness is telling the truth does not preclude cross-examination."[58] This means, in practice, that defense lawyers who believe or know they are representing guilty clients may cross-examine witnesses—known by the lawyers to be testifying truthfully and accurately—in an effort to try to undermine the witnesses' credibility or testimony generally.

Professor Smith, the criminal defense lawyer and Georgetown professor, wrote a 2000 law review article, "Defending Defending: The Case for Unmitigated Zeal on Behalf of People Who Do Terrible Things."

Smith raised what she termed the "burning question" of whether a law-yer's advocacy "crossed an 'ethical line' when he suggested in his opening statement that . . . [a victim's anal] injuries were the result of consensual homosexual sex and not police brutality."

The lawyer, Marvin Kornberg, was representing a New York City po-lice officer, Justin Volpe, who was accused of jamming a broomstick into the rectum of an arrested person in the bathroom of a Brooklyn police precinct in 1997. In the middle of his 1999 trial in federal court, Officer Volpe, after other officers' testimony had implicated him, pleaded guilty and was sentenced to thirty years in prison. Volpe mistakenly believed that the victim had punched him outside a Brooklyn night spot. Pro-fessor Smith wrote that Mr. Kornberg, Volpe's lawyer, "was well within ethical bounds to offer a *flimsy* theory of defense, even if the evidence to support it was largely illusory."[59]

"The more interesting question relates to the propriety of putting forward a theory of defense built on the exploitation of potential juror prejudice," Professor Smith wrote.[60] Smith concluded, "I do not enjoy stirring up or manipulating homophobia or race, gender, or ethnic preju-dice in the course of representing a client. However, my own ideological values cannot be the determining factor."[61] Smith placed responsibility on the prosecution to counter this kind of defense. "A prosecutor is also present. It is the prosecutor's responsibility to anticipate and counter defense strategies—even those that play into juror prejudice. If they fail to do so, why blame the defense?"[62]

Smith wrote that Kornberg, the defense lawyer, "would have been within ethical bounds had he intentionally sought to discredit or dispar-age Abner Louima [the victim by] suggesting that he engaged in homo-sexual sex or was secretly gay—whether or not Louima was in fact gay," though Smith believed this to be a "poor tactical choice."[63]

"There is nothing unethical about using racial, gender, ethnic, or sexual stereotypes in criminal defense. It is simply an aspect of zealous advocacy," wrote Smith.[64] "A trial is theater. . . . Sometimes the exploita-tion of stereotypes is unavoidable."[65]

This approach—defense lawyers' "stirring up or manipulating ho-mophobia or race, gender, or ethnic prejudice in the course of repre-senting a client," according to Smith—seems likely only to exacerbate the lack of trust that exists among lawyers and all the participants in the adversarial system. If prosecutors believe that defense attorneys are trying to manipulate them, they will be less willing to help the lawyers or their clients search for exonerating facts. From this defense approach, innocent people suffer.

In their 1957 book *Not Guilty*, Judge Jerome Frank and Barbara Frank, writing to support innocent people who had been convicted, disapproved of defense concealment of facts:

> The lawyer, these books [dozens of books on trial techniques] advise, has a duty to give the jury, if possible, a false impression of testimony disadvantageous to his side, even if the lawyer does not doubt the witness's honesty and accuracy. If an honest witness is timid, the lawyer, by cross-examination, should play up that weakness in order to confuse the witness and persuade the jury that he is concealing important facts. One of the books, discussing "the truthful, honest, and over-cautious witness," says that "a skillful advocate by a rapid cross-examination may ruin" the witness's testimony.[66]

Lloyd Weinreb, an emeritus professor at Harvard Law School, lamented the techniques of lawyers: "All the arts and, be it said, tricks of persuasion, all the available dust that can be thrown in the fact-finders' eyes, all the obfuscation that may tilt the result in one direction or the other are the zealous advocate's stock in trade. That is what adversariness, as we now think of it, means. Only those who accept adversariness as an article of faith would suppose that such tactics in and of themselves further the search for truth."[67] With the elevation of falsity and obfuscation of truth ever-present goals of lawyers and core conditions of the adversarial legal system, innocent people, who always seek the truth, have few ways to find it.

4

Emergence and Glory of Adversarial Combat

Most people probably find comfort in being open and truthful, which are characteristics that support individual and social progress under almost any view. In contrast, the adversarial legal system supports parties' attempts to remain silent, suppress facts, and avoid revealing evidence, for their advantage, regardless of the effects on society. It seems magical to believe that truth will appear where no one is responsible for finding it and all the parties in litigation (except government lawyers) are devoted to hiding the truth if doing so benefits their clients.

The lawyers' combat ethos and hostility have been assimilated into society. The "virtues of the adversary system are so deeply engrained in the American legal psyche that most lawyers do not question it," wrote Professor Ellen Sward in 1989.[1] It is difficult to measure the value of lawyers because we do not know the extent to which society would benefit if they were not permitted to hide the truth or whether better dispute-resolution methods would have evolved in the absence of lawyers. In contrast to adversarial practice, when the inquisitorial system began evolving in the late 1100s and early 1200s in Europe, lawyers were not an instrumental part of it.

Prior to the inquisitorial system, criminal cases were initiated by private accusers, who were the alleged victims of crimes. Royal courts, municipal courts, and canon courts of the church heard cases outdoors and in public. "Nothing could occur without the active participation of the accuser," and only when offenders were caught in the act of a crime could a judge alone move forward on a case. "Central to many of these prefeudal modes of trial throughout the Germanic kingdoms of western Europe were the ordeals and other divinely inspired interventions," according to Professor Richard Vogler.[2]

Legal systems used any number of methods to try to find facts and evidence, and many of them were destructive. Illogical in every temporal respect, trials by ordeal (by fire or water, for example) required an accused person to walk over hot coals or hold a hot iron or be thrown into a river or lake. If the accused was not infected by the burn injury or did not drown (through God's intervention), though floating could also signal guilt, the accused would be found not guilty. Given the absurdity of the trials, the formal accusation, in effect, was the verdict. Trials by ordeal extended from 800 to the early 1200s and were displaced by the inquisitorial system in Europe and by jury trials in England in 1220.

In addition to seeking advice from God, judges throughout Europe used torture to try to find facts, through the confessions of the accused. In 1210, Roman codes permitted the torture of slaves. In the inquisitorial system, from about 1252, "the Inquisitors were primarily theologians concerned with the salvation of souls," a continuation of law's reliance on religion. Torture was part of the investigation.[3]

Judges, rather than accusers or victims, as in the past, presented charges against the accused person. Torture progressed in the ecclesiastical courts and Papal Inquisition. In 1252, Louis IX permitted torture in France "and the practice spread rapidly across secular courts of Europe" and lasted for six hundred years, but it did not appear as prominently in England or Denmark.[4] (From 1540 to 1640, England used torture in treason cases.)[5]

The judges reasoned that torture should be used to counter procedural defects. Though not reassuring, torture "was not applied in an arbitrary or capricious manner," according to Vogler. The torture in continental Europe "was a direct result of the rigorous method of proof demanded by the Roman-cannon method." That is, the standard of proof before a conviction would stand was "extraordinarily high," as a means to protect the accused against the secrecy of the process.[6]

The proof had to be "certain to sustain a conviction." Two eyewitnesses were required for a conviction to stand. ("A single witness is no witness at all.") Circumstantial evidence alone was never sufficient. According to Vogler, "The stringency of these seemingly humane requirements made it all but impossible for a conviction to be secured. Ironically, therefore, those operating the system felt obliged more and more to have recourse to torture in order to produce the necessary full proof."[7] Torture did not flourish in England because the English did not require the testimony of two witnesses to secure a conviction (except in treason cases).[8]

Judges directed the torture. In France, it consisted of the "rack, the iron horse, heavy weights, the strappado, forced drinking of water, roasting of the feet over a fire or the placing of painful objects in the shoes."[9] The strappado involved tying defendants' arms behind their backs and fastening their arms to a beam and then lifting or dropping them.

A magistrate or procedure was needed to counter the irrational methods used to resolve cases. Judges were an option, but the "most fundamental flaw" of the inquisitorial system was that "the roles of investigator and judge [were] within the same person," according to Vogler.[10] But, in a slightly different form today, that flaw exists in the adversarial system. Prosecutors influence, participate in, or oversee every investigation. While they are investigating and charging someone with a crime, they are also responsible for ensuring that the suspect receives every legal right. Moreover, modern prosecutors have a judicial role, in that their charging decisions determine the outcomes of most cases, given the prevalence of plea bargaining.[11]

The influence of judges eventually waned. From 1660 to 1800, grand juries in one English jurisdiction (Sussex) dismissed what seem to be, by today's practices, a large percentage of indictments (at that time, the prosecution's proposed charges): 11.5 percent of death-penalty-eligible property offenses and 17.3 percent of other property offenses; 14.9 percent of murder charges; 27.4 percent of infanticide charges; 25.8 percent of those for wounding; and 44.4 percent of those for rape.[12]

As its accusatorial system dissipated (the private-person prosecutor versus the accused person), England did not look to the well-established inquisitorial system on the continent because of its use of torture. The first documented appearance of adversarial practice, according to Professor Vogler, "was in the Old Bailey in London in the 1730s," and it presaged a trend toward "human rights" and open trials, with independent actors. In the past, evidence had come from defendants who made statements, jurors who investigated cases, and the ordeals. The newfound presence of accomplices and bounty hunters, as well as disinterested witnesses, required greater scrutiny of the trial.

Lawyers were preferable to torture, but their roles illustrate the haphazard origin of the system. The doctrine of "adversality," "in many ways, was inspired by the market, was pioneered by the men who represented the new capitalists and was imbued with the ideologies of the industrial revolution."[13] Prior to the introduction of lawyers, the criminal process in England "was as rights-free, authoritarian and nearly as brutal as its continental counterparts." The judge decreed the law and controlled the trial.[14] Except for the absence of torture, the prisoner in England was in no better position than a prisoner in continental Europe, in the inquisitorial system. The introduction of criminal defense lawyers in England represented evolving political ideals.

Lawyers helped accused people counter the expertise of solicitors (English lawyers), who were used by the prosecution, which could be a private party, the Bank of England, the Mint, the Treasury, or the Post Office.[15] (At the time, parties in civil cases could use solicitors.) Beginning in 1692, Parliament passed statutes that provided rewards for the apprehension and conviction of thieves, burglars, robbers, and other offenders.[16] Lawyers were needed to confront witnesses who received bounties for their testimony. Lawyers could also confront accomplices who testified in cases of "gang crimes" in return for leniency from the Crown.[17]

Lawyers stepped into a chaotic process. However, English governments did not devote the necessary "thought and resources to the problems of criminal investigation and prosecution in the pretrial phase."[18] As a result, "Adversary trial was the judges' response at the trial level to the dangers of the pretrial process," according to Professor John Langbein.[19]

Political maneuvering contributed to the introduction of lawyers. Toward the end of the English Civil War (1642–1651), the Parliamentarians beheaded Charles I in 1649. Following the Interregnum (1649–1660), the monarchy was restored with the ascension, in 1660, of Charles II, the son of Charles I.

The political class feared that Charles II, with no descendants, would be succeeded by his brother James, a Roman Catholic, who would ally England with France and Spain, Catholic countries. In what became known as the Popish Plot, Titus Oates, an inveterate liar and Catholic convert, falsely claimed a Catholic conspiracy to assassinate Charles II and reintroduce Catholicism into England. His lies led to the execution or death, while imprisoned, of over twenty innocent Jesuits. Tried for treason, the Jesuits were not entitled to defense lawyers.

The last conviction of the Jesuits occurred in 1681, the same year that Charles II dissolved Parliament. This "had the effect of channeling some of the factional strife from Parliament to the law courts, in the form of prosecutions for political crime."[20] Treason trials created the correct perception that innocent people, without lawyers, were being convicted and executed.

James, nonetheless, ascended to the throne in 1685 and ordered that Titus Oates be prosecuted for perjury. Oates was convicted and sentenced to life imprisonment (because execution was not authorized for perjury). When William and Mary, both Protestants, ascended to the throne in 1689 (after the Glorious Revolution of 1688–1689), Oates was pardoned and received a yearly pension. The Treason Trials Act of 1696 permitted defendants to have lawyers, who entered and eventually took control of what became known as the adversarial system.

The appearance of counsel in the Old Bailey, in London, was reported to have occurred in the late 1710s.[21] Lawyers became more prominent in the 1730s,[22] and this "was nothing short of a procedural revolution . . . [because] their presence in the trial produced immediate effects, not only in terms of the radical reorganisation of the procedure but also in the creation of a network of defence rights," according to Professor Vogler.[23]

Professor Langbein is similarly clear about the revolutionary effect of the introduction of lawyers. "We find the judges [in the 1730s] allowing the defendant to have the assistance of counsel at [felony] trial for the limited purposes of examining and especially cross-examining witnesses. This fateful step sent procedure down the path toward what would become the adversary criminal trial."[24]

The passage of the Prisoners' Counsel Act in 1836 allowed lawyer representation in every case. Spurred in part by an anti-death-penalty movement, the act permitted a full defense by lawyers, including pretrial representation and a right to view the depositions of prosecution witnesses.[25]

However, the presence of lawyers created two enormous problems, according to Langbein, the wealth effect and the combat effect, and they remain with us today. Along with the absence of an obligation to search for truth, they are primary reasons why innocent people continue to be convicted. Unlike in the inquisitorial system, where the government funds a neutral investigation, defendants in the adversarial system are responsible for their own defense. Vogler, too, reports that a "combative

style" emerged.[26] Defense counsel "relentlessly fought to evade the restrictions on them and to expand their field of operation."[27]

The new adversarial model subdued all the other participants in the
trial. Judges ceased asking questions of the witnesses. "The active role of
the questioning jury was also diminished by the presence of counsel."
The defendant was "effectively silenced." Vogler believes that "perhaps
the most revolutionary consequence of the intervention of counsel was
the establishment of a network of procedural rights."[28] Subsequently,
lawyers, who controlled the adversarial system and were expert technicians, placed procedure at the pinnacle of law, and the value of truth
diminished.

* * *

Given adversarial conditions—secret government investigations, lawyers' control over procedure, and plea bargaining as the method of case
resolution—the overall influence of juries and judges is now negligible.
Professor Sanjeev Anand concluded that "the one theme that prevails
throughout history is the growing passivity of the criminal jury trial."[29]
Perhaps the apex of the jury trial occurred over nine hundred years ago.
Prior to that time, the methods used to reach verdicts were ordeals,
combat (the accuser and accused, in armor, fighting each other with
batons, some with horns, like a tomahawk), and compurgation (defendants' finding people to swear they didn't commit a crime).[30]

"The most important event in the history of the criminal jury was the
abolition of the ordeal by edict of the Roman church in 1215," according to
Professor Roger D. Groot.[31] In 1215, the Fourth Lateran Council ordered
clerics not to participate in ordeals, such as blessing the water or irons
used to test the accused person. There was no immediate judicial response
and no method with which to resolve criminal accusations. As a result,
judges ordered "medial jury inquests." People accused of major crimes
were imprisoned, those accused of medium crimes were exiled, those accused of minor crimes were "placed under good-conduct pledges," and
the cases of other accused persons were left to the discretion of judges.[32]

From confusion following the Fourth Lateran Council in 1215, ban-
ning trial by ordeal, the English jury was born in 1220. A woman, Alice,
accused five men of crimes. There could be no resolution to the charges
against the men because Alice could not engage in combat with them to

determine whether they were guilty. Two of the men, who would otherwise be imprisoned indefinitely, "put themselves for good and ill . . . upon a verdict and the vills [village] say that they are thieves."[33]

In another case, Roger Wauding failed an inquest; that is, it looked like he was guilty. He should have had the opportunity to engage his accuser, William Smalwude, in combat. However, William, after having accused another person, had lost the combat with that person and, as a result, was hanged. Roger was left "heavily suspected" of a serious crime and facing indefinite imprisonment, with no way of obtaining a final decision. English justices offered him indefinite imprisonment or "the chance for an acquittal via a final jury verdict."

He opted for a jury verdict.[34] Roger "'puts himself upon his neighborhood for good and ill . . . so that if the neighborhood acquits him he is to be quit, if otherwise, he is to be convicted.'" Roger's case appears to be the first instance of a jury verdict, at least a verdict offered by the judges. Roger's fate is unclear. Four of the men Alice accused were hanged; one was "put on pledges."[35]

Through the mid-1100s, victims initiated prosecutions, but the task was taken over by public officials in the latter half of that century (twelfth). The roots of English juries (and twelve jurors) may extend to 1166, when King Henry II, in reforming the public prosecution system, decided "that twelve lawful men of each hundred, and four of each vill, should report to the royal justices or sheriffs those persons reputed to have committed certain serious crimes."[36]

In 1221 and 1222, a jury consisted of thirty-two people. Early jurors were selected from the neighborhood where the alleged crime had occurred. "Self-informing" jurors investigated what happened and reported back to the entire jury. Witnesses did not appear in the courtroom. Judges had no access to facts and were in no position to question jury verdicts.

In the 1300s, as today, accused people were allowed to challenge the seating of potential jurors, and they could exercise thirty-five peremptory challenges, a juror's exclusion for any reason, or dismiss a juror for cause, such as a prior relationship with a party.[37] Majority verdicts were allowed until 1376, when unanimity was required.[38]

By the 1400s, jurors came from outside the neighborhoods and a single jury was responsible for issuing verdicts in several cases. It became necessary for witnesses to appear in courtrooms and jurors to cease their investigations. In the late 1400s and early 1500s, jurors were more dependent on "evidence presented to them than on information they, themselves, had gathered," Professor Anand found. In the latter half of the 1700s, by which time lawyers controlled the trial, jurors were no longer permitted to rely on evidence they collected outside the courtroom.[39]

The cessation of investigations by juries and the subsequent silencing of juries and judges coincided with the rise of lawyers. Several factors lifted the lawyers. First, prosecution offices became more professional and market-based. Lawyers worked on behalf of prosecutors to counter the self-interests of bounty hunters who were hired to search for suspects. Defense lawyers were needed to confront bounty hunters and accomplices who provided evidence in return for pardons.

Second, lawyers used trials to influence political movements, such as antislavery. Third, as an alternative, according to Professor Vogler, the lawyers' "move into criminal law must be seen as an attempt to carve out new monopoly areas to replace those which had been so recently lost." The industrial revolution sprang up in northern England and was serviced by solicitors, as opposed to the barristers in London.[40] (Barristers are lawyers who appear in court; usually solicitors do not, but today solicitor advocates, who have additional training, do appear in court.) Fourth, the law of evidence arose in the 1700s, possibly to equalize new prosecution practices, and lawyers were needed to administer the new rules.[41]

The hope was to reveal "hidden truth," not for innocent people, but rather for the Crown. "More guilty verdicts were confidently predicted under the new procedure."[42] Instead, a truth averting, combat ethos emerged.[43] An English defense attorney, Henry Brougham, defended Queen Caroline against a charge of "adulterous intercourse" in 1820 and expressed the sentiment of a criminal defense lawyer: "'An advocate, in the discharge of his duty, knows, in the discharge of that office, but one person in the world, THAT CLIENT AND NONE OTHER. To save that client by all expedient means,—to protect that client at all hazards and costs to all other, and among other to himself,—is the highest and most unquestioned of his duties; and he must not regard the alarm—the torment—the destruction which he may bring upon any other.'"[44]

Professor Langbein describes the toll that Brougham's outlook took on the adversarial system. "Brougham's self-serving prattle became window dressing for a truth-be-damned standard . . . that served the economic self-interest of the bar. The more latitude lawyers obtained to affect the outcome, the greater would be the demand for lawyers' services . . . the greater would be the inducement for prosecutors to meet fire with fire by hiring lawyers of their own."[45]

The English public became enraged when they discovered that defense lawyers who knew their clients to be guilty alleged police corruption and attacked the character of prosecution witnesses. In one case, a lawyer reminded the jury "of the terrible consequences of convicting him [defendant] wrongfully" (referring to the Courvoisier case, from 1840, in which Charles Dickens objected to the lawyer's duplicity).[46]

Courvoisier, a valet, was convicted of killing his employer, a British aristocrat, Lord William Russell. Courvoisier confessed to having killed Russell, who had discovered Courvoisier's theft of silverware and demanded his resignation. In what is perhaps an early aberrant illustration of how forensic evidence is not available in many cases, Courvoisier claimed to be naked when he slit Russell's throat to prevent blood from being found on Courvoisier's clothes.[47] Courvoisier was hanged in front of an estimated thirty thousand people. Charles Dickens, nonetheless, wrote that he felt the "'large assemblage of my fellow-creatures to be . . . odious. . . . It was so loathsome, pitiful, and vile a sight, that the law appeared to be as bad as [Courvoisier], or worse; being very much the stronger, and shedding around it a far more dismal contagion.'"[48]

Lawyers who knowingly argued against the truth were thought to be engaged in "suspect advocacy."[49] The diminution of truth that their advocacy produced was a price for society to pay in its attempt to protect innocent people who were accused of crimes, according to the lawyers. Lawyers consolidated their authority in England in 1848, when, by statute, a prisoner obtained the right to silence. "These reforms finally completed the process which had been initiated a century before and solidified a form of adversariality with almost no pre-trial phase and in which the defendant remained largely silent," according to Vogler.[50]

The United States came to rely on due process protections and, like the other common law countries, did not develop a model through which to search for truth. In litigation, pretrial hearings are now required to determine whether the police obtained evidence through proper procedures. This requires more participation by investigators and lawyers and less by defendants and juries. It requires an examination of whether government investigators operated properly, not an inquiry into whether an accused person is innocent.

Silence and Falsity—Deterrents to Truth

The adversarial legal system became part of American society, Professor Johannes F. Nijboer wrote.[51] It is a "social system" that is "an integrated part of the American culture ... [and] a commercially organized profession ... [where] lawyers and experts dominate the scene."[52]

In praising the adversarial system, Professor Monroe H. Freedman, in 1998, wrote that "it consists of a core of basic rights that recognize and protect the dignity of the individual in a free society."[53] He found that "the right to counsel is 'the most precious' of rights, because it affects one's ability to assert any other right."[54]

Professor Freedman, who was one of the most prominent ethics experts in the legal profession before he died in 2015, believed that defense lawyers should be allowed to inject falsity into trials. In a 1966 law review article, cited by the Supreme Court,[55] and by seventeen other federal and state courts, including as recently as 2021,[56] he called this "the purposeful deception of the court" and considered it a benefit to society.[57] "The attorney functions in an adversary system based upon the presupposition that the most effective means of determining truth is to present to a judge and jury a clash between proponents of conflicting views," he wrote.[58]

However, Professor Freedman failed to credit sufficiently the historical point behind argumentation: people and societies engage in the unpleasantness of argumentation because they share the goal of finding the truth. Unless representing innocent people, defense attorneys do not search for truth. They try to conceal it. Presenting "conflicting views," the phrase used by Freedman, is different from what he advocated: "purposeful deception of the court." In making this point, he addressed what he called "the three hardest questions" and answered all of them in the affirmative.

1. Is it proper to cross-examine for the purpose of discrediting the reliability or credibility of an adverse witness whom you know to be telling the truth? [Yes]
2. Is it proper to put a witness on the stand when you know he will commit perjury? [Yes]
3. Is it proper to give your client legal advice when you have reason to
   believe that the knowledge you give him will tempt him to commit
   perjury? [Yes][59]

Freedman reasoned that clients will be more likely to communicate fully
if they believe their lawyers will use every means to help them. His three
"hard questions," however, are not difficult to answer if anyone purports
that untruth, the "purposeful deception of the court," somehow leads to
truth. With that mantra as our guide, we'd have only to calculate how
much lawyerly deception to allow. In the end, most people would probably not agree with his conclusion: "The lawyer is an officer of the court,
participating in a search for truth."[60]

In considering how lawyers currently think and act in this area (the
same as when Freedman wrote), the American Bar Association's *Model
Rules* do not prohibit lawyers from trying to undermine witnesses they
know to be truthful and accurate and arguing to judges and juries that
the witnesses are lying and inaccurate. The ABA's *Defense Function* is
a guide for criminal defense lawyers. Under a heading titled "Defense
Counsel's Tempered Duty of Candor," the standard provides, "It is not a
false statement for defense counsel to suggest inferences that may reasonably be drawn from the evidence."[61]

Thus, at trial, if a defense lawyer, during cross-examination, under-
mines a truthful and accurate witness/victim, perhaps by pointing out
in a case dependent on identification that the witness wears glasses,
the lawyer may argue to the judge and jury that the witness's testimony
should not be credited, despite knowing that the lawyer's client/defen-
dant did, in fact, assault the victim (because the client told the lawyer).
So long as a lawyer can discredit a witness sufficiently "to suggest inferences that may reasonably be drawn from the evidence," then the lawyer, according to the ABA, is not making a "false statement," despite
knowing that the inference the lawyer suggests is false. The ABA, the
most influential professional legal institution in America, is redefining

the common meaning of "false statement" so that it does not apply to lawyers who urge jurors and judges to adopt inferences that the lawyers know are false.

* * *

We have a legal system, as Professor Lloyd Weinreb describes, that transcends the lawyers' commercial interests identified by Professor Nijboer. Lawyers find emotional and professional sustenance in their centrality within the system and are permitted knowingly to project falsity onto jurors and judges. "For all their praise of the adversary system, it serves no one so much as the lawyers, whom it glorifies," wrote Weinreb.[62] "In most instances, the canons of ethics provide a shelter of euphemisms that allow lawyers to evade the hard questions with which adversary process confronts them. The questions are so hard because the process imposes on lawyers a standard of behavior that is certainly not right and only with blinkered vision appears to be good."[63]

Seemingly the only workers employed specifically to conceal the truth, the lawyers may lack the peace of mind that comes from openness and honesty. As a result, they may exalt deception and secrecy, normally soul-crushing behaviors, as a form of professional esteem.[64] Secrecy in litigation may represent control and power, in that no other professional possesses it to the extent lawyers do.[65] In criminal cases, lawyers' clients do not have to testify[66] or present any evidence,[67] and they are entitled to have their juries told as much.[68]

Lawyers are comfortable applying procedures, but they have little expertise in creating knowledge, such as searching for facts as a method to find the truth. The Supreme Court, for example in *Taylor v. Kentucky* (1978), described how the umbrella of due process protects the rights of criminal defendants. "While use of the particular phrase 'presumption of innocence' ... may not be constitutionally mandated, the Due Process Clause of the Fourteenth Amendment must be held to safeguard 'against dilution of the principle that guilt is to be established by probative evidence and beyond a reasonable doubt.'"[69]

This broad statement about a procedural requirement appears lofty, but it does not help to measure how many innocent and guilty people are freed through the various procedures mandated by the Court's interpretation of the Constitution. It does not implore anyone to find the truth. We are well past the time, as two scholars wrote, when we should consider how "systems work in practice, [rather] than in how they are supposed to work, as laid down in law and acts of Parliament."[70] What has the adversarial system done to lawyers, innocent people, and society?

In England, where the adversarial system originated, the right to silence has eroded. An adverse inference will be attached to an accused person who declines to testify at trial. In criticizing the English procedure, one commentator, Gregory W. O'Reilly, provided a conventional view of the American adversarial system. "The right to silence is an essential element of the accusatorial system of justice. It prevents the operation of the engine which drives the inquisitorial system—the power to require, encourage, or force individuals to respond to government questioning. By adopting the use of adverse inferences, England has curtailed the right to silence, replaced it with a duty to talk, and moved back toward an inquisitorial system. This trade of tangible liberty for the illusion or symbol of security will transform not only the criminal justice system, but also the character of the relationship between the citizen and the state."[71]

To clarify, the *accusatorial* trial in England, referenced by Mr. O'Reilly, existed from 800 to 1200, when victims carried the burden of accusing defendants. This was replaced by the "formless" *altercation* trial, from the 1400s to the early 1700s. Jurors could ask questions of the parties. "Altercation trials had a wandering quality that resembled ordinary discourse—the judge often questioned the participants, examining and cross-examining them, to fill out the testimony they volunteered. . . . The assumption . . . [was] that if the accused was innocent he ought to be able to demonstrate it for the jury by the quality and character of his reply to the prosecutor's evidence."[72] The *adversarial* trial, to which Mr. O'Reilly was presumably referring, came next and became firmly established in the 1730s.

As O'Reilly demonstrated, there is in America antipathy toward the inquisitorial system and its methods, despite little or no evidence that the adversarial system is superior. Inquisitorial is usually described as a process where "the conduct and control of a procedure is primarily the responsibility of a public, magisterial official, a judge who is committed to neither side, but is positioned, as it were, at the center."[73] Professor

David Alan Sklansky described the lack of substance in the arguments against the inquisitorial system.

> Anti-inquisitorialism is a broad and enduring theme of American criminal procedure. . . . A lengthy tradition in American law looks to the Continental, inquisitorial system of criminal adjudication for negative guidance about our own ideals. Avoiding inquisitorialism is taken to be a core commitment of our legal heritage. . . . All of this could be excused if there were some standard account of what makes inquisitorial process so objectionable. But there is not.[74]

With lawyers in charge of the adversarial system, they should have a greater responsibility to confront the innocent-person-conviction problem. They obtained control over the evidence, "and the questioning of witnesses was eventually wrestled from the other participants in the trial, both judge and jury, by the lawyers," Professor Anand concluded. Jurors became "bystanders," and when "judges lost the ability to detect jury error, they attempted to prevent it by giving more detailed jury instructions and by developing complex exclusionary rules of evidence. Indeed, this legacy of often confusing and counterintuitive jury instructions and rules of evidence is one that remains with us to this very day."[75]

Standards such as the presumption of innocence and proof beyond a reasonable doubt are used to ameliorate the errors arising from adversarial procedures or conditions. These include the incorrect verdicts emanating from investigations imbued with tunnel vision, death penalties that induce false guilty pleas, and the absence of methods through which innocent people can distinguish themselves from those who are guilty. Often unable to find exonerating facts, the adversarial system has relied on lawyers' cross-examination of witnesses at trial, and this has led to an enormous amount of falsity in the legal system, with little or no evidence that the falsity leads to truth.

5

Alone with No Evidence

Scientific testing is an enormous advantage in helping to find the truth, but few legal cases produce evidence that can be tested. Used first in 1989 to help exonerate a man convicted of rape, DNA testing is reliable, but available in only a small number of cases.[1] The U.S. Bureau of Justice Statistics found, "In 2005, 86 laboratories reported completing about 14,000 DNA requests for cases where no suspect had been identified. Ninety laboratories reported analyzing about 25,000 requests from cases that year where a suspect had been identified."[2]

For the same year, the Federal Bureau of Investigation reported 1,390,695 violent crimes and 10,166,159 property crimes.[3] Though there were probably more DNA tests conducted than those noted in the study and more crimes than reported by the FBI, the data from these sources indicate that DNA testing was relevant in approximately 39,000 out of a total of 11,556,854 reported crimes, or only 0.337 percent of reported crimes (3.37 of every 1,000 reports).[4]

Even evidence that can be scientifically tested can be mischaracterized when the defense does not have the resources to challenge the law enforcement personnel who collected or testified about the evidence. In 2012, the FBI started a longitudinal investigation into the trial testimony of its agents on forensic tests they conducted in the 1980s and 1990s. The *Washington Post* spurred the investigation when it reported "that flawed forensic evidence involving microscopic hair matches might have led to the convictions of hundreds of potentially innocent people. Most of those defendants never were told of the problems in their cases."[5] By 2014, an FBI review of the first 160 cases showed that nearly every case included "flawed forensic testimony," according to the *Post*.[6]

The FBI then stopped reviewing cases, and resumed only after an inspector general report criticized the FBI and Justice Department about another investigation from the mid-1990s. The Justice Department then ordered the FBI to review the evidence from 2,600 convictions. "The inspector general found in that probe that three defendants were executed and a fourth died on death row in the five years it took officials to reexamine 60 death-row convictions that were potentially tainted by agent misconduct, mostly involving the same FBI hair and fiber analysis unit now under scrutiny," according to the *Post*.[7] The main problem was that, prior to the introduction of DNA testing, FBI expert witnesses were testifying at trial that hair from a crime scene could be matched to a suspect when, in fact, such a match, without DNA testing, is impossible.

In 2015, the FBI reported on its investigation into its agents' testimony about hair evidence. From trial transcripts, the FBI concluded that at least 90 percent of the transcripts contained "erroneous statements" and that twenty-six of twenty-eight FBI agent-analysts testified erroneously or "submitted laboratory reports with erroneous statements."[8] The hair analysis was based on human eyesight. The analysts would testify that under a microscope the hair recovered from the crime scene, for example, matched, to a certain level of probability, the hair of the defendant. But human hair from different people often cannot be distinguished.

The FBI agents' testimony came from cases in forty-one states prior to 2000, when the FBI began routinely to use mitochondrial DNA to analyze hair samples. But the vast majority of innocent-person convictions from faulty hair analysis will probably never be known because the FBI investigation did not concern state crime laboratories, which employ hundreds of analysts who had been trained for over twenty-five years in the faulty methods used by the FBI.

Scientific Evidence Might Not Lead to Truth

In 1987, in rural Stoughton, Wisconsin, a twenty-eight-year-old mother of two was sexually assaulted in her home. On the bed where the assault occurred, the police found hair that apparently was not from the victim. From the victim's description of the suspect, the police, two years later, arrested Richard Beranek, who was facing sexual assault charges in another Wisconsin jurisdiction. After viewing a number of photos, including one of Beranek, the victim said she was nearly certain Beranek was the perpetrator. She then identified him in a lineup. Despite having no ties to the Stoughton community and the testimony at trial of six witnesses that he was six hundred miles away, in North Dakota, when the assault occurred, a jury found Beranek guilty, and a judge sentenced him to 243 years in prison.

The key forensic testimony in the case came from an FBI hair analyst, Wayne Oakes. Despite the FBI's knowledge at the time that hair analysis had limitations, Oakes testified in the Beranek case that one hair, "to a high degree of probability," was a "match" to Beranek's hair. The suspect's hair and Beranek's hair were "microscopically the same," Oakes testified. He also testified that only "rarely, extremely rarely" could he not distinguish two hairs. Oakes boasted that he had examined "billions" of hairs, which, during his 8.5 years with the FBI, would translate to at least 322,321 hairs per day, according to the *Capitol Times*, a newspaper in Wisconsin. Oakes claimed that a more senior analyst at the FBI confirmed the "match."[9]

Several years prior to the 1987 assault in Stoughton, at a trial in the same jurisdiction in Wisconsin (Dane County), a state crime laboratory analyst testified that hairs from the scene of a crime and on the victim in a rape/murder case from 1981 were "similar" to or "consistent" with (but not definitively) those of the defendant. That defendant was convicted and served twenty-nine years in prison, but DNA testing showed later that he was not the source of the hairs. He was exonerated and received $1.75 million from state and local governments in compensation for his nearly three decades in prison. The crimes were probably committed by his brother, who apparently admitted his culpability to a friend. But the brother was dead and cremated by the time of the DNA testing.

In 1991, a different Wisconsin crime laboratory analyst, in a different case, testified that the defendant's hair was "consistent" with hair that was found at the scene of a sexual assault. That defendant, who served over four years in prison, was exonerated in 1996, after DNA testing showed that the hair was not his. He received $109,000 from the state.

In 2015, the FBI concluded that, in the Beranek case (from Stoughton), the testimony of Oakes, the FBI analyst, contained "erroneous statements" and "exceeded the limits of science." In February 2016, Beranek's attorneys submitted a motion for a new trial. They alleged that DNA testing excluded the possibility that the hair and semen from the crime scene belonged to Beranek.

Prosecutors opposed the motion, arguing, "What hairs got tested for DNA and where they came from simply has not been proved to a degree that would allow this issue to overcome this jury's verdict." The prosecution contended that Oakes's testimony was not "vague, misleading, improper or erroneous."[10]

Common sense indicates that the prosecution's opposition to a new trial is unreasonable if the hair and semen were not from Beranek. But, in the U.S. adversarial system, convictions are extremely difficult to reverse because convicted defendants have to show that they likely would have been found not guilty if the jury had viewed the newly discovered evidence. The prosecutors in the Beranek case apparently reasoned that Oakes's testimony, even if erroneous, was adequately weighed by the jury because Oakes had also testified that "he cannot say with absolute scientific certainty that the questioned hair came from the defendant." Given the high standard for a new trial (a likelihood of a not-guilty verdict), the prosecution argument was legally sufficient despite coming from an apparently unreliable factual basis. Thus, despite the new scientific testing, which constituted a new fact (the hair and semen were not from Beranek), the prosecution could argue ethically that the conviction should not be overturned.

After the DNA testing showed that the hair did not come from Beranek, a judge overturned Beranek's conviction, which provided him the opportunity for a new trial. However, a different judge, in May 2018, at the prosecution's request, dismissed the charges against Beranek, though the victim continued to believe he was the assailant. Despite moving for dismissal, the prosecution asserted a "strong belief" in Beranek's guilt but wanted to spare the victim from testifying in a second trial.

The prosecution may have had a good point. Beranek's lawyers said that DNA testing of evidence at the crime scene "revealed a distinct male DNA profile that was not Mr. Beranek's." DNA testing excluded Beranek as the source of semen from underwear found in the basement of the victim's home. It seems unlikely the perpetrator, however, having committed a rape in the bed upstairs would leave his underwear in the basement before fleeing. (The DNA from the scene has not been connected to anyone.)

Shortly after she was assaulted, the victim described her attacker for an artist working for the police, but her photo and lineup identifications of Beranek did not occur until two years later. The artist's sketch of the attacker is strikingly similar to Beranek's appearance.[11] The sketch spurred the police in Chippewa County, over two hundred miles north of Stoughton, to suspect Beranek, who was at the time facing sexual assault charges in Chippewa County. On these charges, "Beranek was convicted and served time [ten years], including an assault on an 11-year-old girl and another on a 16-year-old girl whom Beranek found riding her bike near the Girl Scout camp where she worked," according to the Wisconsin Center for Investigative Journalism.[12]

At the time the prosecution moved to dismiss the charges against Beranek, it was preparing for a second trial. In that trial, it intended to introduce evidence of prior uncharged domestic violence and sexual assaults allegedly committed by Beranek. Usually, a defendant's prior crimes and alleged bad acts cannot be admitted into evidence (unless he testifies), except when they tend to show a motive, pattern, or opportunity in regard to the charges for which he is now on trial. (This is discussed at greater length in chapter 9, in the context of the trial of Harvey Weinstein, the former movie producer convicted of sexual assault in New York).

Like every defendant, Beranek, with the new plea of innocence, would be permitted to plead innocent and require the prosecution to search for exonerating facts. In a case like this, however, where alibi witnesses testified for Beranek, there would presumably not be much more the prosecution could do to find additional facts. Its obligation to investigate further would be limited. Moreover, in the first place, it is unlikely that Beranek would plead innocent because he would then have to detail for prosecutors his every movement on the night the victim in Stoughton was sexually assaulted, as well as his movements on the days before and following the assault. If his statement indicated the possibility that he was near Stoughton on the night of the assault, he would increase substantially the risk of conviction.

That is, the jury, despite the testimony of six alibi witnesses, found that Beranek was, indeed, in Stoughton on the night of the assault. An additional connection to Stoughton or the possibility that he could have been in Stoughton at the time of the sexual assault, obtained from his statements to investigators, followed by additional investigation, would deter or prevent a suspect or defendant in Beranek's situation from pleading innocent. Moreover, it is unlikely that any judge or appellate court would find the evidence insufficient given the victim's identification and any additional evidence that indicated Beranek could have been in Stoughton on the night of the assault. The new DNA evidence, that Beranek was not the source of the hair on the bed or the semen-stained underwear in the basement, could be outweighed by the testimony of the victim. In summary, forensic evidence, even DNA when it exists, is not nearly as dispositive in the resolution of cases as most people believe it is.

How Many Are Innocent?

The significant legal barriers that prevent the reversal of convictions mean that innocent people, once convicted, will likely never be exonerated. It is, therefore, critical to the reformation of the adversarial system to develop a method capable of exonerating innocent people *prior to trial*. For a 2014 study led by Sam Gross, a law professor at the University of Michigan, researchers analyzed all the death sentences in the United States from 1973 through 2004, a total of 7,482.[13] They compared the number of people sentenced to death with the number of them who were exonerated or who were statistically likely to be exonerated. (Given that exonerations occur years or decades after a conviction, some of those on death row would presumably be exonerated following the conclusion of the study.)

Professor Gross and his colleagues believed their study was relatively reliable because death-penalty cases receive the most attention and resources and, therefore, are more likely than other cases to produce an exoneration after a conviction:

> Almost all [death sentences] are based on convictions after jury trial, and even the handful of capital defendants who plead guilty are then subject to trial-like-sentencing hearings, usually before juries. All death sentences are reviewed on appeal; almost all are reviewed repeatedly. With few exceptions, capital defendants have lawyers as long as they remain on death row. Everyone, from the first officer on the scene of a potentially capital crime to the Chief Justice of the United States, takes capital cases more seriously than other criminal prosecutions—and knows that everybody else will do so as well. And everyone from defense lawyers to innocence projects to governors and state and federal judges is likely to be particularly careful to avoid the execution of innocent defendants.[14]

Defense advocates are much more likely "to pursue any plausible post-conviction claim of innocence" and courts "are much more likely to consider and grant such a claim if the defendant is at risk of execution. As a result, false convictions are far more likely to be detected among those cases that end in death sentences than in any other category of criminal convictions."[15]

The researchers found that 4.1 percent of defendants who remain under death sentences will be exonerated. They reached two additional important conclusions. First, DNA testing will not significantly reduce the number of innocent-person convictions. "One change, however, is unlikely to have much impact: the advent of DNA identification technology. DNA evidence is useful primarily in rape rather than homicide investigations. Only 13% of death row exonerations since 1973 (18 of 142) [12.7 percent] resulted from postconviction DNA testing, so the availability of preconviction testing will have at most a modest effect on that rate."[16]

Remarkably, while sexual assault and, to a lesser extent, homicide are the cases most likely to produce DNA evidence, those cases compose a miniscule number of all cases. The last year the Department of Justice, when calculating the number of arrests per year, included *forcible rape* as a separate category was 2012 (because different agencies around the country classified sexual assault in many different ways). In 2012, the number of arrests was nearly 12 million. The number of arrests for "murder and non-negligent manslaughter" was 11,080, and the number for forcible rape was 18,100, for a total of 29,180 homicide and rape arrests—or only 2.4 percent of all arrests.[17] While forensic evidence is prominent in the mind of the public, virtually all cases are resolved mainly through the reporting or testimony of witnesses (about nonforensic matters).

Second, "With an error rate at trial over 4%, it is all but certain that several of the 1,320 defendants executed since 1977 were innocent," Gross and his colleagues concluded.[18] They believed that the 4.1 percent finding is probably too low. "Capital defendants who are removed from death row but not exonerated—typically because their sentences are reduced to life imprisonment—no longer receive the extraordinary level of attention that is devoted to death row inmates."[19]

The irony is that innocent people "are much less likely to be exonerated than if they had remained on death row." The researchers concluded that "the proportion of death-sentenced inmates who are exonerated understates the rate of false convictions among death sentences because the intensive search for possible errors is largely abandoned once the threat of execution is removed."[20] That is, appellate courts may affirm convictions for murder but replace the death sentences with the next most serious sentence, life imprisonment. (Only defendants who are responsible for the death of a person are eligible for a sentence of death, according to the Supreme Court. "Our concern here," the Court wrote in *Kennedy v. Louisiana*, in 2008, "is limited to crimes against individual persons. We do not address, for example, crimes defining and punishing treason, espionage, terrorism, and drug kingpin activity, which are offenses against the State. As it relates to crimes against individuals, though, the death penalty should not be expanded to instances where the victim's life was not taken.")[21]

The results of the Gross study were consistent with prior estimates of innocence scholars, possibly with one exception. In 2012, Professor Marvin Zalman estimated a wrongful conviction rate of 0.05 to 1 percent and concluded that this translates into two thousand innocent-person incarcerations per year.[22] Professor Zalman recognized the limitations of his estimate given that society is only beginning to confront the innocent-person conviction problem. "At present, the idea of wrongful convictions is too challenging to the legitimacy of criminal justice, and the practical problems are too daunting, for general data collection by the federal or state governments to be minimally plausible," he wrote.[23] In a 2021 article, Zalman and Professor Robert Norris, based on a review of studies concerning the innocent-person conviction rate, concluded that "the estimates that appear the most empirically sound seem to suggest that the rate, at least among certain types of felonies, may reasonably fall in the range of 3 to 6 percent."[24]

One of the other most significant studies on innocent-person convictions was reported in 2007 by Michael Risinger, a professor of law at Seton Hall. Professor Risinger found a "3.3% minimum factual wrongful conviction rate for capital rape-murders in the 1980s," with a possible 5 percent wrongful conviction rate.[25] In 2010, professors Jon B. Gould and Richard A. Leo found that "the several studies on this question cap estimates [of innocent-person convictions] at around 3% to 5% of convictions."[26]

In a recent significant study, released in 2018, three researchers, Charles E. Loeffler, Jordan Hyatt, and Greg Ridgeway, surveyed, over five months in 2015 and 2016, the people who know with certainty whether an individual case produced an innocent-person conviction: state inmates who had been convicted and sentenced to prison. The researchers administered 2,846 surveys; the response rate was 94.1 percent, "with 2,678 complete or partially complete responses received."[27]

The researchers realized that they could not verify whether the inmates were responding truthfully. To test the inmates' veracity, they asked them how many times they had been previously convicted and wrongfully convicted.[28] The researchers concluded that the inmates were forthcoming. "Limitations aside, with a clear majority of inmates indicating complete responsibility for their most recent convictions and a substantial minority indicating partial responsibility for their most recent conviction, these estimates, like those reported previously . . . [in an earlier study] dispel the widespread misconception that all or even most prisoners claim that they are innocent."[29]

The researchers found "that, in a general population of prisoners, two-thirds of prisoners self-report being correctly convicted, a third of prisoners self-report being wrongfully convicted, with 8% making a claim of factual innocence, and 6% making a consistent and plausible claim. We consider this to be an upper bound on the rate of factual innocence within this population and the aggregate of offense-specific point estimates ranging from a low of 2% in DUI convictions to a high of 40% in rape convictions."[30]

The researchers, in concluding, warned that understanding of the innocent-person-conviction problem may be rudimentary because most of the studies in the area have focused on "exonerations in mostly capital cases. Efforts by criminologists and other social scientists to examine the frequency and predictors beyond this population, including general prison populations, non-custodial felony caseloads, as well as misdemeanor convictions, have been more limited and have left scholars and policymakers with an incomplete picture of the extent of the potential problem in this wider population."[31]

The estimates of innocent-person convictions may be too low because convictions for crimes less serious than rape and murder do not receive significant attention or resources. As the National Registry of Exonerations explained, we cannot see the innocent-person convictions emanating from guilty pleas, which produce at least 97 percent of all convictions:

Innocent defendants who plead guilty have an exceptionally hard time convincing anybody of their innocence, or even getting a hearing. Judges, prosecutors, police officers, journalists, friends, lawyers, even innocence organizations are all less likely to believe in the innocence of a defendant who pleads guilty. Procedural obstacles prevent these defendants from filing appeals, petitioning for consideration of new evidence, obtaining DNA testing. And innocent defendants who plead guilty almost always get lighter sentences than those who are convicted at trial—that's why they plead guilty—so there is less incentive to pursue exoneration. In many cases, they would rather put the injustice behind them than engage in prolonged legal battles to prove their innocence.[32]

The registry found that, as of 2015, "drug crimes comprise 40% of all guilty-plea cases (105/261)" (from a total of 1,702 exonerations). These statistics are misleading—but not intentionally so—because, as the registry reported, "since early 2014 there have been 71 drug exonerations in Harris County (Houston), Texas, and the defendants pled guilty in every one of them."[33]

What happened is that Harris County tested the alleged drugs *after* the defendants pleaded guilty and found that the substances tested were not illegal drugs. If this were "done across the country we would no doubt learn of thousands of unknown false drug convictions. And of course hundreds of thousands of additional defendants plead guilty every year to avoid pre-trial detention in non-drug cases. It's anyone's guess how many are innocent, but judging from drug pleas in Harris County it's a lot," according to the registry.[34]

Identifying the number and percentage of innocent-person convictions helps to understand the social costs extracted by them, as well as whether a legal system should be reformed. In 2020, the U.S. Bureau of Justice Statistics estimated that "6,410,000 persons were held in prisons or jails or were on probation or parole in 2018."[35] The number of people incarcerated in state and federal prisons was 1,430,800 at the end of 2019.[36] (Though the studies refer to 2018 correctional populations and 2019 incarcerations, they are used here for illustration because they are recent government studies, which are not usually available simultaneously.) Using an innocent-person conviction rate of 4 percent, this translates into 256,400 innocent people under supervision, with 57,232 of them in prison.

* * *

Data on the number of innocent-person convictions in the inquisitorial system are sparse, and there appear to be no significant studies, clearinghouses, or government agencies that report on such convictions. Many European experts, scholars, and members of the public believe that innocent-person convictions occur only rarely. The inquisitorial system generally uses professional judges, not jurors, as final decision makers; Europeans believe that the outcomes in their system, where investigations are controlled and verdicts are issued finally by the judges, are more accurate than the outcomes of cases in America's adversarial system.[37] In the Netherlands, for instance, "well into the 1990's, only two serious miscarriages of justice—one in 1923 and one in 1984, both wrongful convictions for murder that ended in exonerations—were generally known," according to Professor Chrisje Brants. Between 2002 and 2010, five cases that were reopened resulted in exonerations.[38]

Between 1991 and 2018, Italy, with a hybrid legal system, part inquisitorial and part adversarial, recorded 153 "wrongful convictions." But these included defendants who were "legally innocent" (which might include reversals of convictions of guilty people because of errors by government officials), making the number of factually innocent-person convictions difficult to know.[39]

Germany, in 2017, conducted approximately 720,000 trials, but only 1,300 of them were the result of cases that had been reopened after a prior conviction.[40] A study from 2019 found thirty-one wrongful *sentences* of imprisonment, from twenty-nine cases in Germany from 1990 to 2016. (Convictions that did not result in imprisonment were not studied.) These were cases in which "the proceedings had been reopened and the convicted persons had been acquitted by another court," according to researchers. In that study, "eyewitness misidentification was a leading source for wrongful convictions in Germany (17 cases, 45.8% of all cases)."[41] Other leading contributors were false confessions (five exonerees) and incorrect expert testimony (twelve exonerees). (There can be more than one contributor in each case.)

France, in 2014, revised its penal code to provide greater opportunity for defendants to challenge their convictions, but the effectiveness of the revision is unknown. In France, "The remaining ground for revision [reversal of a conviction] is the existence of a new fact or an element unknown to the court at the time of the initial proceedings, of such a nature as to establish the convicted person's innocence or to give rise to doubt about his guilt. The legislature intended judges to no longer require 'serious doubt.' However, experts question whether judges will comply with this intention of the legislature," according to two researchers.[42] "There is, unfortunately, currently [2020] too little case law publicly accessible to make statements . . . on how the judges of the CRR [Court for Revision and Reopening] interpret the question of doubt."[43] The French revision of 2014 does permit applicants (defendants) "to ask the public prosecutor to carry out the investigative measures that seem necessary to bring to light a new fact or an unknown element before filing a request for revision," according to the researchers.[44]

* * *

In the adversarial system, some may contest whether the 4.1 percent innocent-person conviction rate is correct. Others who conclude that it is correct may believe that the number of innocent people who are under the supervision of a parole or probation officer or incarcerated in a prison or jail is relatively small in comparison with the number of guilty people who are convicted. Regardless of one's perspective, it is a profound condition of society when a large number of innocent people are socially incapacitated or imprisoned. How large must that number be before change is undertaken?

Regardless, as we will see next, the adversarial system appears to have reached a point where it is no longer capable of reducing significantly the number or percentage of innocent-person convictions without increasing the number of guilty people who are acquitted. For example, new identification procedures may prevent eyewitnesses from selecting innocent suspects, but the procedures may also prevent the eyewitnesses from selecting suspects who are guilty.[45] This points to an urgent need to find a method that can more effectively exonerate the innocent while not acquitting the guilty.

PART II

A Deficient Adversarial System

6

Convictions without Truth

An innocent person's most valuable commodity is an exonerating fact, which is most discoverable during the investigation, at the beginning of a case or, at least, at some point prior to trial. In the inquisitorial system, investigators or magistrates are central and expect that their collection of facts prior to trial will resolve cases. Their inquiry must be more neutral and searching because they do not assume that a suspect or defense lawyer will ever be in a better position to find exonerating facts or that a trial will lead to truth. In contrast, adversarial investigators look at the evidence through a more narrow frame. They ask whether the evidence provides probable cause to arrest a suspect or will be sufficient to convict the suspect through a trial or guilty plea and sentencing.

The adversarial culture fosters an uncooperative combat ethos in police, prosecutors, and defense lawyers and does not often emphasize looking at evidence from the perspective of a suspect. The inquisitorial system does. Professor Geraldine Szott Moohr provides an apt comparison of the adversarial and inquisitorial systems and their different emphases and approaches to the collection of facts: "Truth in the adversarial system is a by-product of a competitive process in which the parties put forward evidence and deflect the evidence of the other. In contrast, continental countries adopted an investigatory approach to criminal matters in which governments utilized the state's power to carry out an inquiry. . . . The ultimate issue of guilt or innocence is determined through an official inquiry that is initiated and conducted by the state. In this system, the trial is most accurately characterized as a continuation of the official investigation. The investigation, rather than the trial, is paramount."[1]

Comparing the U.S. adversarial system and the inquisitorial system in the Netherlands, two researchers concluded, "Although, we cannot authoritatively say that the differences in legal practices before and during trial lead to decidedly different outcomes, it is fairly obvious that post-trial justice is much tougher in the United States than the Nether-lands."[2] The *tougher* post-trial procedures in the United States mean that a conviction is unlikely to be reversed. This, in turn, means that even if both systems produce an equal number of innocent-person convictions, the investigation process in the United States should be more thorough and rigorous because the possibility of correcting an error or reversing a conviction later in a case is less likely.

The United States and other common law countries rely on proce-dures to resolve cases, even without knowing whether the procedures satisfy the purpose for which they were created. John Thibaut and Lau-rens Walker recognized in their 1975 book, *Procedural Justice: A Psycho-logical Analysis*, the absence of research on whether due process meets societal goals. "It is indeed surprising that to date procedural justice has not been the subject of much, if any, social science research. . . . Legal practitioners and scholars have generally recognized the great impor-tance of procedural justice but, curiously, very little progress has been made toward developing a conceptual framework."[3]

They wrote that "legal scholars have managed only *ad hoc* investi-gations, perhaps because they have lacked the integrative and analytic concepts."[4] This may have been a polite way of saying that lawyers are not capable of or interested in conducting the research that could quan-tify the value of procedures or lead to the discovery of alternatives to procedures. Since Thibaut and Walker wrote, in at least one area, social scientists have contributed to a greater understanding of misidentifi-cations by eyewitnesses, perhaps the leading contributor to innocent-person convictions.[5]

What to Do about Eyewitnesses

When eyewitnesses mistakenly identify an innocent person, the most effective way for that person to counter them is to find additional, more accurate witnesses. "Under the adversarial model legal proceedings are essentially contests between equivalent rivals. A contest is only a real contest if it is played in a fair way and the essential feature of fair play is the formal equality of the contestants," according to Hans Crombag, of the University of Sussex.[6] But most defendants have few resources, and many are incarcerated while awaiting trial. As a result, they can counter eyewitnesses only with cross-examination, an insufficient method of exoneration.

Introduced earlier, the following case illustrates the danger of a one-eyewitness-identification case in which a defendant does not have resources. A clerk was working alone in a decrepit convenience store in Brooklyn, not the glassy, well-lit, cameras-everywhere 7-Eleven stores or mega gas stations along main roads and highways. This was a modest store, about the size of a living room in a one-story ranch house, packed with dry goods and nonperishables, no cameras, the kind of place offering snacks and canned food that induce poor health.

The robbery was simple and effective. A white man with a gun (no mask) entered the store when no one else was inside and demanded that the clerk, a white Hispanic man, about the same age as the perpetrator, give him the money from the cash register. The clerk handed over the money and the robber fled.

New York City Police detectives collected from their files at the local police precinct photos of people who had been arrested previously and resembled the description provided by the clerk. The detectives prepared a photo array, which is one page of six photos, three across the top and three on the bottom. (Police today often enter the characteristics of the suspect into a computer database to try to identify a suspect as well as to find photos with which to complete the array.)[7] The clerk viewed the array and said one of the photos depicted the man who robbed him.

The detectives found that man and placed him in a lineup with five similar-looking men standing side by side in a row. The clerk watched them from behind a door with a one-way window and selected as the robber the same man he had identified in the photo array. At trial, the clerk's recitation of the robbery and his identification of the defendant in the courtroom constituted the only substantive evidence in the case.

The defendant, who had been arrested previously and convicted of at least one robbery, did not make a statement to the detectives. Rejecting a plea offer, he demanded a trial, but did not testify. If he had testified, the judge would have probably allowed cross-examination about some of his prior convictions, possibly even the prior robbery. It seems inevitable that some jurors will draw an inference of guilt on a current case from a prior conviction for a similar crime. This makes testifying very risky for any defendant with a prior conviction, even if innocent on the current case.

In addition to the defense attorney's cross-examination of the clerk, the defendant called his mother to testify. This probably turned out to be a strategic error. "'Family alibis' are typically seen as weak evidence by jurors under the theory that almost anyone should be able to get blood relatives to lie for them. They . . . are something like indirect character evidence—the value of the evidence is based largely on how impressive or unimpressive the family members are as people more than precisely what they say," wrote Professor Robert P. Mosteller, a former defense lawyer.[8]

In a 2014 study, Professor Jon B. Gould and three other researchers concluded that "our results indicate that family witnesses are associated with erroneous convictions. Family witnesses are among the weakest defense witnesses, usually only providing character evidence or an inadequate alibi. Indeed, defense attorneys may turn to family members in those cases in which there is little additional evidence to offer on the defendant's behalf, or when the attorney has failed to fully investigate other potential witnesses."[9]

In the robbery case, the defendant's mother said he was home with her, watching television, at about the time the robbery occurred. Witnesses' memories of mundane events in the past, liking watching television, can be unreliable, fragmented, or fabricated. The mother said she remembered the day because she asked him to go out and buy cigarettes for her, which he did, she testified. Nonetheless, the jury found her son guilty. About a month later, and moments before the sentencing hearing, the defense lawyer told me his client had admitted committing other robberies, but said that his client told him he had not committed this one. (Later, an appellate court affirmed the conviction.)

Reliable Science: When Should It Be Applied?

Innocent defendants in these types of cases need to find independent witnesses. The problem of mistaken identification is so significant that the top courts in New Jersey (2011),[10] Hawaii (2012),[11] Massachusetts (2015),[12] and New York (2017)[13] concluded that the defense, where eyewitness testimony is crucial, should be allowed to introduce into evidence social science research about the difficulty people have recognizing each other and/or require judges to give jurors instructions about the difficulty witnesses have identifying someone of a different race ("cross-racial identification"). But the value of science depends on how applicable it is to the specific witnesses and facts in a case.

In 2019, federal judges from the Third Circuit (Pennsylvania, New Jersey, Delaware, and the Virgin Islands), professors, and practitioners (nineteen total members) issued a report on eyewitness identifications and described what they believe research shows about cross-racial identification: "Researchers agree that there is generally a disparity in accuracy between identifications of a person of a different race, and those of a person of the same race. But that is not to say that, in *all* circumstances, a cross-race identification is less likely to be accurate. . . . Indeed, researchers have concluded that the prevalence of the effect can vary depending on other estimator variables—such as the amount of time that the witness could observe the perpetrator (exposure duration) and the length of time between the witnessed event and the identification procedure (retention interval)."[14]

In any type of case, of course, scientific findings should be valid and applicable if they are to be admitted into evidence at trials. Scientists recognize "foundational validity and validity as applied."[15] Foundational validity, what may be referred to as *general conclusions*, refers to studies that can be repeated and their results reproduced, and which are accurate to a certain level of confidence, as when DNA scientists conclude that they can, with near certainty, connect a spot of blood to a particular person. Different scientists conducting a similar study will find the same result, that DNA can be used to identify people.[16] However, the lack of proof of the applicability (validity as applied) of scientific findings (general conclusions) to a particular case—to specific victims, defendants, and evidence—usually means that the findings should not be introduced into evidence.

The concepts of validity and reliability (repeatedly obtaining the same result) are clear and satisfying when evidence from a particular case is collected, such as blood from a victim that is allegedly smeared on the shirt of a suspect and then subjected to DNA testing, which is recognized as having foundational validity. In this scenario, trial judges should find that the DNA testing of the blood from the shirt is a reliable method through which to determine its source and allow the blood and the results from the testing of it into evidence at trial.[17] General DNA science is, thus, also valid as applied to this specific case. In legal terminology, the blood and the methods surrounding the collection and testing of the blood are *relevant* (evidence) in determining whether the defendant committed the alleged violent crime.

In federal courts, both foundational validity and validity as applied (to each particular case) are required before evidence can be admitted into a trial.[18] *Kumho Tire v. Carmichael* was a Supreme Court case (1999) in which the plaintiffs alleged that a defective tire caused an automobile collision and the death of a family member. The Court upheld a trial judge's rejection of the plaintiffs' expert on tires because the expert, Carlson, an engineer, could not sufficiently link a possible defect in the tire to the death of the family member. The Court explained:

> For one thing, and contrary to respondents' [plaintiffs'] suggestion, the specific issue before the court was not the reasonableness *in general* of a tire expert's use of a visual and tactile inspection to determine whether overdeflection had caused the tire's tread to separate from its steel-belted carcass. Rather, it was the reasonableness of using such an approach, along with Carlson's particular method of analyzing the data thereby obtained, to draw a conclusion regarding *the particular matter to which the expert testimony was directly relevant.* . . . As we said before . . . the question before the trial court was specific, not general. The trial court had to decide whether this particular expert had sufficient specialized knowledge to assist the jurors "'in deciding the particular issues in the case.'"[19]

Even if a general conclusion is valid, such as that some tires like the one in the *Kumho Tire* case are defective (which is like concluding that some eyewitnesses are mistaken) or even that the specific tire in the case was defective, the conclusion cannot be admitted into evidence unless it helps the jury decide whether the defect contributed to the collision and death. One may infer that a defective tire led to the death, but there must be something more tangible, such as testimony or other evidence, that proves a connection between the defective tire and the death in a specific case before a general conclusion will be allowed into a trial.

In contrast, the state courts' decisions were novel because they allowed general findings to be admitted into trials without proof that the findings (about identification abilities of people, from studies) apply to specific witnesses in a case. The studies on eyewitness identification show that people are less able to identify someone whose race is different from their race compared with someone whose race is the same.[20] That conclusion is even less tied to a specific criminal case because, unlike in *Kumho Tire*, in which the expert witness believed there was a defect in the tire, there is no expert in a criminal case to testify to a *defect* in an eyewitness's perception or that, if the witness has a perceptual defect or impairment (poor eyesight), it contributed to the witness's misidentification of the defendant. Short of subjecting eyewitnesses to batteries of psychological or medical tests before they testify, we cannot know whether the general conclusions (from studies) about the difficulty people have identifying each other apply to the eyewitnesses in a particular case.

Unlike the Supreme Court in *Kumho Tire*, however, the state courts noted above do not require that general conclusions about identification ability be tied to an eyewitness before the conclusions (from the prior studies) may be presented to a jury in a specific case. Indeed, at the request of the defense, the state courts require that the general conclusions *must* be introduced into a case, often through the trial judge's instructions to jurors (despite there being no validity as applied to the eyewitnesses). This means that, without a tangible connection to a particular eyewitness, the general conclusions on identification are not as relevant or valuable as a general conclusion that can be tied to a witness or an issue in a specific case, such as through expert testimony about the value of DNA testing because blood, for example, was found on the defendant. In *Kumho Tire*, a more authoritative expert witness might have been able to conclude, to a certain level of confidence, that a defective tire did contribute to the death of the family member. Unlike such testimony or similar testimony in a DNA case—where expert witnesses tie the defective tire to the death or the blood to the victim—in the kinds of cases described by the state courts there are no expert witnesses or evidence to connect the general conclusions from studies to the eyewitnesses in a case.

Consider an insanity defense, where general conclusions are applied directly to a case (validity as applied). When a defendant pleads insanity, psychiatrists for the defense and prosecution will be asked to examine the defendant and testify as expert witnesses. They might testify about medical studies on brain chemistry and how the use of drugs affects thinking and behavior. Then, they will apply the general conclusions of the studies to opine for the jurors on whether the defendant, who was under the influence of drugs, was suffering from a mental disease or defect (one of the elements of insanity) when the defendant committed the alleged criminal act.

In contrast, and in summary, the state courts (which were concerned with cross-racial identification) now allow general conclusions about identification ability (*error* from the defense perspective) to be presented to juries without expert testimony on whether the general conclusions (from the prior studies) apply to the perceptual abilities of a particular eyewitness. This, the admission of general evidence that cannot be applied to a specific witness and case (no validity as applied), has the potential to lead the defense and prosecution to classify eyewitnesses and defendants according to their race or skin color. Defense lawyers will argue that defendants' race or color makes them sufficiently different from the race or color of the eyewitnesses so as to enable the defendants to receive the benefit of a judge's instructions to a jury on the difficulty of cross-racial identification. Recall that, in *Plessy v. Ferguson*, the Supreme Court, in 1896, in upholding the separate-but-equal doctrine, found that a man who was "one eighth African blood," according to his petition to the Court, may be disqualified from sitting in a train car reserved for white people.[21] The Court's approach, which involved a racial measurement, has been almost universally discredited.

Nonetheless, New York's highest court (Court of Appeals), in 2017, permitted judges and juries to measure the *race* of defendants and witnesses solely by looking at the color of their skin:

We reach the following holding: in a case in which a witness's identification of the defendant is at issue, and the identifying witness and defendant appear to be of different races, a trial court is required to give, upon request, during final instructions, a jury charge on the cross-race effect, instructing (1) that the jury should consider whether there is a difference in race between the defendant and the witness who identified the defendant, and (2) that, if so, the jury should consider (a) that some people have greater difficulty in accurately identifying members of a different race than in accurately identifying members of their own race and (b) whether the difference in race affected the accuracy of the witness's identification.[22]

The New York court did not provide any guidance on how to define *race* or how to determine whether people are of different races.

The New Jersey, Hawaii, and New York courts did not express concern about racial stereotyping or categorization. Neither did the Massachusetts Supreme Court, but it recognized the near impossibility of defining race and identifying racial differences in people. But then, without supplying or suggesting any standard, the court instead permitted jurors in each individual case subjectively to define race and decide whether the eyewitnesses who testify are of a different race than that of the defendant.

The Massachusetts court believed that social science research on identification is valid, but the court did not know how to apply the research findings to an actual case. "The social science research establishing the CRE [cross-racial effect] often does not define race," the court wrote.

The court then cited with approval a conclusion from an academic article. "'Face recognition researchers have investigated the [CRE] for almost [forty] years, but few have attempted to provide a definition of *race*. This is not surprising, since the concept of race is notoriously unclear, with most biologists asserting that it has no defensible definition.'" The court then cited "a leading scholar on the CRE," Professor Roy S. Malpass, for the proposition that race cannot be identified consistently.

Next, the court questioned itself, apparently to show that race cannot be defined. "For example, what is the race of a person whose grandparents on his father's side were an African-American and an Asian-American, and on his mother's side were a Caucasian and a Native American? . . . And what evidence would be admissible to ascertain the person's race?"[23]

Neither finding nor suggesting an answer to its own question, the court decided that jurors on each case should, in essence, have the authority to make and apply law, by accepting or rejecting the concept of race. If they see fit, the jurors may apply a racial construct to the case they are hearing. The court wrote:

> Because differences in race based on facial appearance lie in the eye of the beholder, we shall not ask judges to determine whether a reasonable juror would perceive the identification to be cross-racial. Rather, we shall direct that a cross-racial instruction be given unless all parties agree that there was no cross-racial identification. This obviates any need for the judge to decide whether the identification was actually cross-racial, or whether jurors might perceive it to be. If the jury receive such an instruction but do not think the identification was cross-racial, they may simply treat the instruction as irrelevant to their deliberations.[24]

In every case in Massachusetts, defendants are now subjected to the ad hoc determinations of jurors on whether the concept of *race* exists. If the answer is *yes*, then the jurors will have to decide whether the defendant and eyewitnesses are sufficiently different in race or skin color to justify downgrading the validity of the eyewitnesses' identifications of the defendant.

New Jersey, in its jury instructions, now requires trial judges to inform juries of the general conclusions stemming from research into cross-racial and other identifications, even when the general conclusions have not been shown to apply directly to a specific case (no validity as applied). The jury instruction in New Jersey reads as follows:

> You heard testimony that (insert name of witness) made a statement at the time he/she identified the defendant from a photo array/line-up concerning his/her level of certainty that the person/photograph he/she selected is in fact the person who committed the crime. . . . Although some research has found that highly confident witnesses are more likely to make accurate identifications, eyewitness confidence is generally an unreliable indicator of accuracy. . . . Research has shown that people may have greater difficulty in accurately identifying members of a different race. You should consider whether the fact that the witness and the defendant are not of the same race may have influenced the accuracy of the witness's identification.[25]

The approach of the state courts, allowing general evidence and, essentially, instructing jurors to cast doubt on cross-racial eyewitness identifications, will probably make convictions less likely for innocent and guilty people; require juries, trial judges, and appellate courts to classify defendants and witnesses according to their race; and open the door to prosecutors' using general conclusions, such as that intra-racial identifications are more reliable than cross-racial identifications, thereby elevating the conviction rate. The courts did not discuss the number of guilty people who might go free to ensure that an innocent person is not convicted.

From the courts' reasoning, a next step would be to allow defense and prosecution experts to examine witnesses prior to trial. The reason is that actual examinations of witnesses are more likely than general conclusions to lead to a correct assessment of those witnesses' perceptual abilities. Prosecutors, for instance, knowing that defense lawyers will argue to the jury that general conclusions support the proposition that a particular eyewitness is mistaken, may insist that the witness be examined by experts prior to testifying in an effort to refute the defense argument. Moreover, the courts made no reference to artificial intelligence and, thus, ignored or were unaware of the possibility, or likelihood, that computers have more capacity than humans to arrive at general conclusions and that, therefore, the general conclusions of computers should be admitted into trials. All of these consequences, not considered by the courts, will introduce additional complexity or conflict into the adversarial system.

The Primacy of Procedure

As has occurred over three hundred years of haphazard adversarial practice, the New Jersey, Hawaii, Massachusetts, and New York courts created new rules apparently without full recognition of how the rules will affect future cases and society, particularly whether a decrease in innocent-person convictions will outweigh an increase in guilty-person acquittals. From the courts' reasoning, it is difficult to see how trial judges can avoid having new pretrial hearings when the defense and prosecution disagree on whether the defendant and eyewitnesses are of a different color or race. Will the judges have to allow experts to testify as to the racial and color composition of defendants and witnesses to determine whether there was a cross-racial identification, and thus whether the judges should provide the jurors with a cross-racial jury instruction?

As Professor James Acker noted in 2019, new procedures that benefit innocent people may have disadvantages for society. Professor Acker described what could replace the photo arrays and lineups used by detectives and the results of the replacement: "Studies by and large conclude that when sequential procedures [showing the eyewitness one photo or one person at a time] are used (and when the officer overseeing the identification is 'blind,' that is, unaware who the true suspect is or does not know when the true suspect is presented to the witness), there is a reduction in false positive identifications (the erroneous selection of an innocent person) but also an increase in false negative outcomes (the erroneous failure to select a guilty person)."[26] If this research is valid, then it seems likely that a larger number of guilty-person acquittals than innocent-person acquittals will occur because most of the people who are arrested are guilty.

The state courts' remedy, new jury instructions, obscures the more important need for the discovery of additional facts. The irony is that the courts' new rules, and the new procedures that could ensue, may more securely ensure that the primary reason for innocent-person convictions—the failure to find exonerating facts—will not be reversed. As Justice Antonin Scalia noted in a dissenting opinion in 2009, "This Court has never held that the Constitution forbids the execution of a convicted defendant who has had a full and fair trial but is later able to convince a habeas court that he is 'actually' innocent."[27] With new rules and possibly additional procedures producing *fuller and fairer* trials— even though the new rules or procedures might create greater untruth overall (more guilty-person than innocent-person acquittals)—appellate courts will have even less reason to examine the facts introduced into a trial or found following a conviction. This is a result of elevating procedures over truth.

In *District Attorney v. Osborne* (2009), Chief Justice John Roberts, writing for the majority, restated the rule that innocence may not be a basis for overturning a conviction. That is, even exonerating facts may not be sufficient to allow a federal court to free an apparently innocent person. "As a fallback," the chief justice wrote, "Osborne also obliquely relies on an asserted federal constitutional right to be released upon proof of 'actual innocence.' Whether such a federal right exists is an open question. We have struggled with it over the years, in some cases assuming, *arguendo*, that it exists while also noting the difficult questions such a right would pose and the high standard any claimant would have to meet."[28] In *Osborne*, the Court found that postconviction due process relief will be granted only if state procedures offend a principle of justice "so rooted in the traditions and conscience of our people as to be ranked as fundamental" or "transgresses any recognized principle of fundamental fairness in operation," standards so high that almost no convicted person can meet them.[29]

American courts' reliance on criminal procedures, which proliferated in the 1960s, appears not to have mitigated significantly (possibly not at all) the innocent-person conviction problem. Professor Margaret Raymond summarized the recurring problems: "The causes he [Professor Edwin Borchard] identified [in 1932] for the wrongful convictions—mistaken identifications, inadequate lawyering, police or prosecutorial misconduct, false or coerced confessions, and perjury—are strikingly similar to those offered today [2001] by advocates for the wrongfully convicted. He also advocated the same kinds of relief as today's advocates. Yet we find ourselves, seventy years later, addressing the same problems and the same causes. The lesson is clear: we do not solve this problem merely by identifying it."[30]

Professor John Langbein summarized the key structural defect of the adversarial system and thus identified the critical limitation of procedures: their inability to support a search for truth. "In England, by contrast [to continental systems], the well-meaning reforms of the eighteenth century that resulted in adversary criminal trial had the effect of perpetuating the central blunder of the inherited system: the failure to develop institutions and procedures of criminal investigation and trial that would be responsible for and capable of seeking the truth."[31]

Adversarial legal practice over the centuries has not evolved into a search for truth. Nearly the opposite condition has emerged—acquiescence that truth should not be elevated over procedures and the institutionalization of bias (error) into the U.S. legal system. Professor

Lloyd Weinreb, in 1999, wrote, "I want to say again that this virtue of adversariness, that it encourages the pursuit to the end of whatever may benefit one side or the other, is of first importance, because it is also true that that is its only virtue. All its other attributes, as we are aware elsewhere throughout our lives, are not virtues but vices, which we recognize collectively as bias."[32]

Legal philosopher and former federal judge Jerome Frank, writing in 1949, described bias by a different name, *subjectivity*. Judge Frank said to assume "the notion that there exist some general, immutable and eternal principles of morality or justice. . . . Assume further that these principles can be fairly reliable guides to concrete and definite legal rules." None of this matters, he believed, because "we will not have justice done, in specific lawsuits, in accord with those principles and those subsidiary rules, unless we can eliminate the numerous variable 'subjective' elements in fact-finding."[33] The absence of facts is compounded by "our real problem—the problem of 'subjectivity' in fact-finding."[34]

Through its agents, an institution like the government, which possesses vastly superior authority and resources compared with those of the accused, will naturally develop subjectivity, bias, and tunnel vision, almost always to the benefit of the government. In this environment, the search for facts becomes narrow and circumscribed, as law enforcement agents work within the milieu they know. They are likely to find incriminating evidence, as that is their job, as opposed to searching for the truth, which is a consideration but not a necessary part of their work. We do not have a remedy for human error, whether by witnesses or investigators—and procedures will not suffice—but there is a way to lessen the error, the discovery of additional facts.

7

The Lost Dialectic

Aristotle remarked "that if one wishes to find the truth one must first consider the opinion of those who judge differently."[1] This type of dialectic does not apply to the adversarial legal system because truth is not a goal, the parties in litigation are not searching for truth, and suspects and defendants do not have the right or ability to participate in a meaningful search for evidence. In 1984, in *U.S. v. Gouveia*, the Supreme Court concluded that suspects do not have the right to have their lawyers participate in the investigation because it occurs prior to "adversarial judicial proceedings."

In most cases, an adversarial judicial proceeding does not begin until the suspect sees a judge, which is almost always at the arraignment or initial appearance. (In some cases, the adversarial proceeding begins prior to the arraignment, such as when a judge issues an arrest warrant or a grand jury votes to indict a suspect who has not yet been arrested.) By the time of arraignment, almost all the evidence that will provide the basis for criminal charges has been collected, and almost all the investigation procedures (such as identifications and interviews of witnesses) have been completed.[2] During the investigation, no one on the defense side or any neutral magistrate is present to provide views contrary to those of law enforcement officials.

Poverty

A defendant's constitutional right to a lawyer, even when the government pays the lawyer's salary or fees, creates the illusion of an opportunity for a complete defense. Lawyers who represent indigent defendants work in public defender offices or through contract or appointment systems.[3] They are almost never involved in prearrest procedures and rarely have the resources after a client has been arrested to become fully prepared on a case. In a 2006 article, researchers reported that one county-appointed lawyer had a caseload of three hundred defendants in one year, in addition to his private practice.[4] In 2006, a commission empaneled to examine the indigent defense system in New York reported one county indigent defender office in which each lawyer's average caseload per year was 1,000 misdemeanor cases and 175 felony cases.[5]

This condition produces a "combination of excessive caseloads and inadequate budgets [and] means that defender offices almost never perform out-of-court investigations . . . [and] that many defender offices have no staff investigators or an insufficient number of them and that some public defenders never use investigators in any of their cases," according to Professor Martin Guggenheim. "The lack of resources compels public defenders to enter guilty pleas on behalf of their clients despite the fact that an investigation was never conducted."[6]

Even rudimentary representation after charges have been filed can be elusive. A 2017 investigation by the *Milwaukee Journal Sentinel* found that defense lawyers appointed to represent indigent defendants in Wisconsin rarely use investigators in even the most serious felony cases, including murders. Investigators, too, are paid by the state, with no cost to the lawyer or defendant, and thus there seems to be no reason why lawyers would not hire them. The *Journal Sentinel* examined the billing records of dozens of private lawyers who had represented over five thousand clients from 2010 to 2016. About one hundred lawyers each took over fifty felony-case appointments during this time and never billed for an investigator. One lawyer had three hundred felony appointments and several other lawyers had two hundred appointments without billing for an investigator.[7]

The lawyers' reason for not using investigators might arise not solely or even primarily from incompetence or lack of care for their clients, but rather from a need to support their own livelihoods. In 2017, the state of Wisconsin paid appointed defense lawyers forty dollars an hour, a rate that was unchanged since 1995 (twenty-two years without a raise) and was the lowest in the nation among the thirty states that paid hourly rates for appointed lawyers. If the Wisconsin lawyers received forty dollars an hour, including for their work with investigators, their earnings might be too low to run a legal practice. It seems likely the lawyers were taking appointed criminal cases only when they had spare hours, after billing clients who paid the lawyers' regular fees. At the lower rate, forty dollars an hour, the lawyers may not be willing to spend additional hours working with investigators.

Even if a suspect possessed a right to have a lawyer present during the government's evidence-collection process (prior to arrest), most suspects do not have enough money to enable them ever to hire a lawyer. In 1989, nearly 80 percent of county inmates (in jails) indicated that they were assigned a lawyer to represent them, according to the U.S. Bureau of Justice Statistics.[8] Since then, the financial problems facing indigent defendants seem to have worsened. In 2000, in apparently its most recent report on the subject, the Bureau of Justice Statistics concluded, "Publicly-financed counsel represented about 66 percent of federal felony defendants in 1998 as well as 82 percent of felony defendants in the 75 most populous counties in 1996."[9] In New Jersey, in 2020, to be eligible for a public defender, a person charged with a crime had to have an annual gross income equal to or less than $15,950.[10]

As the *Milwaukee Journal Sentinel* report seems to have shown, impoverished people are represented by lawyers who, themselves, do not earn enough money to provide a complete defense for their clients. "In the 16 States reporting public defender expenditures and criminal caseload, the estimated cost per criminal case was $490" in 1999, according to the Bureau of Justice Statistics.[11] Given that death-penalty cases and other serious felonies are very expensive to defend and increase the average cost, the amount of funding available for the less serious cases must be significantly less, almost surely less than what many lawyers receive from a private-paying client for *one hour's* work.

For example, in 2020, in the top ten U.S. jurisdictions (based on lawyers' fees), the average hourly fee of lawyers ranged from $294 to $380.[12] In 2019, the average hourly fee of partners at large law firms ranged from $1,100 to $1,900.[13] In 2020, the yearly profit for equity partners at the one hundred most profitable law firms ranged from $570,000 to $7.5 million.[14] In their first year, new lawyers at such firms earn $200,000, according to a 2021 report in the *Wall Street Journal*.[15]

The public perception may be that lawyers earn large or, at least, handsome salaries and, therefore, public funding for indigent criminal defendants is unnecessary because defense lawyers can absorb the unfunded costs of litigation. However, most lawyers earn far less, probably a median yearly salary of about $123,000.[16] The average debt of law school graduates (by law school) ranges from $60,000 to $188,000.[17] In 2021, the average yearly salary for a public defender was $60,530 (about $29 per hour).[18] Poor defendants and underfunded defense lawyers create incentives for the lawyers to resolve cases quickly through plea bargaining, rather than through a search for facts, a process that requires significant time.

One might believe that defendants or their families could contribute something toward investigations, but that is often practically or economically impossible. In contrast to state or federal prisons, America's jails are run and funded by counties and cities. Dank, noisy, and crowded, jails hold people (three of every four inmates) who cannot afford bail and are awaiting trial or who are serving sentences for misdemeanor convictions. Inside the jails, where private vendors provide services, inmates or their families are charged an average of $5.74 for a fifteen-minute phone call (cell phones are not allowed), according to the Prison Policy Initiative. The average fifteen-minute phone call in jails in Arkansas is $14.49, the highest in the nation.[19] Incarcerated people cannot afford to call their mothers or try to contact witnesses.

Under these conditions, for poor people and their families, *investigation* is a word with no meaning, an illusion with no hope. One way to visualize the dire situation in which accused people find themselves is to imagine or remember a time when a loved one was in a precarious medical condition. Even the best surgeon working alone, without nurses, anesthesiologists, laboratory technicians, and modern equipment, could rarely save the patient. Next, imagine how the patient and families would feel if the surgeon, working for twenty-nine or forty dollars an hour, like salaried public defenders and fee-based private defense lawyers, did not try to find nurses who could aid in the treatment of the loved one.

Most arrestees will be convicted of some crime, and their families understand that their incarcerated relatives have often traveled the wrong road. Nonetheless, the overall harsh adversarial conditions lead to despair, resentment, and cynicism among inmates and families. The result is disrespect for law and society, which is an additional long-term problem accompanying the adversarial legal system.

In a Brooklyn case, a jury found a defendant guilty of manslaughter for shooting and killing a homeless man, who the defendant believed mistakenly was trying to steal his car. The victim was leaning down into a garbage can, rummaging for food scraps, not leaning over the car, as the defendant believed (and, regardless, stealing a car does not justify killing the thief). For the sentencing, detectives found the victim's only known relative, a brother from New Jersey. The brother, minutes before the sentence was announced, said he didn't want to speak to the judge, who then sentenced the defendant to three to nine years in prison (a mandatory three years before parole eligibility).

After the sentencing, the brother told me, "Shit, three to nine years for killing a man. That's nothing. He wasn't much. But he was my brother." That's how a lot of people feel about the adversarial legal system, whether they're connected to the victim or the defendant. Knowing that their person, whether the defendant or the deceased, received a fair deal from the law is all they want to happen or is as much as they expect.

Secrecy

Almost always during the investigation, government agents act alone and in secret. Through subpoenas[20] and warrants, they have exclusive access to most of the evidence.[21] The resolution of most cases is determined by prosecutors' decisions to charge,[22] which may be premature for "psychological, social, and moral factors,"[23] such as public clamor, and the charging decisions occur prior to the first adversarial judicial proceeding.[24] "The prosecutor . . . is making a determination of guilt or innocence," wrote Gerard E. Lynch, a federal appeals judge.[25] It is only after all this action and rumination by the government that accused people have the right to a lawyer, when they first see a judge.[26]

Even defendants who can afford lawyers have no right to have them present during the investigation, with one exception.[27] At interrogations, suspects have the right to a lawyer if they don't waive the right.[28] But almost no lawyer would recommend that a client speak to investigators at this stage, absent extensive prior independent investigation, if ever. Overall, there is no one present who can argue on behalf of an innocent person or act as a neutral commentator.

After the investigation, defense lawyers spend most of their time trying to deflect or suppress evidence that indicates their clients are guilty. Thus, the primary attributes of the current adversarial system are what led to its deformation in the first place, three hundred years ago: poverty; the presence of defense lawyers and, thus, the silencing of accused people; prosecutors' and defense lawyers' combat ethos; secrecy, unless prohibited by law; and defense lawyers' urging jurors and judges to reach conclusions that the lawyers know are false.

This system was never premised on a genuine, productive dialectic. In litigation, the lawyers, except those who work for the government, are obligated to try to conceal the truth if doing so benefits their clients. "The first point is this: Anyone who considers dialogue, disputation, debate, to be a fundamental method for arriving at truth must already have concluded and stated that arriving at truth is an affair that calls for more power than the autarchic individual possesses. He must feel that common effort, perhaps the effort of everybody, is necessary. No one is sufficient unto himself and no one is completely superfluous; each person needs the other; the teacher even needs the student, as Socrates always held. . . . Dialogue does not mean only that people talk to one another, but also that they listen to one another," according to Professor Josef Pieper.[29] This dialectic, a genuine search for truth, is not required within the adversarial legal system.

Enriching and productive arguments occur when the parties to a dialectic collect and share information. In contrast, the adversarial system is invested in secrecy and conflict. Professor Joseph D. Grano, in 1997, concluded that the "criminal justice system sorely needs major reforms designed to emphasize the importance of ascertaining truth."[30]

Discovering Exonerating Facts: Inquisitorial Methods

A fundamentally different approach should be considered: not every practice in the adversarial system should be adversarial. Indeed, the adversarial investigation did not arise from any scientific finding that it is better than an inquisitorial investigation. Though commentators often cannot agree on how to define an inquisitorial system,[31] generally its characteristics include a "judge [who] is understood and perceived as an active investigator with, consequently, the duty to be active in these interrogations."[32]

Professor David Alan Sklansky concluded that "the broad and continuing legal tradition with which it [inquisitorialism] is identified is

not so self-evidently bad."[33] In inquisitorial systems, "the police in continental countries tend to be seen as investigators for both the prosecution and the defense and thus everyone at trial—the state's attorney, the
defense attorney, and the judge—tends to work out of the same file and
to have roughly the same body of information with which to prepare for
trial."[34]

"Yet the truth is that inquisitorial procedure is neither alien to our
traditions nor inherently unfair," according to Professor Amalia D. Kessler. "As late as the nineteenth century, Anglo-American courts of equity . . . employed a mode of procedure, which like that used in the
courts of continental Europe, derived from the Roman-canon tradition
and thus was significantly inquisitorial."[35] It was as late as 1938 when U.S.
civil law became "fully 'adversarial.'"[36]

European law created "the two classic models of criminal procedure,
the adversarial and inquisitorial, which made their way to most other
countries through European colonization or independent reform processes."[37] The inquisitorial system focuses on a more neutral search for
evidence and is consistent with the values of the less individualistic societies in continental Europe, which elevate cooperation over competition and confrontation.[38] In contrast, the lack of agency of defendants in
the United States—private litigants who are isolated and responsible for
finding exonerating evidence—creates an almost insurmountable burden for innocent people. The consequences are trials without facts, or, at
least, trials without the exonerating facts that exist, as we will see next.

8

Trials without Facts

If the discovery of truth were a formal goal, investigators and prosecutors would have to consider, prior to issuing charges, whether they can find facts that indicate a suspect is innocent. Though in many cases this early search would require more time and resources than in other cases, these costs are far outweighed by the time and resources consumed when an innocent person is convicted and imprisoned or when charges against a guilty person are brought unwisely because, for some reason, the evidence cannot sustain a conviction. Assuming moderately reasonable prosecutors, judges, and jurors, the absence of an adequate number of exonerating facts is the primary conceptual and practical reason why innocent people are convicted. While some defendants might have been *wrongfully convicted* because their truthful confessions to crimes were obtained illegally, for instance, any new procedures or methods should be applied to protect only factually innocent people, to the extent possible. This requires a method to deter guilty people from pleading innocent and availing themselves of new innocence procedures.

"Call Him a Murderer"

Consider who is not factually innocent and should not be entitled to use innocence procedures. In Brooklyn, a defendant was alleged to have intentionally killed a coworker when they were working alone in a small factory on a Sunday afternoon. The victim was a woman who did not return home from her shift at the factory. Her family notified police on the same day, but they could not find her until one detective thought to search the roof of the factory on Tuesday. They found her dead on the roof, strangled, her pants pulled down (though apparently not sexually assaulted). Someone had placed her inside a large plastic bag.

Detectives could not find any evidence other than the body, but they eventually found the victim's coworker from Sunday. They called an assistant district attorney, who went to a police precinct to interview the coworker, a man in his early twenties. The interview was taped by a video technician. The prosecutor informed the worker-suspect of his rights, which he waived, including the right to have an attorney present during the interview. In what turned out to be the only incriminating evidence against him, he described the scene that Sunday afternoon.

He said that shortly after arriving for work at the factory he was leaving to go outside to smoke a cigarette. His coworker, the deceased, told him he hadn't worked long enough to merit a break and then tugged on his arm to urge him to continue working. He said that he put his hands around her neck and then "I saw red." The next thing I know, he said, is that I was standing over her. She was slumped on the floor, dead. He said he pulled down her pants (but didn't say he sexually assaulted her), placed her in a plastic bag, and carried her to the roof, where he left her.

It's not clear he was telling the truth about what happened, though his story was consistent with the placement of the body, or why he would do something like this. But these kinds of human depredations occur every day. In the United States, the prosecution is almost never required to prove the suspect's motive, that is, to explain the seemingly unexplainable. Why does one person kill another for tugging on his arm? Most people will never understand. That is a practical reason why defendants' motive or reason for doing something is not an element of a crime, though it can be used as evidence to prove they committed a crime.

The suspect's statement was very incriminating, but it was the only evidence that would be sufficient to convict him. After seeing the video of his statement at trial, a jury would be likely to find him guilty of committing an intentional homicide (*murder* in New York). A life sentence would be mandatory, with a chance for parole after serving fifteen to twenty-five years, depending on the judge's sentence. However, this suspect had been convicted of committing one prior violent felony and, when the homicide occurred, was out on bail after being charged with sexual assault. If convicted, he would be likely to spend a large part, or all, of the remainder of his life in prison.

From the prosecution point of view, there was some risk that the defendant could escape responsibility if the judge and an appellate court, for some reason, found the defendant's statement inadmissible; the absence of the statement would make a conviction impossible. During pretrial hearings, which were approaching, a trial judge determines the admissibility of evidence, including statements by defendants to police officers or prosecutors. On the day of one court date, a social worker brought the victim's relatives (mother, sister, and daughter) to meet with me. I explained to the family members that to eliminate the risk the judge might exclude the statement from evidence, I would go into court and offer the defendant the opportunity to plead guilty to manslaughter and receive a sentence of 12.5 to 25 years in prison, in return for my recommending to the judge that the charge of murder (and the possibility of a life sentence) be dismissed. The family members understood and were satisfied with the sentence. But, they said they did not want him to be called a "man-slaughterer. He's a murderer." (In the U.S. criminal legal system, private parties, even family members, do not have authority to disapprove prosecutors' decisions.)

We went into the courtroom, and I offered the plea by addressing the judge. The defense attorney wanted his client to take a sure thing and not risk that the statement and a trial would lead to a sentence of life imprisonment. Illustrating the informality of monumental decisions in an overloaded legal system, the defense lawyer turned to his client (everyone in the courtroom could hear) and recommended that the client/defendant plead guilty to manslaughter and accept the sentence. The lawyer and client briefly discussed the advantages and disadvantages of pleading guilty.

Even when defendants know they committed a serious offense, they experience significant emotional pain in admitting what they did, not always because of remorse for the people they hurt; rather, it's difficult to imagine spending months, years, or decades in prison. Somewhere in the back of their minds they believe a jury might find them not guilty. The judge or prosecutor asks, "How do you plead, guilty or not guilty?" When defendants say "guilty," they understand that they will be confined to a small prison cell. This defendant hesitated, but then he agreed to plead guilty.

As part of the formal plea in court, the prosecutor or judge asks defendants whether they are pleading guilty voluntarily and understand the rights they are waiving, such as cross-examination of witnesses and a trial by jury. At one point, defendants confront another difficult moment, when they have to describe what they did so that the judge can be sure there's a factual basis for the offense to which they're pleading guilty.

They must say, for example, "I choked the deceased until she stopped breathing." There's no requirement that defendants explain why (motive) they did this. There's no requirement that they admit they killed the victim intentionally, though intent is an element of many murder charges. Probably all people find it difficult to admit they intentionally hurt another person. Every plea colloquy would consume a great deal of time if defendants were required to utter "I intentionally hurt or killed another person." Fortunately for everyone, defendants' descriptions of what they did and other facts, such as a medical examiner's report that the victim died from strangulation, show an intent to kill. This provides a factual basis for the judge to conclude that a plea to murder or manslaughter is legally sufficient.

As the defendant spoke softly and explained what he had done, the victim's sister stood up in court and shouted at him, "You asshole, you killed my sister. You're a murderer. You're a murderer."

The sister knew that this defendant was not factually innocent. Nonetheless, assume that the trial judge had allowed the defendant's statement into evidence and a jury found him guilty of murder. Then, however, assume that an appellate court concluded that the statement should not have been allowed into evidence at the trial and reversed his conviction. There could be no retrial because the statement, now inadmissible, was the only basis for a conviction.

On this case, the defendant would be free. One could then conclude that he had been *wrongfully* convicted, despite being factually guilty. The point is that procedural changes to the adversarial system, while available to any defendant, must be designed to ensure that they will protect only those who are factually innocent, not those who might be wrongfully convicted based on a legal rule.

The Meaning of Innocence

Somewhat surprisingly, the concept of innocence can be difficult to define and understand. One reason is that the concepts of factual innocence and wrongful conviction are sometimes used interchangeably or difficult to distinguish. To begin, Professor Michael Risinger separates accused people into three groups:

> The term "wrongful conviction" simply cannot be comfortably avoided, but it must always be approached with caution, because it can easily lead to the conflation of three importantly different problems of justice. The first is the problem of convicting those who are factually innocent either because no crime was committed or, more commonly, because a crime was in fact committed, but by someone else (wrongful conviction in the factual sense). The second is the problem of convicting a person who has undoubtedly performed the actus reus of a crime for which they are not culpable, either because of insanity or the absence of some other required indicium of culpability, usually a particular required mental state (wrongful conviction in the culpability sense). The third is the conviction of persons who may very well be both factually guilty and culpable, but who were convicted in trials containing procedural errors not easily dismissed as harmless error (wrongful conviction in the procedural sense).[1]

The concept of factual innocence should apply to the defendants in the first group—no crime was committed or the crime was committed by someone else. Under any moral or legal definition, these accused people are blameless and innocent. Factual innocence, with difficulty, can be applied to the second group—whether the accused person had a culpable mental state when committing the act that is the basis of a criminal charge; but attaching a mental-state label (intentional, knowing, reckless, or negligent) to what someone was thinking is a precarious endeavor. It is very difficult to estimate what someone was thinking. The third group of accused people are not factually innocent under any circumstance.

Determining factual innocence becomes more complicated when we recognize that factually innocent people fall into at least two subcategories. Unfortunately, the people in the first category can almost never be exonerated. In an article, I described the distinction between the two subcategories of factually innocent people: "The first type of factual innocence . . . involves a factual dispute to which the fact-finder must apply a legal rule."[2] In this circumstance, the jurors, for example, might have to determine whether the defendant on trial was reasonable, for which there is a legal definition, when the defendant believed the person he killed was about to unlawfully kill him (self-defense). The jurors might apply the legal definition of reasonableness incorrectly to the facts presented at trial. But, short of reading the jurors' minds, there is no way to determine whether the jurors applied the law of reasonableness incorrectly.

Still within this first subcategory (jury applying a legal rule to the facts of the case), there is another group of innocent people who will almost never be exonerated. The reason is that the fact on which a correct verdict depends cannot be discovered. This could be an exonerating witness who dies before the trial. Probably more frequently, the fact is a process that occurred inside the defendant's brain—reasonable in every respect—that instructed the defendant to kill the deceased before the deceased acted unlawfully and killed the defendant. But this fact cannot be accessed through the defendant's trial testimony, perhaps because the defendant does not communicate clearly or possibly cannot risk testifying and having the jury hear about the defendant's prior criminal convictions. This innocent defendant will be convicted because of human incapacity, the inability of jurors to access the critical fact in the defendant's brain. Recognizing that some innocent people cannot be exonerated because of errors in jurors' brains (misapplication of law) or jurors' inability to access the ultimate fact in a case (whether a defendant's brain processes, in deciding to kill, were reasonable) helps illustrate that the innocent-person conviction problem is probably far greater than anyone realizes.

Only the second category of factually innocent people can be exonerated, and, once charged with a crime, even these people are rarely exonerated for the reasons discussed thus far. "The second kind of factual innocence does not implicate any question of law and is not dependent directly on the fact finder's application of law to facts. Every reasonable person viewing the facts in this type of case would always conclude that the defendant is innocent."[3]

In this kind of case, the determination of whether a defendant is innocent does not in any significant way depend on the mechanics of the jurors' mental processes or their examination of the defendant's mental processes. The defendant has only—and this is difficult to accomplish—to find the exonerating facts that exist outside jurors' and defendants' brains. In some sense, these facts are more *objective* because they exist inside the universe and can be found by anyone, such as by viewing a video recording of a robbery in New York taken at the time we know the defendant was in California.

But even objective facts can be distorted severely by the time the jurors consider them in their deliberations. "We mingle the objective facts with our subjective needs . . . [and] we mistake 'the moaning night-wind for a human cry, an innocent tramp for the escaped convict.'"[4]

Writing in 1949, Judge Jerome Frank found that facts become twisted in all trials. "The facts as they actually happened are therefore twice refracted—first by the witnesses, and second by those who must 'find' the facts. The reactions of trial judges or juries to the testimony are shot through with subjectivity. Thus we have subjectivity piled on subjectivity. It is surely proper, then, to say that the facts as 'found' by a trial court are subjective."[5]

Every factual situation is a new relationship within the temporal world. Witnesses may have no experience viewing a robbery at night. Judges and jurors must apply preexisting statutory or common law to the facts of the new case, the nighttime robbery. In this mind-bending process, jurors hear from witnesses about what the witnesses saw, heard, or otherwise perceived.

Judge Frank believed that this "trial-court fact-finding is the toughest part of the judicial function. It is there that court-house government is least satisfactory. It is there that most of the very considerable amount of judicial injustice occurs. It is there that reform is needed most."[6]

This is a reason why reforms to the adversarial system should be focused on the investigation process, prior to trial, when investigators' errors can be overcome by additional facts that show whether someone is innocent or guilty. A trial is insufficient because the mistaken verdicts of juries are almost impossible to correct. We cannot perceive individual jurors' mental errors (in voting guilty). Appellate courts, if procedural error is not present, virtually always ratify juries' guilty verdicts, including those that may appear to be incorrect, as we will see next.

9

Procedures over Evidence

The inability of appellate judges to exercise omniscient review of cases makes it tempting to conclude that erroneous guilty verdicts are not amenable to review and correction because jurors are in a better position than judges to perceive what happened and infer what was or is in the brains of witnesses and defendants. Therefore, jurors are more able to apply the law to the facts. This mental operation, applying law to facts, is sometimes referred to as a mixed question of law and fact. Appellate courts generally refuse to apply law to facts, leaving the application to designated fact finders, the juries and judges. However, because law and facts are often (perhaps always) indistinguishable, this application can and should be performed by appellate courts also.[1]

An example might be the jurors' application of the law of self-defense, as supplied by the trial judge, to the facts presented at trial. In determining whether the defendant acted legally, in self-defense, when he killed the deceased, the jurors must look into the brain of the defendant to find the ultimate fact—whether the defendant/killer evinced mental reasonableness when he acted (the physical method of killing). This test is used in jurisdictions where jurors determine reasonableness from the defendant's point of view.

Probably most jurisdictions (through juries) determine reasonableness based on what a reasonable person would have done if placed in the defendant's situation. Like the jurors' examination of the defendant's brain, this inquiry is subject to variability because jurors are allowed to conjure what they believe to be a reasonable person in their jurisdiction. Different juries from the same jurisdiction will create a different reasonable person. The arbitrariness associated with this inquiry might be inevitable because human intellect does not seem capable of creating a standard through which to define reasonableness with any precision. We should recognize, therefore, that when facts do not lead to obvious conclusions (a video showing that the defendant did not commit the robbery), the verdicts from trials are based largely on the unpredictable perceptions of jurors.

The usual justification for this scheme is that, with jurors having more ability to determine whether a fact should be found based on the testimony of the witnesses, appellate courts should not consider factual matters. Considering this, Professor Keith Findley, in 2009, described the general futility of innocent people when appealing their convictions. "If protecting against mistaken conviction of the innocent is indeed a primary objective in criminal appeals, it is fair to ask how well the system serves that function. Unfortunately, judging by the recent evidence, especially the empirical evidence from cases in which postconviction DNA testing has proved that an innocent person was wrongly convicted, the appellate process in criminal cases is largely a failure on this most important score."[2]

An empirical study by Professor Brandon Garrett provided the data for Findley's conclusion. Garrett examined the first two hundred people exonerated by postconviction DNA testing. The first exoneration occurred in 1989, the two hundredth in 2007. The exonerated people had been convicted of rape (141), murder (12), rape and murder (44), attempted murder (1), and robbery (2). "These 200 exonerees do not reflect the typical criminal convicts in that very few suspects are charged with rape or murder and even fewer are convicted. According to the Bureau of Justice Statistics . . . only 0.7% of felony defendants are convicted of murder and only 0.8% are convicted of rape," Garrett found. He attributed the difference between all cases and the exoneration cases to the availability of biological evidence in rape cases. Fourteen of the exonerated people had been sentenced to death, fifty to life in prison.[3]

"The vast majority of the exonerees (79%) were convicted based on eyewitness testimony; we now know that all of these eyewitnesses were incorrect. Fifty-seven percent were convicted based on forensic evidence, chiefly serological analysis [the study of body fluids] and microscopic hair comparison. Eighteen percent were convicted based on informant testimony and 16% of exonerees falsely confessed," Garrett reported.[4]

He found that appellate courts affirmed the convictions of the vast majority of the innocent people who were later exonerated. "Courts reversed the convictions of the exonerees at a 14% rate, or a 9% rate if only noncapital cases are included. That rate is much higher than the nominal 1% to 2% reversal rates during criminal review generally. . . . In short, the appellate and postconviction process did not effectively ferret out innocence," Garrett concluded.[5]

The failure of appellate courts to identify innocent-person convictions indicates that the courts should be less eager to defer to juries' guilty verdicts and more willing to weigh, during the appellate process, the facts that were presented at trial or those discovered during postconviction proceedings. Judges should consider whether what appears to them to be a factual issue (which is rarely appealable) may be indistinguishable from what appears to be a legal issue (which is always appealable). Only one state, Wisconsin, according to Professor Findley, makes the introduction of facts, postconviction, a regular part of criminal litigation.[6]

Cognitive Inability

Judges, or anyone, might not have the capacity to classify whether something is legal or factual, and therefore limiting appeals to legal issues may be a less than optimal method of appellate review. For instance, assume that a defendant-father is on trial for perjury because he testified in his child's custody hearing that he had *not* been previously convicted of a felony. His testimony was false (he had been convicted of a felony), but he believed he had been convicted of a misdemeanor, not a felony. (England, where the adversarial system arose, no longer classifies offenses as felonies and misdemeanors.) Under old criminal law rules, he might be guilty of perjury if he made a legal error ("ignorance of the law is no defense"), but not guilty if he made a factual error. The case would turn on whether the condition of being a felon is a legal or factual matter.

First, it can be difficult or impossible to identify a difference between a legal and factual mistake. Second, what is the relevance of determining whether the status of being a felon is legal or factual? The only important issue in this perjury case is whether the father was lying. Criminal law does not now condition the father's mistake-defense on whether he or any defendant made a legal or factual error about an element of the crime (such as perjury). As long as the defendant-father, when he testified at the custody hearing, believed he had been convicted of a misdemeanor, not a felony, he should be found not guilty of perjury, despite having a felony conviction.

The belief in a difference between law and facts predates the beginning of the adversarial system. Toward the beginning of adversarial practice, lawyers in England were permitted to argue about points of law in criminal cases, but they were prohibited from arguing about the facts under the belief that witnesses and defendants were responsible for stating the facts. Naturally, absent a definition that helped judges distinguish between law and facts (and humans might not be capable of making a distinction), lawyers argued that facts were law.

- In 1774, one lawyer argued that his client, a postal worker, should not be convicted of stealing securities from the mail because the postal worker stole money. Is the lawyer's assertion that the thing stolen was money, not a security (paper evincing an ownership interest), a point of law or a statement of fact? If it's a fact, then the lawyer should not have been permitted to argue before the judge. (The lawyer was permitted to argue, and the postal worker was acquitted.)
- Two women entered Newgate Prison and later one of them accompanied a disguised male prisoner to the gatehouse. Should the lawyer for the women, who were charged with a felony for the man's attempted escape, have been permitted to argue that the evidence did not prove the women conveyed women's clothes to the prisoner? Whether the lawyer is permitted to argue depends on whether the term *conveyance* refers to something legal or factual. (The lawyer was allowed to argue, and the women were acquitted.)[7]

It is unlikely there will ever be a consensus on whether the words *security* and *conveyance* in the above cases refer to a legal point or a factual condition. Why continue to try? The existence of a supposed distinction, alone, induced judicial winks and nods. Judges in England sometimes permitted lawyers to argue about what might be facts because of society's increasing revulsion toward the death penalty.[8]

When the English judges were uncertain about a legal point, prior to finally resolving the case, they could submit their questions to the Twelve Judges, which "was a practice that functioned as a species of appellate review."[9] In a meeting in London, the Twelve Judges, from the three common law courts (Exchequer, Common Pleas, and King's Bench), would issue a decision that served as a precedent. Appellate courts today continue to dismiss appeals and affirm convictions on the ground that the convicted defendant-appellant has raised only a question of fact (which is unappealable), as though the courts can define the difference between law and facts. In England, "sometimes counsel's objection about a matter of law was specious, solely a pretext for commenting upon the facts," according to Professor John Langbein.[10]

The lawyers' arguments (law is fact) helped to embed untruth into the core of the adversarial system. "Defense counsel's greater involvement in criminal cases, and the incentive that counsel had to couch his arguments as matters of law, also spurred the growth of the substantive criminal law and of the law of evidence," Langbein wrote.[11]

A trial court judge in Arizona, Randall Warner, while in private practice, concluded, "The whole reason for labeling a question 'law,' 'fact,' or 'mixed' is to determine the standard of review on appeal; thus, any attempt to understand mixed questions must begin with standard of review."[12] The standard of review determines whether the appellate courts will defer to the decisions of juries (about facts) or review a case with more scrutiny (law).

This practice determines how closely, if at all, an appellate court will examine the evidence from the trial. To give defendants who claim innocence an additional opportunity for a meaningful review of their cases, Professor Michael Risinger argues that, under a modified standard of review, trial judges and appellate courts would not be limited in their "ability to evaluate and discount the face value of witness testimony and would be morally obligated to do so when rationally appropriate."[13]

* * *

The Harvey Weinstein case illustrates the difficulty in trying to categorize a thing or event from a trial as a fact or law and thus the importance of considering (factual) claims of innocence even after a guilty verdict. Mr. Weinstein was an acclaimed Academy Award–winning movie producer (*Shakespeare in Love*, 1998). He was convicted in a New York City court in 2020 of committing sexual offenses against two women, both of whom testified at his trial. Four additional women testified that Weinstein committed nonconsensual sexual acts against them, though the district attorney alleged no specific charges regarding those women. The judge allowed prosecutors to introduce the testimony of the four women to show that Weinstein engaged in a pattern of sexual assault, thus buttressing the contention that the sexual contact at issue in the trial was nonconsensual.

Courts in America do not usually allow into a trial evidence of a defendant's prior crimes or bad acts. Their reasoning is that jurors may believe that if defendants committed prior bad acts they are more likely to have committed the acts for which they are now on trial. It is an unreasonable inference, judges conclude, to believe that evidence of a past crime is proof of the commission of a new crime.

There are exceptions to this rule, as in the Weinstein case. Judges will allow evidence of prior crimes and bad acts to show, for example, a method of operation or a pattern of criminal activity. From such a pattern, jurors may infer that the crime for which the defendant (Weinstein) is now on trial is a continuation or part of the pattern, a link in a chain of events. For example, assume that two women testify at trial that the defendant entered their apartments through fire escapes before sexually assaulting them. If the defense lawyer ridicules their testimony as fantastic because the defendant walks with a cane, a judge could allow other women to testify that the defendant somehow entered their apartments through fire escapes, despite the defendant's facing no charges in regard to those women.

Ultimately, eighty-seven women claimed that Weinstein had sexually assaulted or harassed them.[14] Even if the testimony of each woman (whose assault or harassment was a link in the chain) was relevant and supported the prosecution's case, any judge would limit the number of witnesses who would be allowed to testify. One reason for the limitation is that almost no defendant possesses the resources to prepare for the testimony of fifty-nine such witnesses, for example. Another reason is that a large number of witnesses would consume weeks or months of trial time, when, by far, the most relevant witnesses are the two complainants. But assume that a judge allowed fifty-nine of the women to testify. Under the usual approach, appellate courts should not find that fifty-nine were too many and reverse the conviction if the judge's decision, in allowing the witnesses, was based on a fact, such as a finding that, after listening to the defense cross-examination of the two complaining witnesses, fifty-nine additional witnesses were necessary to establish a plan, scheme, or method of operation that was unique to Weinstein.

Nonetheless, under these conditions, most appellate courts would probably reverse Weinstein's conviction because of the trial judge's *abuse of discretion*, allowing too many supporting witnesses (fifty-nine) to testify. It would be difficult or impossible to characterize the trial judge's decision (allowing fifty-nine witnesses) as something *legal*. If four witnesses are not too many but fifty-nine witnesses are too many, what is a proper number above four and below fifty-nine? There is no logical way to know. There is no preexisting rule or law that judges can apply evenly in each case. Their decision to allow four or fifty-nine witnesses to testify is based on their interpretation of facts.

Thus, when reviewing decisions of trial judges, appellate courts necessarily determine whether the number of such witnesses who testified at trial was appropriate, which is a factual determination. In 2018, Bill Cosby, the actor and comedian, was convicted in Montgomery County, Pennsylvania, of three counts of aggravated indecent assault for allegedly having sexual contact at his home with a woman acquaintance who was incapacitated by drugs he had given to her. In the first trial on the same case, in which the jury could not reach a verdict, the trial judge allowed the prosecution to introduce testimony from one other woman witness, who testified that Mr. Cosby had assaulted her.

In the second trial, the prosecution asked the judge to permit nineteen women to testify that Cosby had assaulted them. The judge allowed five of the women to testify to this effect. "Generally, the women averred that, in the 1980s, each had an encounter with Cosby that involved either alcohol, drugs, or both, that each became intoxicated or incapacitated after consuming those substances, and that Cosby engaged in some type of unwanted sexual contact with each of them while they were unable to resist. The dates of the conduct that formed the basis of these allegations ranged from 1982 to 1989, approximately fifteen to twenty-two years before the incident involving [the alleged victim]," according to the Pennsylvania Supreme Court.[15]

According to an intermediate Pennsylvania appellate court, which had affirmed Cosby's conviction, the five witnesses "essentially testified that Appellant [Cosby] had drugged and then sexually assaulted them in circumstances similar to that recounted by Victim [in the current case]."[16] In deferring to the trial judge, that lower appellate court cited a general rule of appellate review: "'The admission of evidence is committed to the sound discretion of the trial court, and a trial court's ruling regarding the admission of evidence will not be disturbed on appeal unless that ruling reflects manifest unreasonableness, or partiality, prejudice, bias, or ill-will, or such lack of support to be clearly erroneous.'"[17]

But an appellate court is just as competent as a trial judge to determine whether the testimony of five or nineteen prospective witnesses is appropriate. Both the judge and appellate court can assess whether a plan or scheme is unique and points to one person and, thus, whether the testimony of the prospective witnesses is relevant to prove Cosby assaulted the alleged victim in the current case. In discussing the admissibility of the witnesses' testimony, the lower appellate court concluded that a "determination of admissibility under the common plan/scheme/design exception 'must be made on a case by case basis in accordance with the unique *facts* and circumstances of each case. However, we recognize that in each case, the trial court is bound to follow the same controlling, albeit general, *principles of law*.'"[18] The court's reasoning is confusing and circular because the *law*—how many supporting witnesses should be allowed to testify in a particular case—is determined by examining the facts.

Without deciding whether five witnesses were too many, the Pennsylvania Supreme Court, in 2021, found a more preliminary error and reversed Cosby's conviction. A previous district attorney had promised not to prosecute Cosby, which induced Cosby to make incriminating statements in a civil case brought by the complainant; that civil case was settled when Cosby paid her $3.38 million. The next district attorney used Cosby's incriminating statements from the civil case in a criminal prosecution. The Pennsylvania Supreme court found that the first district attorney's promise not to prosecute (because he deemed the evidence insufficient) was binding on any later district attorney.[19]

* * *

In contrast to civilian appellate courts, military appellate courts in the United States do review the facts of cases in which service members have been convicted. Possibly the most recent prominent example occurred after a cadet at West Point was convicted of sexual assault in 2017. He testified at his trial that the sexual intercourse between him and the complainant, another cadet, was consensual. It occurred at night in a field on a summer training exercise. He testified not that the other cadet was lying but rather that he, reasonably, viewed her actions as constituting consent to the sexual activity.

In the military, the jurors (termed *trial members*) are service members who are personally selected by the military commander, and generally only the commander can determine whether to bring charges against a cadet or service member in the first place. The system is rife with conflicts of interest and injustice on all sides, and, in another book, I've written about it extensively.[20] (If the commander orders charges, then the commander can be accused of having fostered a climate that leads to sexual assault. If the commander doesn't bring charges, the criticism might be that the commander is not doing enough to prevent sexual assault in the military.) In the West Point case, the five jurors, all Army officers, found the cadet guilty of rape and sentenced him to twenty-one years in prison.

In the U.S. military, the appellate courts for the Army, Navy–Marine Corps, and Air Force have the authority to review the facts of a case, which means that the courts can replace the trial members' view of the facts and verdict with that of a majority of the judges (in the three-judge appellate courts). The inquisitorial legal system contains a similar protection for defendants, in that "the facts of the case may, and often are, considered *de novo* on appeal, thus providing for a second opinion on the merits."[21]

In the West Point case, the three judges on an Army appellate court (officer-lawyers in the Judge Advocate General's Corps) reasoned that the facts supported the convicted cadet's point, that he reasonably believed the complainant consented to sexual intercourse. The court reversed the cadet's conviction and found him not guilty, using the following reasoning: "It is hard to conclude beyond a reasonable doubt that appellant [the convicted cadet] could complete the charged offenses without cooperation or detection. It is even harder to conclude beyond a reasonable doubt that appellant would anticipate that [the complaining cadet] would not make any reflexive noise or movements upon being awakened, which would have alerted multiple others to his criminal activity."[22] The court found that the charges against the cadet were "factually insufficient."

This is the kind of case in which, given the general prohibition on appellate courts' making factual determinations, defendants, whether innocent or guilty, will almost never have their convictions reversed, except in the military. There's one significant caveat. Like civilian appellate courts, the military appellate courts will not generally consider *new* facts, illustrating the importance of finding facts prior to trial. In any event, trials should be recorded so that appellate courts can see and hear the witnesses and be in better position to evaluate the facts.

The Stranger: Law or Fact

Appellate courts' deciding cases by drawing a distinction between law and facts will be difficult to change because the tradition can be traced to Roman Canon law, in the twelfth century. "'Fact' or 'factum' in law implied human actions or events in which human beings participated that might be known even if not directly observed at the time of adjudication. Typically, they were actions, such as a murder or a robbery, that had been committed some time in the past. . . . The distinction between matters of fact and matters of law was found in the law of all jurisdictions that derived all or part of their law from the civil law that had developed in Italy and elsewhere during the medieval era."[23]

The distinction between law and fact has existed in the United States since 1789, when the first seven articles of the Constitution were ratified. Article III of the Constitution provides that "the Supreme Court shall have appellate jurisdiction, both as to Law and Fact."[24] The Seventh Amendment, ratified in 1791, is applicable to civil cases and provides that "no fact tried by a jury shall be otherwise re-examined."[25]

However, the Sixth Amendment, applicable to criminal cases, does not prohibit appellate courts from examining facts. In *Tibbs v. Florida*, the Supreme Court, in 1982, did not object to judges and appellate courts' "weighing" the evidence used to convict a defendant, indicating that judges and appellate courts may reverse a jury verdict based on their view of the facts. An appellate court may sit as a "thirteenth juror," the Court concluded, though this occurs rarely.[26] In *Miller v. Fenton* (1985), the Supreme Court concluded that "at times [the law/fact distinction] has turned on a determination that, as a matter of the sound administration of justice, one judicial actor is in a better position than another to decide the issue in question."[27]

The perceived distinction between law and fact is used to limit consideration of defenses, especially on criminal defendants' appeals. In the 1942 novel *The Stranger*, by Albert Camus, the main character, Meursault, is on trial for murder and considering his options while the jury deliberates on the murder charge. Meursault killed a man he described as an Arab by shooting him five times with a handgun. Though the deceased Arab apparently (but not certainly) possessed a knife and reached for it in his pocket prior to the killing, Meursault's lawyer did not claim self-defense.

This was perhaps Camus's way to illustrate the absurdity of trials and life, which was part of his philosophy. Meursault, who is also the narrator, apparently recognizes the difficulty of overturning a conviction or sentence based on a question of fact. Camus may be satirizing the failure of appellate courts to engage in a meaningful review of convictions.

> My lawyer came to see me [in a holding room near the court]; he assured me that all would go well and I'd get off with a few years' imprisonment or transportation [to a French colony]. I asked him what were the chances of getting the sentence quashed. He said there was no chance of that. He had not raised any point of law, as this was apt to prejudice the jury. And it was difficult to get a judgment quashed except on technical grounds. I saw his point, and agreed. Looking at the matter dispassionately, I shared his view. Otherwise, there would be no end to litigation.[28]

With Meursault, who was found guilty and sentenced to death, agreeing that his appellate issues should be, almost naturally he seemed to say, limited to a "point of law" or "technical grounds," none of which existed in his case, Camus illustrated the futility of the legal process.

A defendant cannot rely on law, which is incapable of producing justice, and cannot rely on jurors, who are incapable of interpreting the law, Meursault seems to recognize. No sentient person facing death, like Meursault, would argue that his grounds for appeal should be anything but unlimited, unless nothing matters, unless the legal system represents a moot process. After all, Meursault, who was in his thirties, recognized that if he were spared death by hanging he would surely die of natural causes within a few decades.

Are Juries Accountable to Anyone?

Finding a distinction between law and fact, the Supreme Court is extraordinarily deferential to the factual findings (verdicts) of juries and judges in criminal cases. In *Jackson v. Virginia* (1979), a state trial judge, sitting as the fact finder, found the defendant guilty of murder. The Supreme Court refused to grant the defendant's habeas corpus petition (asking a federal court to overturn a conviction from a state court), concluding that "the relevant question is whether, after viewing the evidence in the light most favorable to the prosecution, *any* rational trier of fact could have found the essential elements of the crime beyond a reasonable doubt."[29] Because almost all judges and juries are rational, albeit not necessarily correct, their verdicts will almost never be overturned.

Congress's passage of the Antiterrorism and Effective Death Penalty Act of 1996 required federal courts to be even more deferential to the decisions of state courts. The AEDPA now mandates: "An application for a writ of habeas corpus on behalf of a person in custody pursuant to the judgment of a State court shall not be granted with respect to any claim that was adjudicated on the merits in State court proceedings unless the adjudication of the claim . . . resulted in a decision that was contrary to, or involved an unreasonable application of, clearly established Federal law . . . or . . . resulted in a decision that was based on an unreasonable determination of the facts in light of the evidence presented in the State court proceeding."[30]

A federal judge summarized the statute: "Under the amended version . . . a federal habeas court must apply a more deferential standard of review of the state court decision. Thus, the question here is whether . . . [a state court's] application of the *Jackson* standard was reasonable."[31] Further, in 2017, the Court, in *Davila v. Davis*, citing *Jackson*, reinforced the grim prospects of an innocent defendant when appealing a conviction. In denying the defendant's habeas corpus petition, the Court elevated the trial over all other procedures in the adversarial system:

The criminal trial enjoys pride of place in our criminal justice system in a way that an appeal from that trial does not. The Constitution twice guarantees the right to a criminal trial . . . but does not guarantee the right to an appeal at all. The trial "is the main event at which a defendant's rights are to be determined." . . . [The trial is] where the stakes for the defendant are highest, not least because it is where a presumptively innocent defendant is adjudged guilty and where the trial judge or jury makes factual findings that nearly always receive deference on appeal and collateral review . . . [and] under deferential standard of review, "judges will sometimes encounter convictions that they believe to be mistaken, but that they must nevertheless uphold."[32]

There could not be a clearer statement that truth is sacrificed, first, to procedures and then to appellate courts' deference to juries' guilty verdicts, despite appellate judges' belief that the convicted person may be innocent.

The Court's reverence for trials may perpetuate the misplaced belief that a trial is the best adversarial method through which to prevent innocent-person convictions. Despite guilty pleas leading to almost all convictions (at least 97 percent), about 85 percent of innocent-person convictions arise from mistaken verdicts—from trials.[33] This should inform all innocent people and their defense lawyers that trials and appellate courts are not inviting venues through which to find the truth.

* * *

The argument that appellate courts should consider facts is more compelling if we are incapable of distinguishing law from facts or if, by nature, law and facts are indistinguishable. In 2003, two law professors, Ronald Allen and Michael Pardo, argued that there is no distinction between law and facts and that every decision is ultimately based on a factual finding. Allen and Pardo concluded that the "concepts 'law' and 'fact' do not denote distinct ontological [state of being] categories; rather, legal questions are part of the more general category of factual questions."[34] They reasoned: "The even shorter explanation for the chaotic legal landscape is that much of the effort to properly delineate matters as questions of law or fact is animated by the belief that the two terms, 'law' and 'fact,' specify different kinds of entities, that there is a qualitative or ontological distinction between them. This belief is false. Thus, the quest to find 'the' essential difference between the two that can control subsequent classifications of questions as legal or factual is doomed from the start, as there is no essential difference."[35]

Professor Geoffrey Hazard described how facts are constructed, not found, at trials. Like Judge Frank ("the right does not exist unless that proof is available"),[36] Professor Hazard believed that facts come into existence when recognized by the government. He described facts as arbitrary pillars: "A court therefore does not 'find' facts. It postulates them by an official process—a trial, in which the legal system pronounces on the basis of imperfect evidence what will be considered perfect truth. . . . The facts are as the *court* says they are. The ultimate reason why the court's ipse dixit [assertion without proof] prevails is because the pronouncement is ex officio and the political sovereign has said through organic law that judicial pronouncements shall prevail."[37]

The relatively few facts—otherwise innocent people would not be convicted—that are introduced at trial are so refracted and dented, constructed rather than found, by the time they reach the jurors or appellate courts they may hardly seem objectively compelling. Nonetheless, in most cases these imperfect things or events, *facts*, are transformed by a verdict into perfection, which, despite the majestic pitch of *perfection*, exists in law only because of proof beyond a reasonable doubt. Given the fluidity of facts, this is a standard, as we will see, that should be replaced by a more exacting test when defendants make plausible claims of innocence.

PART III

Obtaining Correct Verdicts

10

Neutral Investigations

Reform will be difficult to obtain because judges and lawyers believe the adversarial system is superior to any other legal method and does not require fundamental change. In a 1949 case, *Watts v. Indiana*, the Supreme Court reversed the conviction of a defendant who confessed to a murder during a five-day period of custody, including solitary confinement, before being charged. The Court implied that protections for suspects are unique to the adversarial system. "The requirement of specific charges, their proof beyond a reasonable doubt, the protection of the accused from confessions extorted through whatever form of police pressures, the right to a prompt hearing before a magistrate, the right to assistance of counsel, to be supplied by government when circumstances make it necessary, the duty to advise an accused of his constitutional rights—these are all characteristics of the accusatorial system and manifestations of its demands."[1] But all of these protections are available in the inquisitorial system.

Professor Monroe Freedman, exemplifying the Court's approach, wrote in 1998, "The rights that comprise the adversary system include personal autonomy, the effective assistance of counsel, equal protection of the laws, trial by jury, the rights to call and to confront witnesses, and the right to require the government to prove guilt beyond a reasonable doubt and without the use of compelled self-incrimination. These rights, and others, are also included in the broad and fundamental concept that no person may be deprived of life, liberty, or property without due process of law—a concept which itself has been substantially equated with the adversary system."[2] Except for jury trials, the inquisitorial system provides similar rights and, with its neutral judges presiding over investigations, provides more opportunity to discover exonerating facts.

Despite criticism, adversarial practices in the United States have become almost immovable. Professor Ellen Sward, in 1989, wrote, "The trends away from adversarial adjudication and the difficulty in justifying the adversary system suggest that there are significant failures in the system that we are trying to adjust for. These failures are primarily in adversarial fact-finding."[3] "Adversarial ideology has failed."[4]

Franklin Strier, in 1996, wrote, "The substantial truth-seeking deficiencies of current trial procedure represent a failure of the essential purpose of the trial. Nevertheless, growing public awareness of these problems impels the movement for reform."[5] But there has been no movement and no reform. In 2004, Professor Geraldine Szott Moohr wrote that "the federal white collar criminal justice system not only fails to correspond to our adversarial ideal, it also lacks safeguards that are inherent in the inquisitorial counterpart."[6]

Unlike the United States, continental countries have tried to synthesize characteristics of the adversarial and inquisitorial systems.[7] "Most Continental judges and scholars, along with comparative scholars both in America and overseas, describe Europe's modern systems of criminal procedure as 'mixed,' combining aspects of the old, inquisitorial process with elements borrowed from, or at least convergent with, the common law tradition," according to Professor David Alan Sklansky.[8]

The "continental European preliminary investigation requires a more or less secret investigation by a legally trained official who is duty-bound to ascertain the truth and to officially and impartially collect evidence which will be admissible in court and sufficient to justify a criminal charge. The search for truth, if taken seriously, cannot be partisan and must include an investigation of potentially exculpatory evidence as well. . . . There is a modern trend . . . to permit defense investigations with Italy leading the way," according to another commentator,[9] though there is a "decisive move towards an adversarial model of criminal procedure" in Italy, noted another.[10]

Also, "a significant number of [inquisitorial] countries have eliminated the preliminary investigation judge—a symbol of the inquisitorial process—and have attempted to replace this figure with a pre-trial investigation developed by the prosecution and, in some cases, by the defense. During the pre-trial phase, the role of the judge is now largely limited to decisions about issuing search-and-seizure warrants, arrests, and pre-trial detentions and bails, much like the Anglo-American model," according to Professor Maximo Langer.[11]

In contrast, the adversarial system—which means primarily judges and lawyers—has not adopted inquisitorial methods. Indeed, the Supreme Court has found that police and prosecutorial neutrality are not required by the Constitution. In *Moran v. Burbine* (1986), the Court concluded that there is no Fifth or Sixth Amendment right to counsel at a voluntary interrogation or an identification procedure that occurs prior to judicial proceedings.[12] But "Continental European law . . . often permits the defendant, defense counsel and sometimes even the aggrieved party to be present when investigative measures are carried out," including the presence of counsel during an interrogation, during confrontation with a witness, and during searches and seizures.[13] France allows the parties to submit written motions to the investigating magistrate.[14] Unlike the United States, "nearly all European jurisdictions" require counsel to be present at lineups.[15] Even in England, with an adversarial system, police officers now call defense lawyers to come to the station to represent suspects.

The American adversarial system contains few of the pretrial protections of inquisitorial practice. "Now [in the inquisitorial system] the defendant, defense counsel, the aggrieved party and her lawyer actively participate in the investigative acts and the role of the judge, whether investigating magistrate or judge of the investigation, has become more like that of a trial judge: an impartial arbiter responding to motions of the parties."[16] In the adversarial system, a motion by a defense attorney to a judge during an investigation is almost nonexistent.

The inquisitorial system, dating from 1200, has been more open to change, adopting adversarial methods while retaining the inquisitorial structure. "Inquisitorial methodology has been the dominant model in world criminal justice over the last eight hundred years and, despite the extraordinary advance of adversariality in recent decades, it still exercises a tenacious influence."[17]

In contrast, rather than interpreting law to make investigations more open and neutral, the Supreme Court has required new procedures to counter adversarial investigations.[18] Probably the most prominent and enduring relevant case concerns a suspect's right to remain silent when in custody and being questioned by the police. In *Miranda v. Arizona* (1966), the Court, using anecdotes, described coercive police practices that extended into the middle of the twentieth century: the "third degree" during the 1930s; "beating, hanging, whipping" to obtain confessions; and beating, kicking, and placing "lighted cigarette butts on the back of a potential witness under interrogation for the purpose of securing a statement incriminating a third party."[19]

The relative historical lateness of the decision in *Miranda* (1966) illustrates how adversarial the American investigation had become. In England, about 1730, when defense counsel appeared, some magistrates warned the accused against making any statements, and for a time in 1817 they were prohibited from questioning the accused.[20] England developed rules to prevent "evidentiary participation" by the defense, such as during the investigation, as a way to protect the accused's right to remain silent.[21] If suspects were not required to participate, then they could not be forced into making a statement.

The process had some inquisitorial flavor. The accused could attend the depositions of prosecution witnesses and cross-examine them. "As the new police gradually took over the conduct of the pre-trial from the magistrates during the course of the 19th century, they were bound by even more stringent rules to protect the accused's silence," according to Professor Richard Vogler.[22] The police could not question a person in custody or someone who was about to be arrested.

Defendants' silence became common. "The total silence of the primary evidentiary source [the accused person] completely undermined any claims which the English trial process had to be an objective forensic enquiry." Silence proliferated even as "the adversarial principle itself was tenaciously defended," Vogler concluded.[23] While the accused was excluded from the adversarial process, the process became more inhospitable to the accused. The accused became entirely dependent on the prosecution—the adversary. This remains the formal condition within the American adversarial legal system, in which the prosecution's decision to issue charges largely determines the outcome of cases.[24]

As suspects and defendants spoke less and less, ethics rules, created by judges and lawyers, elevated confidential communications between lawyers and clients. In *Upjohn Co. v. U.S.* (1981), the Supreme Court recognized confidentiality as a way to encourage communication. It noted that the "attorney-client privilege is the oldest of the privileges for confidential communications known to the common law."[25] In *Swidler &*

Berlin v. U.S., in 1998, the Court held that lawyers are bound by this privilege even after a client's death.[26]

As the adversarial system silenced suspects and rejected neutral investigations, it turned to the trial, and specifically defense cross-examination, as the primary method through which to free innocent people. But Professor Roger C. Park declared, "The question of whether cross-examination is the 'greatest legal engine ever invented for the discovery of truth' cannot be answered with any assurance." He concluded, "It seems very likely that the greatest legal engine for discovering truth is discovery and investigation, not trial cross-examination."[27]

Along the way, adversarial rules and practices have institutionalized conflict and distrust. The Supreme Court, in *Moran v. Burbine* (1986), considered the alleged police "impropriety of conveying false information to an attorney" and concluded that it is acceptable: "The challenged conduct [a police officer or detective apparently lying to a lawyer who said she represented a suspect] falls short of the kind of misbehavior that so shocks the sensibilities of civilized society as to warrant a federal intrusion into the criminal processes of the States."[28]

In summary, the Supreme Court's decisions have had the effect of leaving all but the most clever and wealthy suspects completely alone during the entirety of an investigation and preserved the primary reason why innocent people are convicted—their inability to find and collect exonerating facts. The Court, in *U.S. v. Gouveia* (1984), concluded that "our cases have long recognized that the right to counsel attaches only at or after the initiation of adversary judicial proceedings against the defendant."[29] Quoting with approval from a plurality opinion in a 1972 case, *Kirby v. Illinois*,[30] the Court wrote, "'In a line of constitutional cases in this Court . . . it has been firmly established that a person's Sixth and Fourteenth Amendment right to counsel attaches only at or after the time that adversary judicial proceedings have been initiated against him.'"[31] This is after the government has obtained sufficient facts through which to charge and convict suspects and stopped looking for additional facts that could exonerate them.

In contrast, the inquisitorial system allows and even requires participation of defense lawyers and judges during the investigation. "As third-stage adversariality has become entrenched in Anglo-American procedure and projected around the globe, so the common law world has been plunged into a bitter period of domestic self-debate and envy. In England, the possibility of introducing an examining magistrate into the pretrial procedure has been under active discussion since the 1970s."[32] Research over the past twenty years, "although by no means representing a dominant view in either the UK or the US, is clearly evidence of a crisis of confidence in adversarial method in its homelands, at a time when it is expanding across the world as never before in its history," according to Professor Vogler.[33]

The supposed distinctions between the adversarial and inquisitorial systems, mainly the adversarial prosecutor versus the investigating magistrate, can be unnecessarily formal and reflect American misunderstanding.[34] In *Watts v. Indiana*, the Supreme Court described the characteristics of the adversarial system, noting that an experienced prosecutor conducted constant interrogations of the defendant. "Until his inculpatory statements were secured, the petitioner was a prisoner in the exclusive control of the prosecuting authorities. He was kept for the first two days in solitary confinement in a cell aptly enough called 'the hole' in view of its physical conditions as described by the State's witnesses. Apart from the five night sessions, the police intermittently interrogated Watts during the day and on three days, drove him around town, hours at a time, with a view to eliciting identifications and other disclosures."[35]

In suppressing the defendant's confession and reversing his conviction on due process grounds, the Court described the adversarial system. Even as it seemed to disparage the inquisitorial system, the Court did not describe why it believed the adversarial system is better. It cited no empirical evidence. "Ours is the accusatorial, as opposed to the inquisitorial, system. Such has been the characteristic of Anglo-American criminal justice since it freed itself from practices borrowed by the Star Chamber from the Continent whereby an accused was interrogated in secret for hours on end. . . . Under our system, society carries the burden of proving its charge against the accused not out of his own mouth. It must establish its case not by interrogation of the accused, even under judicial safeguards, but by evidence independently secured through skillful investigation."[36] The irony behind the Court's lofty generalizations about the adversarial system is that in an inquisitorial system, with a neutral magistrate replacing or supplementing the adversarial system's prosecutor, who, in *Watts*, was the principal interrogator, the coerced statements—induced, in part, by the prosecutor—would not have occurred in the first place.

Innocent people do not need to be coerced before they will speak. They want to tell their stories as soon as possible, but they should do so only if prosecution authorities are likely to be open to considering and searching for exonerating facts, not pouncing on and taking advantage of a suspect's truthful disclosures. The coercion inherent in the endurance test to which authorities subjected the suspect in *Watts* is akin to the dangers faced by innocent people who speak up when the prosecution is guided by proving guilt beyond a reasonable doubt, in contrast to having truth as a goal. The consequences of this structure are undesirable and frequently dire.

11

A New Procedure

The Search for Truth

A new procedure through which defendants who plead innocence and are required to consent to an interview with the prosecution in return for an innocence investigation would allow accused people to have a more central role in their defense. In England, felony trials were conducted without the full participation of lawyers until the 1730s, and defendants were expected to speak, according to Professor John Langbein, who examined the *Old Bailey Sessions Papers*.[1] Beginning in the 1670s, when the adversarial system started to form in England, the "*Sessions Papers* were contemporaneously published pamphlet accounts of the trials at the Old Bailey. As the Court with jurisdiction over cases of serious crimes in metropolitan London, the Old Bailey was the most important criminal court in the Anglo-American world throughout the eighteenth century."[2]

The *Sessions Papers* were presumably unknown to the Supreme Court in the 1960s, when it interpreted the Constitution to provide various procedural rights to suspects and defendants in criminal cases, and to early scholars of adversarial history, including Professor John Henry Wigmore (1863–1943). Over the past century, Wigmore has been the most influential authority in the United States on the law of evidence. The Supreme Court, every federal appellate court, and courts in every state, in over seventeen hundred cases, have cited Wigmore's work, especially his treatise on evidence.[3] Langbein, inadvertently, found the *Sessions Papers* when conducting research at the Bodleian Law Library at the University of Oxford, in 1977. His important book, *The Origins of Adversary Criminal Trial*, reporting on the *Sessions Papers*, was published in 2003.

The *Sessions Papers* show that Wigmore was incorrect about the state of criminal procedure at the beginning of the adversarial system, and his errors have informed the modern rules of evidence, to what extent we will probably never know. For example, in *Miranda v. Arizona* (1966), perhaps representing the pinnacle of process-based decision making in law and one of the most prominent cases in U.S. history, the Supreme Court's majority, concurring/dissenting, and dissenting opinions cited, with approval, Wigmore's writings.

However, as the *Sessions Papers* show, Wigmore's view that the right to remain silent applied to defendants early in the adversarial system was incorrect. Indeed, Langbein found that Wigmore was incorrect in his analysis of five of the most critical rules in an adversary trial. The rules pertain to character evidence, confessions, corroboration, hearsay, and, as noted, the privilege against self-incrimination (silence). Wigmore's errors are significant because modern judges and legislatures have relied on his work to include or exclude from trials legally relevant evidence of innocence and guilt.

First, according to Langbein, "In 1684, the year of the decision in *Hampden's Case*, which Wigmore saw as the turning point in disapproving the use of character evidence, we find Old Bailey cases in which character evidence was not only admitted, but was said to have been central to the outcome."[4] In trials in the United States today, the prosecution may not introduce evidence of character unless defendants place their character into issue. Though rarely, this occurs when a witness for the defense testifies that the defendant is known to have a peaceable nature when the charges pertain to assault or a history of honesty when the charges relate to theft or fraud.[5] In England, the jury was allowed to consider the character of accused people even if they did not raise the issue.

Second, Wigmore believed that the prohibition on allowing involuntary confessions into trials was formulated in 1775 and solidified in 1783. In contrast, "The *Sessions Papers* make it clear that the confession rule . . . was formulated in the early 1740s and settled by the 1760s," according to Langbein.[6] If English judges curtailed the use of involuntary confessions earlier than previously believed, then part of the basis for some of the modern, judge-made rules on the exclusion of defendants' statements might be unsound.

That is, toward the beginning of the adversarial system, not later during the American Revolution, as Wigmore believed, English judges had already accounted for coerced statements. The U.S. Constitution, ratified in 1789, and its Bill of Rights, ratified in 1791, might not require what modern judges believe. The Constitution's Drafters might have been aware that the English judges, as early as the 1740s, in accounting for involuntary confessions, created rules to prohibit them. The English rules, rather than the modern American rules, could be more in accord with what the Drafters intended.

Third, the corroboration rule prevented a defendant from being convicted based solely on the testimony of an accomplice. According to Langbein, Wigmore believed the corroboration rule "dated from the 1780s" and that it was "'no rule of evidence,'" only a caution given by the judge to the jury. "Wigmore was wrong on both points. The corroboration rule came into force in the 1740s . . . as a rule of exclusion, not a mere caution," Langbein wrote.[7]

Regarding corroboration, the point is the same as in regard to English judges' rejection of involuntary confessions earlier than what Wigmore believed: the judges, early on in the adversarial system, recognized some of its infirmities and tried to correct them. The U.S. Supreme Court, as well as lower courts and state and federal legislators since then, perhaps relying on Wigmore and others and thus unaware of the English judges' recognition of the problems, created new rules to deal with problems that may have already been considered and addressed or resolved, at least according to the original thinking behind the adversarial system. Perhaps this informed the Drafters of the Constitution. This is not to argue against change, but the modern changes—and recall that the adversarial system is not the result of an organized plan or structure or any document that describes how to make changes—might be more haphazard than necessary and without some of the foundation that judges and legislators believe existed when they made the changes.

Fourth, the rule against hearsay evidence is central to the adversarial legal system today. Unlike the prior three rules for criminal cases (character, confessions, and corroboration), the hearsay rule—a witness's testimony in court about what someone said outside court is usually inadmissible—applies in both criminal and civil cases.[8] Wigmore believed the hearsay rule was settled by the early eighteenth century, but, according to Langbein, the rule "was not settled until well into the early nineteenth century."[9] The English judges allowed hearsay evidence into cases far longer, one hundred years, than U.S. judges and legislators may believe, thus making less supportable reliance on Wigmore as justification for prohibiting some hearsay evidence.

The question surrounding hearsay is how much of it to allow, under the rationale that some hearsay is reliable, despite that the hearsay (a statement) occurred outside a formal courtroom. To make the discussion more concrete, one exception permits the first person to whom a complainant reported a sexual assault to testify in court about what the complainant told that person. The rationale is that complainants who make prompt reports of sexual assault are unlikely to be fabricating. What we may never know is how many of such rules or parts of them were created by modern judges and legislators without a complete assessment of adversarial history.

That is, have judges and legislators permitted the adversarial system and its processes overall to become unforgiving and rigid, at least from the perspective of innocent people, because modern evidentiary rules lean toward the protection of guilty suspects through courts' misreading of adversarial history? For example, even the lofty notion that the American legal system does not allow involuntary confessions into court cases seems quaint. The *Alford* plea, in which a defendant who claims to be innocent pleads guilty to avoid going to trial and being found guilty and sentenced to death, is probably far more mentally and emotionally coercive than a police officer's verbal threats to or physical beating of a suspect.[10]

Presumably almost everyone would prefer a moderately severe beating, or worse, to a prosecutor's credible threat of execution. On a continuum, with voluntary and involuntary on opposite ends, a guilty plea induced by the threat of death would be considered one of the most involuntary events in anyone's life. Moreover, even a suspect's body is not absolutely protected today from physical invasion by the government, especially when prosecutors obtain warrants, but even without warrants. In 2019, the Supreme Court, in *Mitchell v. Wisconsin*, approved, at a police officer's request (and without a warrant), medical personnel's drawing blood from an unconscious drunk-driving suspect and using the blood to convict him.[11]

The government's use of involuntary statements and manipulation of suspects' bodies either never left the adversarial system or perhaps returned after the exclusionary rule expanded, when the Supreme Court applied the rule to state cases in 1961, in *Mapp v. Ohio*.[12] Since then, as discussed in chapters 7 and 10, the Court has approved a wide range of severe government investigative procedures, such as mostly secret investigations, in which detectives are permitted to lie to suspects and witnesses. We do not know how much of this rebalancing, if that's what it is, occurred because of courts' and legislatures' mistaken views of the nature of the early adversarial system.

England's adversarial system has evolved to provide more protection for suspects during the investigation, but less protection for defendants at trial. Suspects in England must be provided a lawyer while at the police station. At trial, English courts require defendants to speak; if defendants refuse, their juries may draw adverse inferences against them. Also, prosecutors in England may introduce evidence of bad character against defendants. In these changes, England has returned to early adversarial practice.

Fifth, perhaps Wigmore's most significant error concerns the privilege against self-incrimination, which he believed existed early in the adversarial system. Judges then were concerned about coercive interrogations, but their concern had nothing to do with the common law adversary trial. "What became the privilege [against self-incrimination] had its origins as an effort by the common law courts, using the writ of prohibition to restrain practices of the ecclesiastical and prerogative courts, most prominently the Court of High Commission, in the seventeenth century."[13] These religious courts did not follow common law criminal procedure. They would force oaths on accused people, such as the Puritans, "who were typically quite guilty of the nonconformist religious practices being investigated."[14]

When an accused person is forced to take an oath prior to making a statement, the right not to make a statement (silence) helps ensure that authorities will not try to mentally or physically coerce suspects. When suspects want to speak, the absence of an oath ensures that authorities cannot prosecute them for perjury (both innocent and guilty people lie or may appear to be lying) as a method through which to obtain a harsher overall sentence. In the absence of an oath, authorities cannot prosecute suspects for lying as a method to punish them when the evidence of an alleged underlying crime is insufficient for a conviction.[15]

The English common law courts did not require accused people to take oaths, but they expected them to speak. (Defendants' testifying is the practice in the inquisitorial system today.) Common law courts prohibited oaths even when accused people wanted to take them. Parliament sided with the Puritans and banned the ecclesiastical courts from using oaths. This allowed the courts to continue to require accused people to tell their stories without being punished for speaking. The belief was that the accused, innocent or guilty, harbors the most relevant evidence.

How, then, did the oath requirement and the right to remain silent seep into the common law courts and become a central component of the adversarial system, especially in the United States? The answer is *defense lawyers*. Professor Langbein explains:

> So long as the rule against defense counsel required the accused to conduct his own defense, there could be no effective privilege against self-incrimination. In common law criminal procedure, therefore, the privilege against self-incrimination was the creature of defense counsel. . . . Without defense counsel, a criminal defendant's right to remain silent was the right to forfeit any defense; indeed, in a system that emphasized capital punishment, the right to remain silent was literally the right to commit suicide. . . . The privilege we know in modern Anglo-American law was fashioned across the nineteenth century, by extension of an earlier privilege that had protected third-party witnesses, but not the criminal accused.[16]

Langbein wrote, "I have examined most of the *Sessions Paper* reports from their beginnings in the 1670s through the 1780s. In these thousands of cases I have not noticed a single instance in which the accused refused to speak at trial on the asserted ground of a privilege to remain silent."[17]

Contrary to Wigmore's belief, English judges did not recognize a right to remain silent. Yet in Miranda, concerning the right to remain silent prior to trial and the requirement that investigators inform suspects of their rights, all three Supreme Court opinions (majority, concurring/dissenting, and dissenting) cited Wigmore for various propositions, a total of seven times. But, without access to the *Sessions Papers*, Wigmore's views on early adversary procedure could not have been well formed. "I have elsewhere shown that the authorities on which Wigmore based this account [of the origins of the privilege against self-incrimination] do not support the claim that the common law courts recognized a general privilege against self-incrimination by the end of the seventeenth century," Langbein found.[18]

In summary, it is difficult to identify and would be equally difficult to wring from the law of evidence the current practices that have arisen from Wigmore's misreading of the evolution of adversarial practices. But recognition of Wigmore's errors helps us understand that many of today's legal practices may not be well-formed pillars of an adversarial legal system. What is perhaps most significant is that Wigmore's errors, depending on the extent to which courts and legislatures followed Wigmore, may have had the effect of *decreasing* the number of relevant and probative facts that are allowed into trials today.

The English common law courts prohibited involuntary confessions and uncorroborated accomplice testimony decades earlier than what Wigmore believed. But why, then, do false confessions and accomplice testimony remain two of the primary contributors to innocent-person convictions today? Relying on Wigmore, modern judges may have believed false confessions and accomplice testimony, among other evidentiary matters, were larger problems than they actually were and instituted exclusionary rules to restrain the police collection of evidence. Perhaps recoiling from new and unnecessary procedures that benefit mostly guilty defendants, the modern judges became comfortable with, and approved, authoritarian police investigations, which, ironically, produce false confessions, false guilty pleas, and reliance on accomplice testimony.

The English judges permitted evidence that is prohibited in U.S. courts, but which would often be beneficial in convicting guilty, as well as some innocent, people. The judges permitted the prosecution to introduce evidence of a defendant's character longer than what Wigmore believed, permitted hearsay evidence one hundred years longer than what Wigmore believed, and required defendants to testify, which Wigmore believed they did not require. The modern exclusionary rules limit the number of facts introduced into a trial, which, as a practice, is contrary to the desire of innocent people, who almost always benefit from the introduction of facts.

Indeed, if all defendants in America were required to testify, jurors would have access to a far greater number of facts and society would be in a better position to distinguish the credible claims of innocent people from the incredible claims of those who are guilty. But the Fifth Amendment of the Constitution, for good reasons—to limit the power of government and to protect the innocent, whose truthful testimony might make them appear guilty—prohibits the government from compelling a defendant, but not anyone else, to testify. But is there a way to allow innocent people to testify without increasing the risk they will be convicted?

* * *

With the introduction of defense lawyers, the adversarial system evolved so that it became acceptable practice for an accused person to remain silent. Guilty people do not want to be required to admit they committed a crime and will almost always exercise the right. Therefore, aside from a political reason (restraint on government), there can be only one primary reason for the right to remain silent—to protect innocent people who, if required to speak or testify, would tend to incriminate themselves. For example, it would be very precarious, indeed, for an innocent person who resembles the actual robber to admit to a police detective, "Yes, I was at the donut shop last night near the time the robbery occurred."

The theory of the common law courts on why an accused person should be required to speak was borne of practical experience. "The innocent àccused will be as able to defend himself on 'a Matter of Fact, as if he were the best Lawyer,' whereas 'the Guilty, when they speak for themselves, may often help to disclose the Truth, which probably would not so well be discovered from the artificial Defense of others speaking for them.' Hence, by speaking at trial, the accused would clear himself or hang himself."[19]

Unlike the United States, England today expects to find more facts by questioning defendants and evaluating their behavior prior to the alleged crime. In 1995, after generations of permitting defendants to remain silent, England changed course and required them to testify under oath at their trials. If they decline to testify and remain silent, judges instruct juries that they are permitted to draw adverse inferences against the defendants, including that they are guilty of the crime charged.[20]

While investigations in the United States have become more secretive, in England they have become more open. After a suspect is arrested, police officers are required to contact a solicitor. The solicitor, paid by the government, will come to the police station to represent the suspect. Before recommending whether the suspect should make a statement to the police, the solicitor will examine the police officer's *custody file* and request other documents regarding the evidence that has been collected.

Suspects will decide on one of three options: speak with the police officer; submit a short, written statement for the officer and file; or remain silent. In America, if a suspect were ever represented by a lawyer prior to charges, the lawyer would almost always tell that person to remain silent. The reason is that, in the United States, there is no downside for a defendant to remain silent because, at trial, the prosecutor may not comment on the defendant's prior silence. This allows a defendant to have ample time (from arrest to trial) with which to forge or fabricate a defense that is most in accord with the evidence.

However, in England (and Wales), suspects are far more likely to speak to the police. If they do not speak at the police station but go on to testify at trial, the prosecution is entitled to cross-examine them and imply that they remained silent earlier because they needed time to fabricate a defense. The reasoning is that innocent people do not need to wait until the trial to speak because they know by the time of an arrest they are innocent.

The Criminal Justice Act of 2003 permitted prosecutors in England to introduce evidence of a defendant's bad character. For example, in burglary cases, the prosecution may introduce evidence of prior convictions for burglaries to show defendants' propensity to commit them and permit the inference they committed the burglary for which they are on trial.[21] The common law judges, too, allowed character evidence, and longer than what Wigmore believed. They also required defendants to speak, which Wigmore thought the judges did not require. In all of these changes—solicitors at police stations, suspects' speaking to the police, expectations that defendants testify, and the use of character evidence—England realigned itself with the early judges. It is, therefore, a significant question to what extent U.S. courts, because of their possible misreading of adversarial history, deviated from the early thinking behind the adversarial system and implemented procedures inconsistent with it.

Unnatural Evolution

Adversarial practices developed because England and its judges tired of capital punishment and harsh treatment of suspects. "By the sixteenth century in England . . . intentional killings as a result of drunken brawls and breaches of honor had become all too common. The death penalty was viewed as an inappropriate and excessive response to deaths occurring in such fights."[22] Nonetheless, Britain, in 1723, established the "Bloody Code," which allowed the death penalty for over two hundred offenses, many of them related to theft and misuse of resources. Some of the crimes leading to execution included "forgery," "stealing from a ship wreck," "deer-stealing," "cutting down trees," "stealing from a rabbit warren," and "wrecking a fishpond."[23]

Any such punitive ethos will inevitably produce dishonesty. "To understand how a system so flawed [with truth-defeating tendencies] could gain acceptance, we need to bear in mind the growing aversion to capital punishment that characterized these years [later eighteenth and early nineteenth centuries]," according to Langbein.[24] The typical defendant who confessed to a crime and needed to be saved from a severe penalty was "a young and vulnerable domestic servant (often female), or an apprentice, hireling, or lodger . . . charged with taking food, clothes, housewares, tools, or stock of the trade."[25] Prosecutors and juries downgraded charges from burglary to theft to ensure that defendants would not be convicted of a felony and receive the death penalty.[26] The heat-of-passion defense provided that a husband who intentionally killed his wife after being surprised and seeing her having sexual intercourse with another man could be convicted of manslaughter rather than murder,[27] a defense that exists today.[28] (Because most people do not kill for any reason, the heat-of-passion defense protects the most hot-headed spouses.)

England's primary method of execution was hanging, but it also employed burning, beheading, and the firing squad.[29] In 1861, England abolished the death penalty for all crimes, except murder, treason, piracy, and arson, and ended public executions in 1868. In 1965, it suspended and then abolished, in 1969, the death penalty for all crimes, except treason. In 1998, it abolished the death penalty for treason as well.[30]

In summary, as its sentences became less severe, England implemented practices that produced additional facts. In contrast, the United States retains the death penalty, as well as extraordinarily long sentences of imprisonment compared to other Western countries. As a result, Americans experience the accompanying truth-defeating practices, such as innocent people who plead guilty to many crimes, including murder, to escape long terms of imprisonment or execution (detailed in chapter 3).

In England, "the judges developed the exclusionary rules of evidence, especially corroboration and confession rules, and the beyond-reasonable-doubt standard of proof, rules whose breadth assured that not only some innocent defendants would be spared, but also many culpable ones."[31] The trial evolved from an "accused speaks" trial to an adversary trial that "largely silenced the accused."[32] "Trial became what it has remained, a proceeding whose primary purpose is to provide defense counsel with an opportunity to test the prosecution case," not a search for truth.[33]

The Limitations of Trials

Trials, indeed, are not optimal places to search for truth; there are very few trials, and most of them result in convictions. A 2009 study by the Bureau of Justice Statistics of felony defendants in the seventy-five largest counties in the United States showed that 66 percent of felony arrests result in a conviction (54 percent felonies and 12 percent misdemeanors). Nine percent of the arrests had "other outcomes," such as "diversion and deferred adjudication," indicating that probably about 75 percent of the people arrested are formally responsible for some offense. About 25 percent of the cases were dismissed. Guilty pleas constituted 97 percent of the convictions. Only 1 percent of people who were arrested were acquitted at trial.[34] In federal courts in 2018, for all defendants who went to trial (from drunk driving to homicide), the acquittal rate was 17 percent, according to an analysis by the Pew Research Center (a total of 1,879 verdicts, 1,661 by juries and 218 by judges).[35]

Scholars and practitioners have recommended improving virtually every procedure in the adversarial system, but few have proposed significant structural change since the system took root in the late 1600s and early 1700s. Even without considering the new plea of innocence, many structural changes could be made to promote the discovery of exonerating facts and deter untruth from seeping into the system.

- The most beneficial reform would involve making the investigation more neutral and open.
- Defendants could be encouraged to tell their stories by eliminating oaths for them.
- Lawyers could be prohibited from knowingly undermining truthful and accurate witnesses and urging judges and jurors to adopt inferences the lawyers know to be false.
- Appellate courts could be open to considering whether jury verdicts are correct, especially when a defendant presents a plausible claim of innocence.

Yet almost every proposed modification thus far accepts a fixed adversarial system and is limited to nipping only at the corners of centuries-old procedures.

Beginning with prosecutors, the central actors in the system, one recommendation was that they should consider the "psychological, social, and moral factors" that influence their decisions.[36] Also, prosecutors should be more attuned to ethical rules[37] and more subject to ethical charges,[38] with new ethical rules established to require prosecutors (postconviction) to seek truth.[39] Prosecutors should be more amenable to trying to "resolve postconviction justice issues" through new ethical standards.[40] They and defense lawyers should work more cooperatively where DNA evidence is at issue.[41]

Defense lawyers should receive additional funding.[42] Witnesses who work in law enforcement should not receive absolute immunity.[43] Witness perjury should be easier to attack via habeas corpus.[44] Jurors could be permitted to ask questions.[45] Cross-examination might not be limited to the lawyers.[46]

Judges, it has been suggested, could be more active at trial so that a defendant may assert a political position.[47] One commentator argues that "until state and federal judgeships are depoliticized . . . judges should be held personally, directly and openly accountable for the violence they initiate with the words they speak and write" or "they will continue to inflict egregious harm on multitudes of innocent people with scant regard for the human consequences of their actions."[48]

Professor Craig Bradley, in 1996, was an exception and went further. He suggested that a "short, *mandatory*, nonjury trial in the continental mode, with few of the evidentiary restrictions that inhere in the usual jury trial" would be a "sensible alternative" to trials in the adversarial system.[49]

One commentator summarized the recommendations about the current procedures. "In response, a multiplicity of procedural protections have been proposed: improved eyewitness identification procedures and independent corroboration; protective jury instructions; videotaped interrogations . . . [evidence] 'reliability hearings'; strongly regulated forensic labs and examiners; independent case reviews; limiting 'anecdotal' forensic testimony; better lawyer training, funding and oversight and stronger lawyer ethics rules."[50]

Identification procedures, which are probably the most common procedures connected to innocent-person convictions, should employ double-blind protections.[51] "In a double-blind procedure, neither the eyewitness nor the officer conducting the identification procedure are [*sic*] aware of who the suspect is within the photo array or lineup. This straightforward procedure protects against witnesses looking towards the administrator of the photo array or lineup for cues as to which person to choose, or for confirmation of their selection. It also prevents against the administrator giving unintended or express reinforcement of the witnesses' selection."[52]

One commission recommended that identification procedures include recording witnesses' initial descriptions; telling witnesses the person they are viewing may not be the one who committed the crime; presenting photos or live suspects in a sequence, one at a time, rather than on one page (photos) or in a lineup; and ensuring double-blind procedures.[53]

These recommendations, almost all of them valuable, have come from accomplished professionals. But most of the recommendations have not been mandated by courts or legislatures or adopted by the various state and federal agencies and prosecution offices. Moreover, even if every recommendation were adopted, there would still not be a new method through which to find additional exonerating facts or by which innocent people could tell their stories without increasing the risk of conviction. Human error would continue its pervasive, debilitating influence.

The piecemeal process of implementing all these nonstructural recommendations could consume decades or generations of time, and maybe never occur. No matter what—because the recommendations do not contain a specific method through which to find additional facts— every case would remain adversarial and have to be decided through grueling, costly, time-consuming litigation. Innocent defendants, still receiving no benefit from speaking up, would continue to remain silent with the truth. To the world and, more importantly, jurors, they would appear guilty, and they would continue to be lumped together with all those who are, in fact, guilty.

The Innocence Movement

Since DNA testing revealed the certainty, and, to a lesser extent, the frequency, of innocent-person convictions, the *innocence movement* (perhaps beginning in 1989 with the first DNA exoneration) has been a phrase used broadly to represent the work of scholars and defense lawyers (often working in innocence projects at law schools) and a few district attorneys who have tried to reverse innocent-person convictions. The movement has been important in ensuring the release of hundreds, possibly two to three thousand, innocent people and focusing public attention on the problem of the convictions.[54] However, the movement can assist only a small percentage of innocent people because of two fundamental limitations: it offers no new method through which to find additional facts, and almost all its work occurs only *after* convictions and appeals, by which time innocent people, even if exonerated, have spent years or decades suffering in prison. It is not sufficient to hope the current adversarial process will work and then, if it does not, get into high gear following a conviction.

Moreover, probably the primary method through which innocence projects have helped obtain exonerations has been DNA testing. But even according to the most prominent innocence project, at the Cardozo School of Law, the number of DNA exonerations in the United States from 1989 through early 2022 was only 375, or about 11 per year.[55] The project's data show the number of *postconviction* DNA exonerations is dropping, down to 5.7 per year from 2015 to 2021, probably because DNA testing is now a staple of investigations.[56] In short, postconviction exoneration is rare.

As early as 2005, Professor Andrew Siegel summarized the dissipating utility of the resource-draining, case-by-case-litigation, postconviction approach of the movement:

> While the second generation evidence-related law reform activities of the wrongful convictions movement rightfully continue to occupy its members, the scholarly work on false confessions, faulty eyewitness identifications, and other predictable problems of proof is largely complete. As a result, the academic allies of the wrongful convictions movement are, to some extent, adrift without an agenda. . . . [The] wrongful convictions scholars should shift their focus from post-conviction strategies and evidence-related flaws in our system of criminal justice to broader questions about the structure and administration of the justice system, both because of the intrinsic importance of the knowledge they will create and in preparation for future litigation and law reform campaigns.[57]

Professor Siegel, focusing on one state, described what he viewed as the misdirection of the movement. "While readily accessible post-conviction DNA testing, innocence commissions, double-blind lineups, and videotaped confessions are all worthy reforms that would no doubt improve the operation of the South Carolina criminal justice system, none of these reforms would have nearly the impact on the quality of justice—including the prospect for wrongful convictions—as the simple alteration of a single procedural rule [regarding docket control by prosecutors]."[58]

In 2006, North Carolina created the Innocence Inquiry Commission, which is probably the most prominent and well-funded public agency in the United States (not including courts) devoted to correcting innocent-person convictions.[59] Like the innocence projects, the commission is limited to investigating claims of innocence only after someone has been convicted. Consisting of eight commissioners and a staff of nine people, the commission is authorized to search for exonerating facts and recommend that an outside three-judge panel convene to consider whether the convicted person is "factually innocent." Defendants who make their way to the three-judge panel must prove by clear and convincing evidence that they are innocent of the charges.[60]

The North Carolina commission instructs claimants (convicted people), "In order for the Commission to review your claim there must be . . . credible and verifiable evidence of innocence . . . [or] new evidence of innocence that the jury did not hear or that was not available prior to a plea."[61] This is surely a benefit to innocent people who have been convicted, but, with DNA testing now routine, almost all exonerating evidence (except recantations by witnesses) exists prior to convictions. Why not look for it then? Facts are fresh and more available, investigators are more open-minded, suspects and defendants are presumed innocent, and the prosecution is required to prove guilt beyond a reasonable doubt. Following a conviction, almost everyone presumes the defendant is guilty.

Unlike with a plea of innocence, which provides defendants a right to require the government to search for potentially exonerating facts, the commission in North Carolina has no obligation to do anything. The statue creating the commission provides, "The determination of whether to grant a formal inquiry regarding any other claim [compared with those automatically barred because the defendant filed a late claim] of factual innocence is in the discretion of the Commission. The Commission may informally screen and dismiss a case summarily at its discretion."[62] The commission reported 3,033 "cases closed" and fifteen exonerations through early 2022, which is a very significant benefit to innocent people and society.[63]

* * *

The deepest crack in the adversarial system, now more like a vast crevice after three hundred years, is the absence of a mechanism devoted to the search for truth. "The lawyer-dominated system of criminal trial that emerged in eighteenth-century England was not premised on a coherent theory of truth-seeking," Professor Langbein wrote. "Adversary procedure presupposed that truth would somehow emerge when no one was in charge of seeking it."[64] Professor Lloyd Weinreb reached the same conclusion:

> The adversary system, as we call our criminal process, is far too adversarial. We should not regard it as in the nature of things and not to be altered. Nor should we suppose that the Constitution requires the extreme, destructive manifestations of adversariness that are now common. Rather, at each stage in the process, we should ask, with no presumption either way, "Ought we to entrust this to the lawyers?" Unless we can reasonably conclude that the outcome overall is likely to be better if lawyers of varying ability, committed only to one side, and employing all the arts and tricks of their profession have control, we ought to displace them and adapt a more neutral procedure.[65]

Still bereft of neutrality, the adversarial system designates prosecutors, the government's advocates, as its chief gatekeepers and decision makers, with little or no opportunity for plausibly innocent people to request additional consideration.

Gerard E. Lynch, the federal appeals court judge, recognized that cases are decided when the prosecutor decides whether to charge a person with a crime. Judge Lynch, in 1998, wrote: "Americans . . . need to recognize first, that most defendants in the United States are effectively convicted by government officials rather than independent judges and lay juries, and second, that our failure to acknowledge this fact helps to perpetuate a situation in which those officials are encouraged to view themselves as partisan adversaries of the defendant rather than as neutral adjudicators."[66]

Some changes to the adversarial system, according to Judge Lynch, might concern its informal processes, which cannot be contested by defendants. "In many cases . . . the process internal to the prosecuting agency . . . [is] the 'real' trial or procedure by which society adjudicates the case," not the guilty plea or trial.[67] Accordingly, "the two strongest candidates for formal recognition involve greater discovery rights, and the formalization of the opportunity to be heard before prosecutorial decisions are made."[68]

Another federal judge, Jed S. Rakoff, in his 2021 book *Why the Innocent Plead Guilty and the Guilty Go Free*, also recognized the disparity in power between prosecutors and poor defendants.[69] He recommended that magistrates supervise the plea-bargaining process to lessen the disparity. Both of the judges are former federal prosecutors; their recommendations could be implemented with relatively little cost and would make the government's evidence more available to defendants.

Professor Darryl K. Brown takes a broad view as to why cases are resolved through defendants' guilty pleas. He notes the asymmetric power of prosecutors, who have far greater access to the evidence than do defendants and thus more knowledge about the likelihood of a conviction. Professor Brown notes two other conditions that induce defendants to plead guilty. Prosecutors, who determine the number and severity of charges, engage in "hard-bargaining" tactics. Defendants face "severe trial penalties," the large increase in terms of imprisonment when they are sentenced following a jury's guilty verdict, compared with the more lenient sentences accompanying a negotiated guilty plea.[70]

Professor Geraldine Szott Moohr advocates the integration of inquisitorial principles into the adversarial system.[71] "In sum, the quasi-inquisitorial federal system, dominated by the prosecutor, is not an entirely effective vehicle for achieving deterrence and may ultimately impair the deterrent effect that aggressive enforcement is supposed to achieve. This prospect justifies and gives force to efforts to restore a better adversarial balance. Such efforts might begin by examining characteristics of the inquisitorial system that could be adapted most readily to the federal criminal justice system."[72]

Professor Ellen Sward asked whether the adversarial system should be scrapped. "The trends away from adversarial adjudication and the difficulty in justifying the adversary system suggest that there are significant failures in the system that we are trying to adjust for. These failures are primarily in adversarial fact-finding. Thus, we might ask whether adversarial ideology is correct or even useful."[73]

Professor David Alan Sklansky concluded, "My prescriptive claim will be more modest: not that we should try to copy civil law systems, but simply that we should not go out of our way to differentiate our own system from theirs, and that we should stop treating differentiation of that kind as a paramount constitutional value."[74]

One final recommendation is that it would be valuable if defendants could comment to prosecutors formally prior to charges being lodged against them, as Judge Lynch suggested. But being heard in this manner means only that the prosecutor will listen to the defense lawyer, a practice that already exists in federal cases, but only rarely in state cases, where arrests are made on the streets. For street-crime suspects in the United States, the retention of a defense attorney is not a realistic possibility until after an arrest and at the arraignment, when the defendant first sees a judge, by which time all or most of the facts that will be the basis of a guilty plea, dismissal, or trial have already been collected.

From the defense perspective, innocent suspects should not speak at this point because prosecutors, who believe already that the suspects are guilty, will use their statements to connect them to the crime or to narrow their defenses at trial. Despite a dire need for facts, an innocent suspect or defendant in the adversarial system appears not to have ever had the opportunity to plead innocent and compel the prosecution to search for facts. In 2003 and 2004, three professors at universities in England led a project, *The Proceedings of the Old Bailey: London's Central Criminal Court, 1674 to 1913*, which culminated in a computer database with the written record of all the trials in the Old Bailey, from the beginning of the adversarial system to the early twentieth century, a total of over 197,700 trials.

It does not appear that a formal plea of innocence has ever appeared in the adversarial system. In the Old Bailey, apparently no cases contained the phrase *plea of innocent*, although two cases, one from 1685 and the other from 1762, contained the phrase *plea of innocence*. In the first case, presumably recorded by a court clerk, "Robert Brooks and Charles Cuckin, were Tryed for stealing Ten Gold-Rings" and "found guilty of the Felony: They being known to be Notorious Theives, their *plea of innocence* availed them of nothing."[75] In the second case, according to the chaplain of the prison where all three defendants were held, "all these, together . . . confirm this material part of the evidence of Joseph against his brother John: so that his *plea of innocence* must fall, and can only send to prove him obdurate in his guilt."[76] The records of these two cases indicate the defendants claimed they did not commit the crimes, not that there existed a plea of innocence.

In the first case, Brooks was sentenced to transportation (the location is not indicated), and Cuckin was sentenced to branding, which was often on a finger to indicate a previous conviction if he were arrested again. (Branding was also done on a cheek, but that practice was discontinued because the obvious stigma prevented convicted people from being employed.) In the second case, the defendants were sentenced to death and executed, two of them for robbery and one, John Kello, whose brother (Joseph) testified against him, for forgery.

In a stirring account, particularly from a religious point of view, the chaplain described the two killers' last moments, and how, in contrast, John Kello, who insisted he was innocent, spent his last moments:

> GOING in to visit the convicts, I was informed by the men who watched, that Whem and Collins had been very earnest in their devotions, for the greatest part of the night, and were now preparing, in their cells, to come to chapel. Mr. Kello was in bed . . . and I found myself still mortified with a disappointment, as he still persisted to deny his guilt, (with this reserve, "in the manner I am 'charged'") adding, he knew nothing of the forgery till it was too late to prevent it. . . . They were all three carried out in one cart about nine, and brought to the place of execution about ten; where a numerous mixt multitude were met to see them suffer. . . . Mr. Kello now at last declared his sorrow for all his offences against God. . . . At a proper pause, Kello was asked whether he would join in confessing and repeating the creed? to this he agreed; but as he did not speak out, either in this or in the prayers, his joining could only be internal. He was further asked whether he was not grieved for not being admitted to the holy communion? he answered, that he had joined with us in his heart, and spirit, as far as he could. This gave me good hope of some better dispositions within him, now at last, than we could hitherto discover by his outward behaviour. He was again desired to declare he forgave his brother; he answered, that his brother knew his sentiments in that respect, by his behaviour and conduct towards him, referring to some secrets between themselves. He added, "As far as humanity can, I forgive him;" to which I subjoined, "may the grace of God help all your human infirmities." . . . The convicts being humbly and earnestly recommended to the divine mercy and protection, took leave of each other very affectionately, by joining of hands, as well as their cords would permit, they behaved with

an intrepid and calm resignation; and about a quarter before Eleven were turned off. May they now be partakers and witnesses of the power of divine mercy unto Salvation.[77]

Except in salvation, innocent people, unable even to rely on their brothers, are, like John Kello, alone, and to save themselves they must have a way to discover exonerating facts.

Conclusion

The Plea of Innocence

For a society considering innocent-person convictions, the most preliminary question is whether the rate of conviction, probably about 4 percent or higher, is too high or too low (necessitating change), or tolerable because any legal system will produce some erroneous convictions. Regardless of whether there's agreement on the rate of error or need for change, the only approach acceptable to most people would be to create a method that reduces the number of innocent-person convictions but does not increase the number of guilty-person acquittals. Because such a method may be available, the premise of this book is that the adversarial system should be reformed because it is not capable of collecting the facts that will lead to a sufficient or significant reduction in the number of innocent people who are convicted. Inevitable human error will continue to cause innocent-person convictions, but, as in any endeavor or discipline, error can be mitigated through the discovery of facts.

In their 2021 book, *Noise: A Flaw in Human Judgment*, three professors, Daniel Kahneman, Olivier Sibony, and Cass R. Sunstein, describe studies that illustrate the sentencing disparities that come from judges, over generations, even when the judges view the same facts. Because judges' sentences and juries' verdicts rarely receive meaningful review from appellate courts, the errors committed by the fact finders at trials are rarely correctable. Professor Kahneman and his colleagues show that judicial sentencing is arbitrary, a large, recurring error in the adversarial system.

Lenient and harsh sentences on the same case or facts cannot both be correct. The authors noted a 1974 study, in which fifty judges issued sentences in hypothetical cases. "Most startling of all, in sixteen of twenty cases, there was no unanimity on whether any incarceration was appropriate." A heroin dealer could receive a prison sentence from one to ten years, a bank robber from five to eighteen years, and an extortionist from three to twenty years.[1]

A 1977 survey of forty-seven judges found that prison sentences for the same burglary (hypothetical) ranged from three months to five years. In a 1981 study of 208 U.S. judges, there was unanimous agreement in only three of sixteen hypothetical cases on whether to sentence a defendant to prison. In one case, the average prison sentence recommended was just over one year, but one recommendation was for fifteen years. In a fraud case, the average prison sentence was 8.5 years, but one recommended sentence was life imprisonment.[2]

Beginning in the late 1980s, federal sentencing guidelines, mandated by Congress, reduced the sentencing disparities, but the guidelines were struck down, as unconstitutional, by the Supreme Court in 2005 and are only advisory now.[3] "After the guidelines became advisory, judges became more likely to base their sentencing decisions on their personal values," which resulted in "law without order," according Kahneman and his coauthors.[4]

Where people, including judges, have discretion, which is unavoidable in many areas of life, probably the only way that their errors can be reduced or mitigated is through finding facts that do not require significant interpretation. An example would be a jury's reaching a not-guilty verdict after watching a video that showed the defendant was in California when the robbery for which he is on trial occurred in New York. In the same case, assume that all the facts are the same, except that no one knows the video exists or, if it is known to exist, no one can find it. The only substantive evidence is the testimony of an eyewitness who (mistakenly) identifies the defendant as the robber. In this circumstance, the jury has fewer facts, but, ironically, more discretion. Without the video, the jury can comfortably and legally find the innocent defendant guilty by deciding to credit the testimony of the mistaken eyewitness.

An exonerating video is rare, and, given the implacability of human error, it is likely that we are underestimating the number of innocent people who are convicted. The National Registry of Exonerations found only 2,809 exonerations in the United States from 1989 to 2021, an average of 85 per year.[5] Each year, there are more than 10 million arrests in the United States.[6] The conviction rate, based on all arrests, is probably about 66 percent.[7] This translates into a lot of convicted people, and many of them are almost certain to be innocent.

A New Adversarial System

To reduce error in the legal system, five fundamental changes should be considered. First, the purpose of the legal system should be to search for truth. Law enforcement officials and prosecutors should integrate that concept into their ethos and think about whether a suspect is innocent, not only about whether the evidence supports probable cause for an arrest or will establish guilt beyond a reasonable doubt. This search for truth includes recognizing that a legal system cannot retain legitimacy when lawyers are permitted to argue that a fact is true or false when they know the opposite to be true. The example used in this book concerns defense lawyers who know their clients are guilty but tell juries and judges that prosecution witnesses they know to be truthful and accurate, in identifying their clients, are lying or inaccurate. This infirm practice by lawyers is the essence of the American adversarial system.

Therefore, second, ethics rules should be changed so that lawyers are not permitted to urge upon judges and juries something the lawyers know to be false. The legal system and society should abandon the fiction that this false practice contributes something to a search for truth. With everyone knowing that this is how lawyers operate, almost nobody believes lawyers when they claim a client is innocent or when the client-defendant proclaims innocence. It is misguided to believe that an effective dialectic exists in the adversarial legal system when at least one of the parties is trying to hide the truth. It is one thing to try to prevent the truth from percolating to the surface, but it is another, more despairing condition for society when its lawyers are legally authorized knowingly to assert that truth is false and falsity is truth, the current operating norm of litigation lawyers in the American adversarial legal system.

Third, scientific research should be an integral part of legal education and legal decision making and a primary basis for the reformation of the adversarial system and the trials within it. Law schools throughout the world are guided by faculty members who have PhD degrees and are focused on producing knowledge. More like scientists than technicians, these faculty members are inclined to reserve judgment until their own research findings are scrutinized by other scholars.

American law schools, in contrast, require that almost all faculty members have a JD degree, while some also have PhD degrees. Learning in the United States is based on studying procedures and cases, which are the result of adversarial litigation. The procedures are not often based on scientific studies. To deemphasize the adversarial culture and introduce new methods of learning into U.S. law schools and the legal profession, social scientists should be fully integrated into the schools. Their presence would help prevent lawyers from generalizing despite a lack of empirical proof. Policy choices will always be required, such as determining whether it's better to free ten guilty people to ensure that one innocent person is not convicted. But it would better, first, if social scientists could help determine the harm that will be caused by the ten guilty people who are freed.

Fourth, the adversarial legal system should implement a method through which to search for truth on behalf of people who plausibly claim and are willing to try to prove they are innocent. The adversarial combat ethos is so ingrained in lawyers and the legal system that it is unlikely to change anytime soon. Where the parties have to be truthful to each other and are not allowed to urge falsity upon judges and juries, competition between the defense and prosecution can be beneficial. It can lead them to discover evidence and arguments to counter the other side and resolve cases. However, this competition starts only when a suspect has been arrested and then arraigned before a judge. Prior to then, the police and prosecutors control every aspect of an investigation and operate in secrecy. The legal system should work to offset the tunnel vision that can develop from one-sided investigations, especially because the majority of all accused people are impoverished and do not have the resources to find exonerating facts.

Fifth, especially if prosecution offices do not develop a truth-seeking ethos, the office of neutral magistrate should be established to recommend to the prosecution avenues through which to find exonerating evidence. The defense would have equal access to the magistrate. Most prosecution offices know well how to search for facts, but many will not do it unless they have an incentive and additional resources. If the prosecution proceeds to trial, and when the trial judge must determine whether a prosecution office made a diligent and reasonable search for exonerating facts, the judge may ask whether prosecutors consulted with the magistrate and to what extent they followed the magistrate's reasonable recommendations.

The magistrate's response will inform the judge in determining whether to instruct the jury to draw adverse inferences in favor of the defendant from the prosecution's failure to make a good-faith effort to find exonerating facts. Some states have one primary laboratory through which to test forensic evidence. Similarly, only one magistrate's office per state would be necessary, with satellite offices in more populous states. In reality, the magistrate's office would be relatively small and require modest funding because most people who are arrested are guilty of some crime and the last thing they want to search for is the truth.

While practicing lawyers do not have the time and expertise to conduct social science research, they and judges can help reduce error by using checklists based on scientific studies. Checklists are the distillation of the findings and reasoning of generations of scientists and scholars. With this in mind, a guide for judges and practitioners, as well as a practical plan through which to reform the adversarial system, can be organized around the principles within the headings that follow.

The Psychology of Error and Correction

Improvements in current criminal procedures, while important, cannot affect the large majority of cases, which depend on witnesses' testimony for resolution. Unfortunately, the most that witnesses can offer, given everyone's perceptual limitations and subjectivity, is an estimate of what they saw, heard, or otherwise perceived. Worse, people try to organize what they've perceived, which is a mental step beyond perception. This increases error. "The integration of evidence in complex decision tasks lies at the core of the body of research on the *coherence effect*. This psychological phenomenon can be encapsulated by the Gestaltian notion that what goes together, must fit together," Professor Dan Simon found.[8] But this is a psychological creation, not a description of a fact or what actually occurred in the past, at the scene of a crime.

In the checkerboard illusion/experiment, for example, two squares are labeled A and B. The A square appears to be darker than the B square, but both squares are exactly the same (darker) shade. Two variables make the B square appear to be lighter: it is shaded by a cylindrical object, and it is in the place on the checkerboard where the square should be light, not dark.

As in every instance in which witnesses view crimes and, later, when jurors view witnesses describing what they saw, "your perception of the degree to which a surface is light or dark tracks not the *amount* of light that is reflected to your eyes by the surface but the *proportion* of the light falling on that surface that is reflected by it."[9] The shade of the B square is distorted because the cylinder prevents light from shining onto it (counterintuitively making it appear to be light), and everyone expects the B square to be light because of its position on the checkerboard.

Cognitive scientists Hugo Mercier and Dan Sperber considered how the brain tracks this *reflectance* accurately, the light that the brain perceives. Their answer is disturbing because it shows how people gather extraneous information to help them interpret what they see. "To do so, [the brain] has to use contextual information and background knowledge and infer that other relevant quantity, that is, the amount of light that falls on the surface."[10] People rely on personal experience to determine what happened. Their report of what they perceived may not reflect what actually happened because their perception is formulated by considering their prior experiences, as well as other variables that are peripheral and unrelated to the facts of a case.

While people may conjure facts to provide context and interpret what they perceived, they may also make a decision by fixating on a single fact or a limited number of facts, when an event actually involves many facts. Mercier and Sperber offered that "if there are dark clouds in the sky and you want to go out, you might intuit, 'It might rain. This is a strong reason to take my umbrella.'"[11] From personal experience, you could act on the basis of dark clouds, but your decision to purchase or deploy an umbrella would be better informed by checking the latest radar and measuring the speed and direction of the wind. One's intuition about rain descending from dark clouds is as useful as a witness's identification of the person who robbed the victim—somewhat indicative of rain or guilt, but at the lower end of conclusiveness when other more authoritative facts, like radar images, are available.

Professor Simon identified five types of faulty reasoning, all of which provide people with a sense of real, but misplaced, completeness. These typologies increase the incidence of human error. The first type of faulty reasoning is *framing* an inquiry to support a hypothesis; a more effective inquiry would try to prove that your hypothesis is wrong. The second is *selective exposure*, in which "people tend to selectively expose themselves to information that confirms their focal hypothesis and shield themselves from discordant information."[12]

The third is *selective scrutiny*, in which people "scrutinize information that is incompatible with their conclusion, but apply lax standards when assessing the validity of compatible information." The fourth is *biased evaluation*, such as concluding that your preferred political candidate won the debate or interpreting a shove as "either jovial or aggressive depending on the race of the actor." The fifth is *selective stopping*, in which "people tend to shut down inquiries after having found a sufficient amount of evidence to support their leading hypothesis."[13]

Until investigators and prosecutors understand the concepts that lead to errors, we will not devise or implement a method to reduce truth-defeating practices. For example, if police detectives and prosecutors understood how "selective stopping" occurs (not looking for more evidence once they have probable cause to arrest a suspect), they might create an additional entry on their checklist: whether "a member of our force or office has searched for plausible evidence of innocence." Unfortunately, premature and incorrect decision making might be almost innate. As Professor Kahneman explained in another book, people are unrealistic in believing they can achieve their "best-case scenarios," the "planning fallacy."[14]

Kahneman and his coauthors, in synthesizing social science research, recognized some of the origins of human error and the importance of selecting competent people to mitigate error. "There is reason to believe that some people make better judgments than others do. Task-specific skill, intelligence, and a certain cognitive style—best described as being *open-minded*—characterize the best judges."[15] But Kahneman and his coauthors understood that even presumably competent and well-vetted people, such as judges, will not agree on what is a correct outcome or, in legal cases, a correct sentence.

They suggest six principles through which to minimize error, all of which lead to people looking outside themselves or their organizations for guidance. Their first principle is that the "goal of judgment is accuracy, not individual expression," because "judgment is not the place to express your individuality." They recommend "algorithmic evaluation" and, through statistics, taking "the outside view of the case," the second principle.[16] They believe "the outside-view principle favors the anchoring of predictions in the statistics of similar cases."[17]

To avoid "*excessive coherence*, which causes people to distort or ignore information that does not fit a preexisting or emerging story," judgments should be separated into "independent tasks," a third recommendation.[18] For example, witnesses should not be allowed to consult with each other, and the police and prosecution should employ double-blind identification procedures. In the current adversarial system, one detective or agent usually controls an investigation. In a reformed system, different detectives or units would collect forensic evidence and interview witnesses. Other detectives or units would conduct lineups and interviews of suspects.

Their fourth recommendation is to "resist premature intuitions," a concept we encountered previously. Recall the high error rate (higher than 50 percent) of most judges and college students who took the Cognitive Reflection Test. "(1) A bat and ball cost $1.10 in total. The bat costs $1.00 more than the ball. How much does the ball cost? [The ball costs five cents and the bat costs $1.05.] . . . (2) If it takes 5 machines 5 minutes to make 5 widgets, how long would it take 100 machines to make 100 widgets? [One hundred machines would produce 100 widgets in only five minutes, and 200 machines would produce 200 widgets in five minutes.] . . . (3) In a lake, there is a patch of lily pads. Every day, the patch doubles in size. If it takes 48 days for the patch to cover the entire lake, how long would it take for the patch to cover half the lake? [Forty-seven days.]"[19]

The test's creator, Professor Shane Frederick, described how intuitive decisions lead to more error than deliberative decisions. Similarly, Kahneman and his colleagues found, "An intuitive choice that is informed by a balanced and careful consideration of the evidence is far superior to a snap judgment. Intuition need not be banned, but it should be informed, disciplined, and delayed."[20]

Continuing with the same approach—looking outside and collecting additional viewpoints—the authors' fifth and sixth recommendations are that we should "obtain independent judgments from multiple judges" and "favor relative judgments and relative scales."[21] Such decision making could be fostered by permitting defense lawyers to argue on behalf of suspects prior to the prosecution's issuance of charges, as in the federal criminal system. However, most criminal cases originate as street crimes and are handled in state courts, such as relatively spontaneous assaults, thefts, and property damage, in which arrests are made soon after the crimes and before suspects obtain lawyers.

This is why investigators—all law enforcement officers, including those patrolling the streets—should view their roles differently, as neutral actors, and recognize that society depends on their conducting an independent investigation that is devoid of tunnel vision and the understandable emotion behind the desire to aid victims and clear cases by making an arrest. An investigation, while sometimes complicated and extending over months or years, frequently involves one police officer or detective finding as many witnesses as possible and questioning them with an open mind.

In other words, try to avoid the pressure of groupthink by stating your judgment prior to the discussion of a case, and try to place the current case on a continuum of prior cases, including those in which suspects were guilty and innocent. Where does the current suspect lie on that sliding continuum or scale? Professor Carrie Leonetti, in a 2021 article, proposed an "innocence checklist," with twenty-seven variables that have been shown to contribute to innocent-person convictions. The variables fall within three "clusters": "constitutional-esque errors affecting accuracy"; "material new evidence"; and "others," a potpourri of variables, all of which have been discussed in this book.[22] The presence or absence of such variables and the collection of additional facts will slide the marker of the scale to the left, toward innocence, or to the right, toward guilt.

The approaches above emphasize investigation and employ the moderating effect of experience and prior learning (knowing how prior cases were investigated and resolved, including exonerations). Through consideration of additional facts by other viewers—almost always consult viewpoints outside one's organization—they moderate or reduce the number of incorrect decisions made by less competent decision makers. They also help to reduce the number of incorrect decisions made by more competent decision makers who lack an adequate number of facts.

Pleading Innocent

After establishing truth as its primary goal, a reformed legal system should provide accused people with the right to plead innocent, which is a method through which to find exonerating facts. Prior to a judge's acceptance of the plea, defense lawyers will have to affirm their clients' innocence. Further, with an actual emphasis on truth, the lawyers will no longer be permitted to imply or argue that witnesses they know to be truthful or accurate are lying or inaccurate. Continuing along an axis of truth, scientists and reliable studies should have larger roles in the legal system, all toward the goal of creating an ethos of discovery and the displacement of the combativeness of the lawyers.

If a defendant makes a reasonable or plausible claim of innocence, then prosecution offices will be required to conduct good-faith searches for exonerating facts. If the new structure does not lead prosecutors to search sufficiently for exonerating facts, then neutral magistrates should preside over innocence investigations. In any event, magistrates should be available as a resource to prosecutors to help ensure that tunnel vision does not limit their search for evidence. Most cases, at least 97 percent, are resolved through guilty pleas, including many cases within twenty-four hours of an arrest, at the arraignment, when defendants may plead guilty to misdemeanors. In these cases, and probably most cases, magistrates are less necessary or unnecessary. The advice of the magistrate in serious or complicated cases will help to lessen the combative ethos of prosecutors and defense lawyers, who may have different views about how to conduct an innocence investigation.

The office of the magistrate might be similar to what Lewis Steel, a civil rights lawyer, envisioned in 2003, when he proposed innocence bureaus, independent of prosecution offices, to help impoverished defendants.[23] He believed that

the mild pretrial reforms considered fail to address the deeply entrenched problems of our criminal justice system that often lead to false
convictions—especially the pressure police feel to cut corners in order to
"solve" heinous crimes and the disadvantages faced by indigent defendants who almost always have to rely on grossly underfunded public defenders with limited access to investigators, crime laboratories and even
the witnesses against them. Conducting reviews after convictions and appeals are exhausted is too little, too late. Instead, the search for truth must
begin shortly after police hand the case over to the prosecutor's office. To
reduce the possibility of wrongful convictions, prosecutors should establish "innocence bureaus."[24]

This approach is insightful and valuable. However, the magistrate,
innocence bureaus, and public defenders all have the same inherent
limitation: they lack the authority of prosecutors. Responsible for deciding whether charges will be issued, prosecutors, when open-minded, are
in the best position to evaluate the facts and assess whether a suspect is
guilty or innocent.

In Germany, as long ago as 1978, the defense could make a motion
to ask a judge to require the prosecution to investigate "defense claims
and evidence" that the prosecution has overlooked.[25] Today, however,
a defendant in Germany remains dependent on the judge, who may
reject the request to "take further evidence."[26] These limitations and
truncated processes show why defendants, who are responsible for their
defense, as in the adversarial system, should have more autonomy and
the right independently to activate innocence procedures by pleading
innocent. If defendants waive the right to remain silent, they will be entitled to a more thorough investigation—a search for exonerating facts—
conducted by a prosecution office.

* * *

The exoneration of innocent people—without freeing those who are
guilty—cannot be undertaken effectively only by providing additional resources to public defenders. First, criminal defense lawyers
do not have ethical or moral obligations to search for truth. Second, as
described by Professor Robert P. Mosteller, a former public defender,

defense lawyers may not have the inclination or ability to pursue claims of innocence.

> A special focus cannot be given to innocence because defense attorneys have no special and reliable ways to know innocence. They usually have no means to establish innocence definitively. Like others in the criminal justice system, they principally rely on the absence of proof of guilt to mark innocence and, at their peril, use intuition and subjective judgment as problematic guides. To let special care about innocence matter in representing clients would be to deny a full defense to the innocent who lack either readily available objective proof or a compelling persona. . . . Defenders who search among their clients for those who are innocent are inviting personal and professional destruction. A defender's belief in her client's innocence must be backed by evidence; otherwise, it largely only torments the defender and interferes with the performance of the attorney's professional duty to all of her other clients. Furthermore, because this can become disabling, it can harm even a client the defender believes to be innocent.[27]

Perhaps the only way defense lawyers emotionally can navigate through the adversarial system is not to venture to make difficult cost-benefit decisions that would lead to expending more time and energy on cases in which clients claim to be innocent.

Nonetheless, clients with plausible claims of innocence should not suffer because of the inability or unwillingness of their lawyers to expend the emotional energy necessary in pursuing claims of innocence. Physicians and nurses in emergency rooms in hospitals, for example, and medics on the battlefield allocate more time and resources to the injured people who have a greater chance of living. If these professionals can make split-second decisions in crises, which lawyers in offices do not have to do, it is not too much to ask the defense lawyers to overcome their sensitivities and prioritize clients who have plausible claims of innocence. We would not say that a defendant with an alibi witness should not be permitted to have the witness testify because other defendants do not have alibi witnesses. Why should defendants with plausible claims of innocence not have additional opportunity for acquittal, whether arising from the efforts of their lawyers or from a new structure in the adversarial system?

Third, neither public defenders nor private defense lawyers who represent wealthy clients possess the authority of prosecutors. Prosecutors know the whereabouts of victims and witnesses who provided the basis for charges and, unlike members of the defense team, have an obligation to try to protect witnesses and obtain correct verdicts. Prosecutors supervise identification procedures, issue subpoenas, obtain search warrants from judges, provide immunity to cooperating witnesses or accomplices, and convene grand juries. Defense lawyers do not engage in any of these activities.

Moreover, some prosecution offices have created conviction integrity units. The prosecutors working in these units, if convinced of a convicted person's innocence, may ask a judge to vacate a conviction and release the person from prison immediately. The conviction integrity units plumb the legal system for innocent-person convictions in their jurisdictions, but they do this only after a conviction. Their work often does not begin until after all defense appeals have failed, usually years or decades after the incarceration of an innocent person.[28]

* * *

The urgency for reform of the adversarial system is illustrated by how little some of the conditions have changed over the past three hundred years. Professor Richard Vogler, of the University of Sussex, in England, found that the "pre-modern criminal process in England, before the intervention of lawyers, was as rights-free, authoritarian and nearly as brutal as its continental counterparts. The accused was very much the passive object of the procedure and only in very rare instances had enough courage or skill to participate in any significant way."[29]

Judges controlled the process then, but their responsibilities have been overtaken by prosecutors, who are the adversaries of accused people. A rule dating to the twelfth century prohibited defense attorneys in felony cases (though later they could argue legal points) under the "principle that no man should have counsel against the King."[30] In the United States, the right to an attorney, at state expense, for a poor person, was not guaranteed until 1963, about 233 years after defense attorneys began regularly representing accused people in England.[31]

In premodern time, a prosecutor would present witnesses and evidence to a justice "with a view to establishing the basis of a case against the accused," who "enjoyed few rights in this process and was not told precisely what the evidence was against him or her, nor allowed to be present when depositions were taken from the accusers."[32] This is similar to investigations and grand juries today, which are secret proceedings through which twenty-three states and the federal government determine whether to bring charges and what the charges will be. An additional twenty-five states have the option of using what is similar to a grand jury procedure.[33]

"The situation of the [accused] prisoner," in the premodern era, "was an extremely difficult one. He or she was routinely incarcerated in gaols notorious for squalor and where the disease and mortality rates were extremely high." Vogler found that "it was not unheard of for prisoners to spend nine months in gaol awaiting trial."[34] Many defendants in the United States spend a year or more in jail before their trials. As of July 2021, more than 2,700 inmates in jails, prisons, and immigration detention centers in the United States had died from COVID-19 infections during the pandemic, and many other COVID-19 deaths remain uncounted because detention facilities released infected inmates who died outside their walls.[35]

"It is not too much to see pre-trial incarceration (with the prisoner usually shackled in leg-irons up to the moment of arraignment) as a species of torture aimed at cowing the prisoner into passivity and submission. . . . What emerges from these accounts is the image of a trial process in which the accused enjoys almost no procedural rights other than the bare right to trial," Vogler concluded.[36] Defendants have more procedural rights today, but the conditions they encounter in investigations and jails and at trials can be similarly difficult.[37]

* * *

In 2015, two professors, Marvin Zalman and Ralph Grunewald, identified five proposals, from five researchers, for changing various parts of the criminal legal system.[38] In comparing the proposals, Zalman and Grunewald identified fourteen reference points. The only point common to all five researchers was the need for increased discovery of facts. Three proposals would modify a defendant's right to remain silent. In their conclusion, Zalman and Grunewald advocated providing more discovery, modifying prosecutors' roles with defense attorneys, permitting judges to discuss cases with attorneys and produce fact summaries, and giving defendants a limited right to reinvestigations.[39]

In contrast to the researchers, Professor Paul Cassell, a former federal judge, argues that innocence procedures "offer no real safeguard against guilty criminals taking advantage of them."[40] Professor Cassell concludes, "The upshot is that if [Bakken's] scheme was implemented in this country, it would likely block the convictions of at least tens of thousands of dangerous criminals every year, causing grave harm to public safety."[41]

When he wrote in 2011, Professor Cassell could not have known of the 2014 study that found an innocent-person conviction rate in death-penalty cases of 4.1 percent.[42] Nonetheless, in 2018 he claimed to have synthesized empirical studies. He concluded that "it is possible to construct a plausible error rate for violent crimes somewhere in the range of 0.016%–0.062%."[43] Needless to say, the lower end of Cassell's range (a rate of 1.6 innocent-person convictions per 10,000) is far lower than the findings of the 2014 study (more than 400 per 10,000).

* * *

Regardless of the percentage, few of the innocent people who are convicted will ever have an opportunity to discover exonerating facts after their convictions, pointing to the importance of more searching and neutral pretrial investigations. In *Herrera v. Collins*, the Supreme Court summarized the bleak outlook for convicted people who claim that the Constitution prohibits innocent-person convictions. "Claims of actual innocence based on newly discovered evidence have never been held to state a ground for federal habeas relief absent an independent constitutional violation occurring in the underlying state criminal proceeding," the Court wrote.[44]

The Court said it would assume the Constitution prohibited the conviction and execution of an innocent person, but it found Herrera's claim of actual innocence to be "far short of that which would have to be made in order to trigger the sort of constitutional claim which we have assumed, *arguendo*, to exist."[45] Though it is difficult to imagine that any judge or appellate court would allow an obviously innocent person to be executed, the Supreme Court, since deciding *Herrera* in 1993, has never held that a freestanding claim of innocence is a basis for relief under the Constitution.

In his concurring opinion in *Herrera*, Justice Antonin Scalia ridiculed what he seemed to believe was the weak-kneed notion that the Constitution might prohibit the execution of an innocent person who received all the process he was due. (The defendant in *Herrera* was later executed.) "I nonetheless join the entirety of the Court's opinion . . . because there is no legal error in deciding a case by assuming, *arguendo*, that an asserted constitutional right exists, and because I can understand, or at least am accustomed to, the reluctance of the present Court to admit publicly that Our Perfect Constitution lets stand any injustice, much less the execution of an innocent man who has received, though to no avail, all the process that our society has traditionally deemed adequate." Justice Scalia noted the "unhappy truth that not every problem was meant to be solved by the United States Constitution, nor can be."[46]

Justice Scalia also ridiculed what he viewed as the whimsical notion that a convicted person who is obviously innocent would ever be executed. He must have believed that every governor of every state would act in a just and fair manner. "With any luck, we shall avoid ever having to face this embarrassing question again [possibly allowing the execution of an innocent person], since it is improbable that evidence of innocence as convincing as today's opinion requires would fail to produce an executive pardon," he wrote.[47]

Justice Scalia's view, however, does not seem to reflect political reality. We observe politicians, including governors, who are incapable of making evidence-based decisions or who selfishly defy logic and reason to appeal to a voting bloc in an effort to retain their positions. Thomas Bilbo, who had taken classes at the University of Michigan Law School, was the governor of Mississippi when, on July 29, 1929, Marlin Drew was shot dead, through the heart, while sleeping in his marital bed in Ashland, Mississippi. Alcoholic and frequently angry and abusive, Drew had constantly beaten his wife. After the police considered the possibility that he had unintentionally killed himself while drunk (a pistol was found near the bed), suspicion fell on his father-in-law, Thomas Gunter.

Marlin Drew and his wife, Pearl, and their children lived with Pearl's father (Thomas Gunter) and mother. After his arrest, and in late August, fewer than thirty days after the killing, Thomas Gunter was tried, found guilty of murder, and sentenced to five years in prison.[48] One newspaper, in January 1930, reported that Gunter's sentence was life in prison.[49] If the lenient five-year sentence applied, it was because local people did not view the deceased, Marlin Drew, favorably. A World War I veteran who returned home with alcoholism, he had recently been fired from his job as a railroad section worker for being drunk and fighting with coworkers.

The witnesses against Thomas Gunter were his daughter, Pearl, and his seven-year-old (possibly eight) granddaughter, Dorothy (Pearl's daughter), both of whom testified that Gunter shot Drew. For the defense, Gunter's wife testified that she heard a gunshot and rushed to the bedroom, only to see Pearl, her daughter, standing with the pistol over the deceased, Marlin Drew. Mrs. Gunter testified that her husband, the defendant, was passed out, drunk, when the killing occurred.

By November, Pearl had a change of heart. She wrote to Governor Bilbo to say that she had killed her husband and coached her (and Drew's) daughter to testify against Gunter. In her letter to Bilbo, Pearl included a poem, which was also her confession. It began as follows:

> Down in a lonely graveyard,
>   Where flowers bloom and fade,
> There lies my darling sleeping
>   In a cold and silent grave.
> Down on my knees before him
>   I pleaded for his life
> But deep in his bosom
>   Had plunged a forty-five.
> But O how sad the ending
>   To sit beside my dear
> For I have often told him,
>   "Darling, don't you fear."

In the poem, Marlin Drew, the deceased, then speaks to Pearl:

> No, my darling,
>   Your words can never be,
> For I soon will be sleeping
>   In a grave away from thee.
> I know I've been a rambler,
>   I know I've done you wrong:
> But don't forget me, darling,
>   Whenever you sing this song.

Pearl then summarized what she hoped her husband was thinking just before he died:

> The time has come, my darling,
> When you and I must part,
>   The bullet of that forty-five
>   Has surely plunged my heart.
> But kiss our little children,
>   And tell them I am gone,
> Don't let them follow my footsteps
>   For I have led them wrong.[50]

Pearl included a stanza about her father:

> To prison went my father
>   All innocent of this crime;
> I could not long endure this,
>   My father doing time.[51]

One newspaper from the day, the *Evening Journal*, reported that Pearl's poem did, indeed, become a song. "Her poetic confession has been converted into a song—of mournful and dismal tune—by negro cotton pickers and is being sung by thousands of them on Mississippi's plantations."[52]

After confessing to the sheriff, county attorney, and district attorney, Pearl was indicted and charged with murder and perjury. As a result, Governor Bilbo issued a ninety-day suspension of the sentence of Thomas Gunter, who was released from prison. The *Evening Journal* reported, "Nobody in Mississippi believes Mrs. Drew will be convicted. Public sentiment is with the mother."[53] Pearl Drew spent Christmas in jail with her five children, one of whom was born four days after she killed her husband, who had claimed that Pearl conceived the child with another man.

In February 1930, Pearl pleaded guilty to manslaughter and the judge suspended her sentence. She was released from jail, after serving about three months while waiting for the resolution of her case. Everyone believed that Governor Bilbo, of course, would issue a pardon for Thomas Gunter. But Bilbo would have none of it.

The whole affair had been an embarrassment for the state of Mississippi. Governor Bilbo ordered Gunter back to prison and issued the following statement: "Somebody ought to be in the penitentiary all the time for the murder of a sleeping man. If Judge Pegram does not believe Mrs. Drew is guilty enough to serve her term, then the man convicted of the murder will have to serve his term. Husbands ought to have some protection."

Amid the turbulence of this unconventional case, Thomas Gunter reconciled with his daughter, Pearl, and granddaughter, Dorothy. He never returned to prison, as ordered. All of them fled, presumably relieved, to Tennessee; he died in 1939, in Trenton, Tennessee. Pearl remarried and moved with her new husband, Jack Kelly, to his hometown, New York City, where Justice Scalia (born in 1936, in Trenton, New Jersey) grew up. Pearl died in New York, in December 1986, the same year that President Ronald Reagan appointed Justice Scalia to the Supreme Court.[54]

It's doubtful Justice Scalia was aware of Governor Bilbo's refusal to pardon Thomas Gunter, the innocent man. Scalia, who died in 2016, overestimated the capacity of governors to free innocent people and underestimated the incidence of human error in the adversarial system.

Six Reasons to Tell the Truth

To assess the plea of innocence, consider what is possibly the most dangerous situation for an innocent person, the one-eyewitness identification, in which the only significant evidence of guilt comes from the testimony of the complainant or another eyewitness.[55] The testimony of one witness, assuming the witness is not a former accomplice whose testimony must be corroborated, is sufficient, if believed by a jury, to convict any person of any crime, from shoplifting to capital murder.

Assume that this one-witness identification case is more treacherous than usual for an innocent person because the victim's background and characteristics show that she possesses acute perception, especially under stress. In a sequential photo array and lineup conducted under the most rigorous and modern (double-blind) conditions on the day after the crime (an assault), the victim immediately, but mistakenly, selected the defendant. Only he knows that he was home alone at the time of the assault. He has no way to show this, except his assertions, if he testifies at a trial.

In the current system, the man's entire defense will be based on discrediting the victim's identifications of him in the photo array and lineup and later at trial. In pretrial hearings and during the trial, the defense lawyer will try to show that the detectives' identification procedures were somehow defective or suggestive of the defendant and that the victim's opportunity to view her attacker during the assault was obscured by darkness or other conditions. Assuming that these avenues do not call the mistaken identification into question, the defendant's only chance for acquittal is to testify and hope that his truthful assertion he was home alone raises reasonable doubt in the jurors' minds.

To make a not-guilty verdict more difficult for him to obtain, assume that, like many others, he cannot risk testifying because, despite what would be truthful testimony ("I'm innocent"), he has prior criminal convictions that the prosecutor would use to discredit him, and which the jury would use to conclude (mistakenly) showed a propensity to commit an assault. This innocent person is very likely to be convicted. Aside from the victim's credibility, the two main reasons are that he cannot locate exonerating facts and tell his truthful story.

In contrast, if this defendant pleaded innocent, he could compel the prosecution or police to search for facts. Nonetheless, assume that no one can find additional facts, such as an alibi witness (because he was home alone) or a cell phone call (because he made no calls) that pinged off a tower near his home at the time of the assault, which occurred twenty miles away. By pleading innocent, he will have to tell prosecutors that he was home alone when the assault occurred. This kind of statement is virtually always a significant benefit for the prosecution. The defendant cannot later change his defense without appearing to have lied during the interview.

While lawyers should not be permitted to argue that a witness they know to be truthful is lying, they should be permitted to argue, even if they know their client is guilty, that the evidence, including the testimony of witnesses, does not establish guilt beyond a reasonable doubt.

This point helps identify what, on the surface, seems to be a difficult ethical question in lawyers' representation of innocent people in identification cases. A legal ethics professor, Monroe H. Freedman, posed the problem in a 1966 law review article, "Professional Responsibility of the Criminal Defense Lawyer," as justification for allowing lawyers to attack the credibility and reliability of truthful, accurate witnesses. Professor Freedman proposed the following hypothetical:

> At the [robbery] trial, there are two prosecution witnesses. The first mistakenly, but with some degree of persuasion, identifies your [innocent] client as the criminal. At that point, the prosecution's case depends on this single witness, who might or might not be believed. Since your client has a prior record, you do not want to put him on the stand, but you feel that there is at least a chance for acquittal. The second prosecution witness is an elderly woman who is somewhat nervous and who wears glasses. She testifies truthfully and accurately that she saw your client at 15th and P Streets at 10:55 p.m. She has corroborated the erroneous testimony of the first witness and made conviction virtually certain. However, if you destroy her reliability through cross-examination designed to show that she is easily confused and has poor eyesight, you may not only eliminate the corroboration, but also cast doubt in the jury's mind on the prosecution's entire case. On the other hand, if you should refuse to cross-examine her because she is telling the truth, your client may well feel betrayed, since you knew of the witness's veracity only because your client confided in you, under your assurance that his truthfulness would not prejudice him.[56]

Professor Freedman did not address many reasons why lawyers should *not* be permitted to project such falsity. First, to have legitimacy, a legal system should not accept falsity as an everyday method of lawyers' practice. Second, the hypothetical case, while remotely possible, is anecdotal and should not be a basis for constructing a legal system. No scientist, engineer, or physicist would construct a theory around one anomaly. In fact, there might not be any other profession or occupation in which the workers and leaders, like lawyers in the legal profession, have the authority to mislead everyone else in their company, institution, or society.

Third, a legal system should not encourage falsity to benefit one innocent defendant when an ethos and practice of truthfulness will benefit a vastly larger number of them. Fourth, an even larger number of guilty people want their lawyers to have the right and opportunity to engage in such truth-defying practices, which lead to incorrect verdicts (guilty-person acquittals). The guilty want their lawyers to discredit truthful and accurate witnesses. Fifth, some innocent people will always be convicted. Otherwise, the burden on the prosecution would be so high that almost all guilty people would escape.

Sixth, defense lawyers in the Freedman hypothetical, for the benefit of innocent clients, will always have the option of trying to undermine the witness who truthfully and accurately testifies for the prosecution that the client/defendant was at the scene of the crime, "at 15th and P Streets at 10:55 p.m." Legal ethics authorities, if they discovered this gambit, could try to discipline the defense lawyer, such as suspending the lawyer's license to practice law. However, lawyers could successfully defend themselves against ethics charges by arguing that it is better for society to undermine a truthful, accurate witness than not to do so and allow an innocent person to be convicted.

* * *

In cases where defendants plead innocent and consent to being interviewed by prosecutors, the burden of persuasion should be higher than beyond reasonable doubt to compensate for the advantage obtained by the prosecution and ensure that defendants will not be dissuaded from telling their stories. Varying the burden of persuasion depending on the significance of a case is not unusual. Courts in the United States employ three burdens: beyond reasonable doubt in criminal cases; clear and convincing evidence in family law and other matters where the treatment of people is involved, such as child custody and institutional placements due to mental health; and a preponderance of evidence, which is used to resolve most financial disputes among people. Some judges in England, to protect defendants who did not have lawyers (as few did in felony cases until the 1730s) and, if convicted, would be executed, imposed high burdens of persuasion before allowing a jury to find a defendant guilty.

One high burden of persuasion allowed a guilty verdict only if "'the evidence . . . should be so manifest, as it could not be contradicted.'"[57] As the adversarial system did not arise from a central plan, there was nothing sacrosanct about the beyond-reasonable-doubt standard; it was not a link in a chain or a domino that, if nudged, would lead to the collapse of other dominos. It was not established in England until the second half of the 1700s, and then only in general terms.[58] It was not a requirement in all state criminal trials in the United States until 1970, when the Supreme Court decided that the Constitution required it.[59]

The critical point is that the beyond-reasonable-doubt standard is not a mythical or inalterable burden of persuasion. It's not a standard with even internal coherence. Professor Dan Simon, in his 2012 book *In Doubt: The Psychology of the Criminal Justice Process*, described the confusion about the standard: "The criminal process's signature standard of proof—beyond a reasonable doubt—has received a fair amount of scholarly attention over the years, yet it remains elusive and deeply disputed. For one, there is considerable disagreement as to whether the standard should pertain to the fact finder's subjective state of mind or to a property of the evidence itself. . . . There is also disagreement about the appropriate meaning of the reasonableness criterion, namely, whether it pertains to the strength of the doubt or to a substantive judgment of its underlying rationality."[60]

The beyond-reasonable-doubt standard was not, according to Professor John Langbein, "invariably applied, hence we still find different judges formulating the standard of proof differently."[61] In English cases in the late 1700s, the various burdens of persuasion, as compiled by Langbein, were a mishmash and included the following:

- "Jurors should convict if 'fully satisfied on your conscience,' but not 'if a doubt remains in your mind'" (1776).
- "'If the scale should hang doubtful, and you are not fully satisfied that he is guilty, you ought to lean on the favorable side and acquit him'" (1781).
- "If, upon 'considering the evidence that has been laid before you, and all the circumstances of the case, you should err on the innocent side of the question, I am sure your error will be pardonable'" (1783).[62]

At about the same time and later, the burdens of persuasion focused on some semblance of reasonable doubt, including the following:

- "'If on viewing the evidence any reasonable doubt remains . . . he will be entitled to your acquittal'" (1783).[63]
- "'If there is a reasonable doubt, in that case that doubt ought to decide in favor of the prisoner'" (1784).[64]

Importantly, the burdens of persuasion should be higher when the risk of error is higher, such as when defendants, via pleading innocent, tell a plausible story of innocence and reveal their entire defense to the prosecution. The burdens in England were, in fact, sometimes higher than beyond reasonable doubt, including the following:

- "'If you have doubts . . . of course you will acquit the prisoner'" (1783).
- "Acquit 'if any doubt whatever remains in your minds'" (1785).[65]

These latter two standards are more protective of defendants than the reasonable-doubt standard used by courts in the United States today. In New York State courts, for example, a judge on a criminal case will instruct a jury (in part) on reasonable doubt, as follows: "A reasonable doubt is an honest doubt of the defendant's guilt for which a reason exists based upon the nature and quality of the evidence. It is an actual doubt, not an imaginary doubt. It is a doubt that a reasonable person, acting in a matter of this importance, would be likely to entertain because of the evidence that was presented or because of the lack of convincing evidence."[66] Given the amorphous, circular nature of this New York jury instruction, and that the beyond-reasonable-doubt standard started percolating about two hundred fifty years ago, it appears that human intellect cannot yet create a more precise standard.

Note in the jury instruction the vague words (*reasonable, honest, nature, quality, convincing*). The circularity and imprecision of the instruction are illustrated by the repetition of the word *doubt* five times. The instruction leaves jurors to interpret broad, malleable words and apply them to the facts, according to the jurors' preferences.

Moreover, a significant amount of research indicates that jurors do not comprehend the instructions that judges give them. Professor Simon found that studies on how well jurors comprehend judges' instructions range "from 13 to 73 percent, levels that are not always better than chance. The data are mixed as to whether the instructions actually improve jurors' understanding of the law, with some studies finding modest improvement, and others finding the instructed jurors are no more knowledgeable than their noninstructed cohorts. . . . A study conducted in England found that people tend not to acknowledge their limited levels of knowledge. While only 31 percent of respondents understood the judge's instructions, two-thirds of them maintained they comprehended them correctly."[67]

A basic hypothetical illustrates the point that jurors may not understand how to apply the law that judges explain to them and that they will disagree about the meaning of judges' instructions. Assume that you are a guest at someone's home and scheduled to have dinner at seven o'clock. At five o'clock, you are hungry and see freshly baked and apparently delicious cookies on a platter and unattended in a room. You grab several cookies and lift one toward your mouth. At that moment, the baker, who is also preparing dinner, sees you. The baker, the lawgiver, says, "Don't eat the cookies. They'll spoil your appetite."

Someone who interprets the law strictly may say that the sentence "Don't eat the cookies" prohibits eating any cookies. The second sentence, about "spoiling your appetite," is an explanation for the prohibition on eating the cookies. Someone who interprets the law broadly may say that, read in context, the two sentences mean, "Don't eat the cookies if eating them will spoil your appetite." In response, the strict interpreter will say the baker would have said that if the baker meant that. This back-and-forth will go on and on, and the jurors will never agree on the baker's edict or the meaning of the law about the cookies.

The wide discretion of jurors may be unavoidable given judges' inability to instruct jurors more precisely. If so, this points again to the arbitrary nature of jury verdicts and the importance of finding facts prior to trials. A burden of persuasion that is higher than beyond reasonable doubt might not be more precise, but it would signal to the jurors that they should be especially vigilant because the case concerns an unusual risk of an innocent-person conviction. Yes, the remaining defendants who plead *not guilty* instead of *innocent* would not benefit from this signal, but they would retain all the rights they currently possess; nothing would be lost. It makes no sense, in the name of *equality*, to deny plausibly innocent people additional opportunity for acquittal because other defendants who appear more culpable and more likely to be guilty cannot plead innocent.

* * *

That prosecutors would receive a significant benefit from an interview illustrates the increased likelihood of a conviction for a defendant who pleads innocent, which, alone, is a strong indicator of innocence. Almost no one who is guilty and represented by a lawyer would ever consent to disclosing information to the prosecution in an interview. If unconvinced by the defendant's story and unable to find exonerating facts, prosecutors could proceed to trial and introduce the defendant's pretrial statements, if they are inculpatory. Defendants would not be allowed at trial to introduce their (presumably self-serving) pretrial statements for the same reason they're not allowed to do so today—because the prosecution would not have the opportunity to cross-examine defendants at trial.

To help offset the advantage obtained by the prosecution through an interview, defendants who plead innocent will not be required to take an oath when they testify. The absence of an oath will allow defendants to tell their stories to juries without fear that prosecutors, who did not believe the stories they asserted in the interviews, might charge them with perjury even if the jury finds them not guilty on the underlying charge. An oath is an especially significant deterrent to testifying in less serious cases because the penalty for perjury (imprisonment up to five years under federal law) may be more severe than the penalty for the underlying crime.[68] In England in the 1700s, a defendant's statement under oath was not permitted because "'an Oath is a Compulsion; and consequently that no Man is obliged to swear against himself in Cases where it affects his Life.'" For their protection, defendants were not allowed to speak under oath in England until 1898.[69]

Another indicator of innocence is the defense-lawyer affirmation, which, in some form, is a requirement of lawyers in all civil cases. Under the Federal Rules of Civil Procedure, lawyers are required to make "claims, defenses, and other legal contentions [that] are warranted" and "factual contentions [that] have evidentiary support or . . . will likely have evidentiary support after a reasonable opportunity for further investigation or discovery."[70] With criminal defense lawyers having the same obligation, society will be alerted that some criminal cases merit additional scrutiny.

In considering the behavior of criminal defense lawyers, one question is whether their affirmations of innocence will reflect an actual belief. Another question is whether lawyer-client communication will be hindered because the lawyers may not affirm innocence if, in private, their clients conceded they committed the crimes charged. A corollary to these questions is the defense practice of directing clients not to fully disclose to the lawyers. "I will not ask you" or "I don't want to know," the lawyers will say in their first meeting, "whether you committed the crime. If you tell me you did, then I cannot assert all defenses or question you if you decide to testify."

The rationale behind this willful ignorance is that if defense lawyers know their clients committed the crime they cannot ethically call alibi witnesses or allege that someone else committed the crime, for example. Plainly, whatever the lawyers' rationale for these behaviors and society's rationale for allowing them, guilty defendants (and lawyers know this if their clients have told them) should not have additional opportunity for acquittal. The guilty will have to choose between lying to their lawyers to enable the lawyers to affirm innocence and enable them to assert the plea (and the many negative consequences attached to lying to your lawyer) or tell their lawyers the truth and forego pleading innocent.

Experienced defense lawyers will have greater ability than those of less experience to evaluate the truthfulness of a client's claim of innocence and determine whether pleading innocent will provide an overall benefit to the defense. This disparity in experience exists in all of law and every profession. But because of the high costs of defense lawyers' failure—an innocent client's loss of freedom—this illustrates the importance of adequate funding for public defenders. No ailing patient would be comfortable with a physician who is only a few years removed from medical school undertaking a complicated surgery alone in an operating room. But, in courthouses throughout America, public defenders of similar experience are trying felony cases in which convictions can lead to years or decades in prison for their clients. The young surgeons will always be supervised by a physician who is more experienced, but, for lack of funding, the young public defender is often alone.

Similarly, judges in England, in the 1700s, used the beyond-reasonable-doubt standard or higher burdens of persuasion because they feared that two conditions then—which prevail prominently now—would lead to the conviction of innocent people: inadequate investigation procedures and the silencing of defendants.[71] The English judges increased the burdens of persuasion because they feared also that defendants would receive undeserved, almost automatic, death penalties for many felonies. Given the 2014 study (4.1 percent of defendants sentenced to death are innocent), this is a reasonable fear in America.

The Right to Speak Truthfully

The adversarial system's silencing of innocent people who want to tell the truth is in opposition to their natural inclination to speak up and profess innocence when confronted with a false charge. However, in the current system, an innocent person's urge to tell the truth should be suppressed for any number of reasons, previously discussed. In some circumstances, even silence can be indicative of guilt when speaking up would be natural or expected. In a 2013 Supreme Court case, *Salinas v. Texas*, police officers, for an hour, questioned a suspect about two murders. Without asserting a right to remain silent or requesting a lawyer, the suspect, Salinas, denied involvement in the killings.

Salinas, who owned a shotgun, was eventually asked "whether his shotgun 'would match the shells recovered at the scene of the murder.'"[72] He then looked at the floor, shuffled his feet, bit his lip, clenched his hands, and tightened up.[73] The Court concluded that Salinas's verbal silence and downcast demeanor could be used by the prosecution to argue that the silence indicated his consciousness of guilt. The Court reasoned that "someone might decline to answer a police officer's question . . . because he is trying to think of a good lie, because he is embarrassed, or because he is protecting someone else."[74]

Similarly, if the prosecution may argue that speaking, silence, or body movements indicate consciousness of guilt, then, in some instances, the judge should instruct the jury that other evidence may indicate a defendant's consciousness of innocence. Two examples of such evidence would be a suspect's prompt claim of innocence following an accusation and a defendant's answering completely the questions of prosecutors or investigators pursuant to a plea of innocence.

Courts throughout the country have long permitted this kind of practice in sexual assault cases, in favor of the prosecution. Prosecutors may introduce evidence of complainants' pretrial statements to imply to the jurors that the complainants are telling the truth. To support this contention, prosecutors routinely introduce evidence that a complainant told someone of an alleged sexual assault promptly after it occurred, though several states do not even require that the statement be made promptly.[75]

A 2011 decision by New York's highest court (Court of Appeals) illustrates the theory that someone's prompt response may be indicative of truthfulness. This case, involving the sexual assault of a child, is possibly the most difficult to litigate. From the prosecution perspective, children are vulnerable and inexperienced in communication. On the other side, defense lawyers have to be wary of questioning children sharply and alienating jurors. At the same time, the defense lawyers recognize that if the jurors credit the child's testimony and find their clients guilty, the clients may be sentenced to decades in prison. In two of the three cases where the state supreme courts (Connecticut and California) approved the use of prior statements, even though the child-complainants did not make them promptly, the courts approved sentences of imprisonment of twenty years and twenty-six years for each of the defendants.[76]

The New York case will be discussed in detail because it illustrates many of the points in this book and how trial judges and appellate courts focus almost exclusively on procedures, not on whether the jury was correct in finding defendants guilty. In a trial in New York City, in 2007, an eleven-year-old female testified that an adult, male babysitter, the defendant, Luis Parada, sexually assaulted her at various times when she was six or seven years old, from mid-2002 to early 2004. At the trial, the prosecution introduced what is known as *outcry* evidence: "While defendant was still babysitting her . . . [the] complainant [female] disclosed to a female cousin, who was one year older, that defendant had 'put his front private part in[to her butt].' Complainant made her cousin 'pinky promise' not to tell anyone because she 'thought they wouldn't believe [her],'" the court wrote.[77] (The child-complainant testified to this; the cousin did not testify.)

This kind of evidence, a complainant's statement prior to a trial, which is consistent with a complainant's trial testimony, is rarely admitted into evidence in cases. The court explained why: "In general, the hearsay rule prohibits the admission into evidence of out-of-court statements [such as the child's statement to her cousin] to prove the truth of the matter stated. This rule applies even to prior statements of a testifying witness that are consistent with the witness's testimony . . . [and] the reason generally given for the exclusion of prior consistent statements is that 'an untrustworthy statement is not made more trustworthy by repetition.'"[78]

In an exception to this rule, courts permit evidence of a prompt outcry, such as the child's informing her cousin of an assault, to support the prosecution contention that the complainant is telling the truth when she testifies in court. The presumption is that a prompt disclosure, combined with later, similar trial testimony ("he assaulted me while babysitting"), is a measure of truthfulness. In this case, the child informed her cousin of the assaults within the time period in which they allegedly occurred.

After the trial judge allowed the testimony, the "defendant [who had no prior criminal record] took the stand and professed innocence.[79] His expert, a psychiatrist with experience in evaluating child victims of sexual abuse, testified that children may allege molestation to get even with someone in their environment, and sometimes 'confabulate' or 'introduce fantasy' into their statements," the court wrote.[80] The jury found the defendant, Parada, guilty, the judge sentenced him to twenty years' imprisonment, and the Court of Appeals affirmed the conviction and sentence.

New York, like most jurisdictions, permits the trial judge, at the request of the prosecution, to instruct jurors on how to view evidence of outcry. The current New York jury instruction reads: "You may consider whether . . . [the complainant] complained of the crime promptly or within a reasonable period of time after its alleged commission. If you find that the complaint was made promptly or within a reasonable time, you may consider whether and to what extent, if any, that fact tends to support the believability of the witness's testimony."[81]

This instruction, combined with outcry evidence, may provide a significant benefit to the prosecution's case. First, the instruction alerts the jury to evidence that supports the prosecution's arguments. Also, according to the rules of evidence, the child's trial testimony about what she told her cousin, absent the outcry exception, should not be allowed because the testimony refers to hearsay (an out-of-court statement introduced in court for its alleged truthfulness). Generally, the legal system considers hearsay evidence to be less reliable than trial testimony because the conditions under which hearsay statements were made, as well as the statements themselves, cannot be observed and scrutinized by the jurors.

Downplaying the significance of introducing a trial witness's prior consistent statements (hearsay), the concurring judge in the case wrote that courts disallow it only for a minor reason, because "it is generally a waste of time"; it is "rarely prejudicial."[82] Despite the judge's perspective, a child's testimony about her consistent pretrial statements may have a cumulative effect and create in the minds of jurors the perception of an additional layer of evidence. This is more likely to have occurred in this case than others because the child's aunt and mother, and a nurse who examined the child, and a detective who investigated the case all testified about what the child told them, in the past, about the sexual assaults.

In a sexual assault case, the prosecution often has only one eyewitness, the complainant, who, in this case, was six or seven years old when the alleged assaults occurred, ten years old when she testified in the grand jury, and eleven years old when she testified at trial. The prosecution's introduction of the outcry evidence, from the testimony of the child and the four other witnesses, was based on a general theory (prompt statements indicate truthfulness); the theory was not shown to apply to this complainant.

Similarly, the defense's introduction of the psychiatrist's testimony, about children's "confabulation" and "fantasy," was not shown to apply to the complainant. The testimony about the theory, even if proven through studies, does not lead to the conclusion that a particular child-complainant would fabricate a story or imagine that she was sexually assaulted. That both the prosecution and defense resorted to general evidence, without any applicability to this case (no validity as applied), shows the difficulty of finding facts in sexual assault cases. Both sides look to general principles, which exist outside the case. When applied to cases, these principles are less valid than the conclusions drawn from a personal examination of witnesses by experts.

During the trial, the judge mistakenly permitted the child's aunt to testify about disclosures the child made to the aunt, more than two years after the last alleged assault. "In mid-May 2006," according to the court, the "complainant revealed to her paternal aunt that defendant had 'touched her' when he babysat her. At complainant's insistence, her aunt agreed to keep this a secret. On another occasion, complainant again talked to her aunt about 'what [had] happened to her.'"[83]

These disclosures were not *prompt* and should not have been allowed into evidence at the trial, according to the court. Nonetheless, the court concluded: "The admission of complainant's disclosures to her aunt was *harmless error.*"[84]

In other words, the court believed the jury would have found the defendant guilty even if the improper evidence, the aunt's testimony, had not been considered by the jury. The "harmless error rule is probably the most cited rule in modern criminal appeals," concluded Professor William M. Landes and Judge Richard A. Posner, formerly the chief judge of the U.S. Court of Appeals for the Seventh Circuit.[85]

New York's highest court is rejecting Parada's appeal by making factual findings beneficial to the prosecution (that the jury would have convicted Parada if the statement to the aunt had not been admitted). In rejecting Parada's other points, the court wrote, "Defendant's remaining arguments, to the extent preserved, are without merit."[86] That is, the court was apparently referring to the same arguments Parada made in his appeal previously to one of New York's lower, intermediate appellate courts. In affirming Parada's conviction, that court denied his claims on procedural grounds, without considering the sufficiency of the facts of the case. That court wrote:

- "Although the victim's disclosure to her aunt did not qualify under that exception [prompt outcry], *any error in admitting that evidence was harmless.*"[87]
- "Defendant *did not preserve* his other challenges to prior consistent statements by the victim, and we decline to review them in the interest of justice."[88]

- "Defendant's challenges to the People's summation *are unpreserved*, and we decline to review them in the interest of justice."[89]
- "While the prosecutor improperly cited expert testimony to suggest that the victim's change in behavior was indicative of her having been abused, we find no basis to disturb the jury's determination regarding the credibility of the victim's strong testimony, and *find the error to be harmless* in any event."[90]

By the end of the trial, the only substantive evidence of the defendant's guilt came from the child-complainant. The judge on the Court of Appeals who concurred referred to the evidence that should not have been admitted (testimony of the aunt), but which the court held was harmless error. "I do not find it as hard as the majority does to imagine an acquittal if the evidence had been kept out. . . . Defendant [Parada] testified, in what seems from the transcript a straightforward and convincing way, that he had never done and never would do any of the things the victim accused him of. It seems possible to me that a juror could have thought his denial raised a reasonable doubt; that the victim and her mother might for some reason (perhaps to protect the true abuser) have concocted a false story."[91]

The two dissenting judges from the intermediate appellate court (three judges in the majority) were skeptical that the evidence supported a conviction. "Given that the only evidence of defendant's guilt was the testimony of the 11-year-old complaining witness and that there was no physical evidence, I believe the errors were not harmless and that defendant is entitled to a new trial."[92] The dissent added, "The majority acknowledges it was error for the prosecutor to use the expert testimony of the psychologist to prove that abuse occurred, but concludes this error was harmless. . . . I am not persuaded that this unduly prejudicial testimony did not affect the outcome of the trial."[93]

This case illustrates how different emphases lead to different results. The dissenting judges focused on whether all the facts (including those that should not have been allowed) supported a guilty verdict. On the other side, the majorities in both appellate courts used procedural rules (harmless error and unpreserved claims) to avoid the holistic scrutiny of facts employed by the dissent.

The case also illustrates that one way to measure truthfulness is to determine whether a sexual assault complainant made a prompt outcry. But defendants who claim to be innocent do not have any similar pre-trial test through which to measure their truthfulness. In a 2016 chapter for a book on sexual assault prosecutions, I described how an innocence interview, attended only by law enforcement officials and the defense team, would promote a search for truth and "would cause no trauma, no embarrassment, no public scrutiny, nor any kind of harm to an actual victim. After the prosecution questions the defendant, it could show his (or her) taped interview to the complainant. The defendant would not be present. The complainant would become aware of probable defence questions and could prepare for his or her cross-examination at trial. Actual victims in sexual assault cases are sometimes confused by the locations of furniture and objects. They sometimes have difficulty estimating time or distance. From the defendant's recorded statement, the complainant could try to recollect time and place facts prior to his or her testimony at trial."[94]

In a 1990 case, the New York Court of Appeals explained why outcry evidence is admissible; the same reasoning could apply to the pretrial statements of a plausibly innocent person: "Evidence that the victim of a sexual attack promptly complained of the crime has long been deemed admissible as an exception to the hearsay rule, the premise being that prompt complaint was 'natural' conduct on the part of an 'outraged female,' and failure to complain therefore cast doubt on the complainant's veracity; outcry evidence was considered necessary to rebut the adverse inference a jury would inevitably draw if not presented with proof of a timely complaint."[95]

Probably the most disbelieved person in the adversarial legal system is the defendant who claims to be innocent. Like complainants who promptly, naturally, or under any other truth-producing conditions tell someone they suffered a sexual assault, defendants who plead innocent and divulge their stories prior to trial (especially because this increases their risk of conviction) may be similarly likely to be telling the truth. Defendants' consent to the innocence interview, as well as a prompt assertion of innocence upon becoming aware of a criminal accusation, should be brought to the attention of juries on the same basis as complainants' reports are brought to the attention of juries.

The End of Silence

The most necessary changes to the adversarial system are that the investigation should be more neutral and innocent people should have the opportunity to tell their truthful stories to investigators and jurors without suffering adverse consequences. In England, "The principle [that criminal defendants need not accuse themselves] seeped into the common law trial primarily as a protection for witnesses rather than for the accused, especially to shield prosecution witnesses against the growing aggressiveness of cross-examination by defense counsel in the second half of the eighteenth century," according to Professor Langbein.[96] Defendants' testifying was a natural part of adversarial practice.

In England, the right to remain silent was made necessary not by government abuse, but rather by practice and legislation in the late eighteenth and nineteenth centuries that provided criminal defendants with lawyers who could speak for them.[97] Langbein, in examining most of the reports from the *Sessions Papers*, from the 1670s through the 1780s, did not find in "these thousands of cases" even one case "in which an accused refused to speak at trial on the asserted ground of a privilege to remain silent."[98]

The silencing in the adversarial system occurred because accused people obtained the right to counsel. Silence and confidentiality are valuable because they promote communication between lawyers and clients, as well as individual autonomy. However, the English judges believed that when defendants do not have an obligation to speak there is a much greater likelihood that guilty people will be acquitted because the primary source of evidence in almost all cases is the accused person. While witnesses and victims can be mistaken, all defendants know whether they committed the alleged crime.

Professor Gordon Van Kessel, in 2002, summarized the increase in silence, especially at trial. "In colonial America, virtually all defendants testified at trial, and this trend continued throughout the first half of this century. Studies of trials in the 1920s and the 1950s show that very few defendants refused to testify at trial and that few were helped by such refusals. However, following *Griffin* [no adverse inferences if a defendant does not testify during the guilt-stage of a trial] and the Supreme Court's decisions of the 1960s and 1970s which strengthened the right to silence, fewer and fewer defendants are testifying at trial. . . . The failure of American defendants to testify has become so common that even the public rarely notices when the defendant does not take the witness stand."[99]

Professor Van Kessel cited studies showing, with one exception, that most defendants do not testify. One study showed that in thirty-seven capital trials only 27 percent of the defendants testified at the guilt phase and 22 percent testified at the penalty phase.[100] In contrast, in "continental Europe, nearly all defendants choose to testify. Likewise, in England, it is the rare case in which the accused does not take the stand and give evidence."[101]

In the American adversarial system, suspects and defendants who waive the right to remain silent and speak to law enforcement agents, thereby helping them do their jobs, receive nothing in return. This is not a bad deal for society when those who speak up are guilty, but even many of them face overcharging by police and prosecutors, which may be made possible by use of their incriminating statements. Worse, from the perspective of an innocent person, upon a waiver of the right to remain silent, suspects' statements are often used to incriminate them.

Professor Edwin Borchard, in 1932, suggested that the privilege against self-incrimination does not serve either the defendant or society. In producing what is probably the first exposition of the factors that contribute to innocent-person convictions, he examined sixty-five cases. He believed the main contributors were police and prosecution practices, eyewitness misidentifications, questionable expert-witness testimony, lack of resources for poor defendants, and the inadequacy of defense attorneys.[102] Borchard found little to recommend an absolute right to remain silent:

> It seems probable that the privilege [against self-incrimination] is not an essential condition of the impartial administration of justice and that it does not afford to the accused the protection assumed. On the contrary, it is probably responsible for many abuses, not least of all the "third degree," which subjects accused persons to far more brutal and intolerable ordeals than any obligation to tell the truth in open court. Refusal to take the stand—under circumstances where an explanation from the accused is naturally expected—even if it cannot be commented upon by judge or prosecutor, inevitably affects the jury unfavorably; but in addition, the

accused's known privilege of refusing to testify influences the police to exact "confessions" which, whether true or not, stigmatize the system of obtaining them as a public disgrace.[103]

It is ironic that the Supreme Court, in *Miranda v. Arizona* (1966), cited Professor Borchard's book, *Convicting the Innocent: Sixty-Five Actual Errors of Criminal Justice*, a quotation from which is excerpted above, in supporting its decision to require that police officers inform suspects in custody that they have the right to remain silent.[104] Professor Borchard, who died in 1951, probably would not have been in favor of expanding the right.

Many point to the right to remain silent as a way to exalt the American adversarial system. While discussing the right, the Supreme Court, despite citing no empirical evidence, used it as a reason why the inquisitorial system is inferior. "The privilege against self-incrimination . . . reflects many of our fundamental values and most noble aspirations . . . [such as] our preference for an accusatorial rather than an inquisitorial system of criminal justice."[105]

Other than the formal constitutional requirement, the rationale for the right to remain silent must be that innocent defendants, if forced to speak, could tend to incriminate themselves. But, in practice, the right to silence benefits mostly people who are guilty. Of the people who are arrested, 66 percent plead or are found guilty and 9 percent are placed in diversion or deferred prosecution programs.[106] Society endures a significant cost in providing the right to remain silent to a large number of guilty people, given more than 10 million arrests each year in the United States.[107]

A voluntary statement by defendants pursuant to their pleas of innocence would not create what the Supreme Court, in *Murphy v. Waterfront Commission of New York* (1964), characterized as the "cruel trilemma" of self-accusation, which occurs when a suspect or defendant is required to speak.[108] Such compulsory speech may result in a charge of perjury for guilty defendants, who are likely to lie, and for innocent defendants, who appear to be guilty; a greater likelihood of conviction for innocent defendants, who must admit, for example, they were near the scene of the crime; or a contempt citation for defendants who refuse to speak.

The trilemma can occur only when a defendant is compelled to speak under oath and is, therefore, subject to perjury charges for lying. In contrast, "At common law, the accused was not examined under oath, indeed, he was forbidden to testify on oath even if he wished," Langbein found.[109] The trilemma cannot apply to defendants who plead innocent; they are speaking or testifying voluntarily and do not have to take an oath.

"The slogan that a criminal defendant need not accuse himself . . . emerged as a revered principle from the constitutional struggles of the mid-seventeenth century. It has been formulated to strike at the oath-based investigative procedures of the non-common law courts but had no determinate meaning when applied to the common law criminal trial, at which the accused was forbidden to speak on oath," Langbein found.[110] The common law courts "came to internalize a principle of hostility to self-incrimination, which they had originally developed to counteract the radically different, oath-based procedures of the ecclesiastical and prerogative courts."[111]

European inquisitorial systems do not require defendants to speak under oath. Professor Stephen Thaman wrote that "in most continental European countries an accused or a criminal defendant is never placed under oath, whether he is declaring to a public prosecutor, a magistrate or judge, or in a trial before judge, jury or mixed court."[112] Thus, American defendants' speaking to prosecutors as a requirement of a plea of innocence is consistent with prior adversarial practice, current practice in England, and current inquisitorial practice throughout the world.

Some may claim that social and public recognition of the plea of innocence would make defendants who plead not guilty seem to be guilty. Though not addressing an innocence plea or procedures when she wrote in 2001, Professor Margaret Raymond illuminated the reasoning behind this kind of contention: "Focusing as it does on factual innocence, the wrongful convictions movement places a premium on it. It creates, in effect, a supercategory of innocence, elevating factual innocence over the other categories. My concern is that our jurors, thoroughly schooled in the importance of factual innocence, may conclude that anything short of factual innocence is simply not good enough to justify an acquittal."[113]

However, jurors bring innumerable, unseen biases into all cases, and, as a result, judges direct the jurors to decide each case on the law and facts before them. The exclusion of a "supercategory" of innocence cases for more rigorous examination would prohibit additional protections for people who can make plausible claims of innocence. Without a new plea, they will continue to be lumped together with all those who are guilty.

Professor Daniel S. Medwed is not concerned that recognizing a category of factually innocent defendants will harm the legal system.

> First, defendants will not inherently be disadvantaged by having jurors who have been exposed to tales of wrongful convictions. That is, defense lawyers normally must make a choice early on in a case, prior to trial, regarding whether to pursue one of several theories. . . . [A] lawyer might be legitimately wary of jurors for whom factual innocence is the benchmark for a not guilty verdict. And this is exactly what *voir dire* during jury selection could achieve: allow that lawyer to clarify to all potential jurors that factual innocence is not a *sine qua non* for an acquittal and, in the process, seek to exclude those who believe otherwise.[114]

Similarly, defendants are already entitled to special jury instructors when they decide *not* to testify. The Supreme Court, in *Carter v. Kentucky* (1981), held that defendants have a constitutional right to a jury instruction that they have no obligation to testify.[115] In the same way, defendants who have not pleaded innocent may ask the trial judge to direct the jurors to draw no inference from their not-guilty pleas and/or failure to assert innocence.

Moreover, defendants might be in a better position by not requesting such an instruction. "A number of psychological reasons warrant suspicion about the curative potential of judicial admonitions," according to Professor Simon. "Research on ironic mental processes has shown that instructing people to suppress a thought is a difficult mental feat, which can even backfire by increasing the salience of the thought. Likewise, research on reactance theory suggests that people respond negatively to restrictions on their freedom."[116]

Exonerating Facts

Research continues to indicate the arbitrariness of jury verdicts and the validity of one of the conclusions at the beginning of this book: the most important part of a criminal case is the investigation and the discovery of exonerating facts. In summarizing a 1986 study on thirty-eight sexual assault cases, professors Daniel Givelber and Amy Farrell, in a 2012 book, point to jurors' rendering verdicts based on "hard" factors (legally relevant evidence), as well as factors that jurors should not consider (irrelevant evidence). The hard evidence consists of "eyewitness testimony, physical evidence, recovered weapons, and physical injuries to the victim."

In contrast, when jurors believe that the evidence presented to them is "weak," they may tend to "liberate" defendants. Jurors then consider the attractiveness of defendants, whether they are employed, negative comments about the victims' character, and the victims' (presumably alleged) responsibility for the assaults.[117]

In analyzing several major studies from the United States and United Kingdom, Givelber and Farrell did not indicate that jurors consider such nonrelevant evidence as the formal titles attached to the legal parties in a case (defendant, accused, prosecution, or district attorney) or the formal procedures of a case (grand jury and indictment).[118] Similarly, it seems unlikely that jurors would disfavor a defendant who pleads *not guilty* instead of *innocent*. Whether jurors base their verdicts on hard, legally relevant evidence or weak, irrelevant evidence, their biases will remain, neither fewer nor greater in number given the formal plea of a defendant.

In conclusion, we should recognize the importance of a search for truth and that the discovery of facts will contribute to correct outcomes in cases. Law enforcement officials should recognize that more neutral and open investigations will produce more facts. Prosecution offices should have rules designed to lessen individual prosecutors' combativeness. Legal ethics rules should prohibit defense lawyers from arguing that truthful and accurate witnesses are lying and inaccurate. Appellate courts, especially when defendants have presented plausible claims of innocence, should be willing to review the facts from a case and the correctness of juries' guilty verdicts and, in some cases, reverse convictions and acquit defendants.

The plea of innocence will require new jury instructions. Over time, the instructions will have to be calibrated, but they should contain a number of fundamental parts, with the trial judge instructing the jurors as follows:

Members of the jury, by virtue of the defendant's plea of innocence, you are required by law to consider the following. The plea required the defendant to waive his right to remain silent and answer any questions put to him by the prosecution prior to trial. Moreover, the defendant claims that he made a prompt disclosure of innocence and that his actions prior to being charged with the crime in this case indicate innocence. Therefore, if you find that the defendant, from the point of view of a reasonable person [not the defendant's point of view], fully answered the questions of the prosecution, or communicated innocence to a person when it would be first natural to do so, or that his demeanor or actions reasonably implied innocence, then you may consider any one or all of these factors a credit to the defendant in deciding whether to find him guilty or not guilty of the crime charged. However, if you find that the defendant did not fully answer the questions of the prosecution then you may infer that the defendant was concealing relevant information or evidence. Similarly, if you find that the prosecution did not fully investigate the defendant's reasonable or plausible claims of innocence, then you may infer that, if the prosecution had fully investigated the defendant's claims, it would have found some facts or evidence indicating his innocence.

Finally, from prior learning or experience, you may know that one burden of persuasion in criminal cases is proof beyond a reasonable doubt. That is, jurors may find a person guilty only if the evidence proves guilt beyond a reasonable doubt. I will provide that definition to you in a moment. However, because the defendant in this case has pleaded innocent, he is entitled to a higher burden of persuasion, but only if you find that he fully answered the questions of the prosecution and made a reasonable or plausible claim of innocence. Otherwise, you must apply the beyond-reasonable-doubt standard. Therefore, if you find that the defendant complied with his obligations under the plea of innocence, you must find him not guilty if any doubt as to his guilt remains in your mind or conscience. This does mean you must be certain. If your mind or conscience does not provide you with a doubt about his guilt, then you may find him guilty.

* * *

The adversarial system, including the U.S. Constitution, provides no method through which people who make a plausible claim of innocence can distinguish themselves from all the other defendants who cannot. Yes, all defendants have the right to require the government to comply with the procedures provided by the Bill of Rights. Remarkably, however, guilty defendants use the Constitution to *exclude* evidence that indicates they are, indeed, guilty. Innocent defendants will, of course, sometimes want to exclude guns and drugs to which they have been mistakenly linked. But, in almost all cases, innocent people, unlike those who are guilty, want to introduce into evidence as many facts as possible. It is, indeed, a cruel and illogical irony that there is nothing in the Constitution or law that provides an innocent person with the right to obtain exonerating evidence in the way the Constitution and law provide guilty people with the right to exclude incriminating evidence.

A more rigorous search for truth, through the plea of innocence, can be implemented immediately. When professors Zalman and Grunewald, in 2015, commented on five proposals for adversarial change, they described how, through the plea of innocence, a demonstration project could be implemented: "It would take just one district attorney with a good working relationship with the police, a willing judge, and a defendant willing to waive the jury right to create a quasi-inquisitorial court and trial experiment that might be well worth trying. It is somewhat surprising that in the two decades since the American innocence movement was born, very little trial-procedure innovation has happened even at the county level."[119]

Our knowledge of the breadth of the innocent-person conviction problem shows the need for the reformation of the adversarial legal system. Most innocent people about to be pushed against the wall of conviction and imprisonment will not want to relinquish opportunities to fight back, a strong reason to ensure that defendants retain an adversarial right. However, especially when impoverished, they need help.

The right of defendants to plead innocence will encourage government agents to conduct more thorough investigations and provide innocent people a meaningful opportunity to find exonerating facts. The resources consumed during this search will be far outweighed by the resources saved from eliminating unnecessary trials, appeals, and collateral proceedings involving innocent people who have been prosecuted, convicted, imprisoned, or executed. It makes little difference how this system is characterized—adversarial, inquisitorial, or truth-based—so long as its primary purpose is to discover exonerating facts and truth at the earliest possible moment.

ACKNOWLEDGMENTS

Many people have provided support and guidance, and I want to express my deep appreciation. Clara Platter, senior editor at NYU Press, has extraordinary insight and recognized the importance of developing new ways to help innocent people. Clara guided me and supported the book at every point along the way. Her remarkable vision will be an enduring contribution to the literature and scholarship in law and criminal justice. Martin Coleman, the Editing, Design, and Production Director at NYU Press, was a steady, professional influence. Martin was instrumental in the completion of this book. Joseph Dahm was an expert copy editor for the book. Joseph was precise in his work, generous in his comments, and respectful of the author's intent. Jeff Ourvan, of the Jennifer Lyons Literary Agency, provided unwavering support and mentorship, and I am very grateful for his belief in this project. Marvin Zalman, one of the leaders among innocence scholars, provided invaluable commentary on the manuscript, and he has inspired me for many years. Marvin's work, vision, and mentorship to many students, lawyers, and professionals will undoubtedly be a central part of the history of how the legal and criminal justice systems evolved.

NOTES

Some of the internet links in the endnotes may have been broken, and some websites may have been taken down or revised. The views expressed in this book are those of the author and do not reflect the official policy or position of the Department of the Army, the Department of Defense, or the U.S. government.

INTRODUCTION

1 Office of Justice Programs, *Statistical Briefing Book* (2019), www.ojjdp.gov.

2 Ryan J. Owens and David A. Simon, "Explaining the Supreme Court's Shrinking Docket," 53 *William & Mary Law Review* 1219, 1231 (2012). See also Supreme Court of the United States, "Granted and Noted List: October Term 2021 Cases for Arguments" (as of January 14, 2022), www.supremecourt.gov.

3 Jon B. Gould, Julia Carrano, Richard A. Leo, and Katie Hail-Jares, "Predicting Erroneous Convictions," 99 *Iowa Law Review* 471, 479 (2014).

4 Gould et al., 492.

5 Gould et al., 492.

6 Gould et al., 489, 490.

7 Gould et al., 494.

8 Gould et al., 494, emphasis added.

9 Daniel Kahneman, *Thinking, Fast and Slow* (New York: Farrar, Straus, 2011), 28.

10 Gould et al., 504.

11 Gould et al., 505.

12 Hugo Mercier and Dan Sperber, *The Enigma of Reason* (Cambridge, MA: Harvard University Press, 2017), 25.

13 Mercier and Sperber, 26.

14 Mercier and Sperber, 21.

15 Rachel E. Morgan and Barbara A. Oudekerk, "Criminal Victimization, 2018" (U.S. Bureau of Justice Statistics, September 2019), 1, https://bjs.ojp.gov.

16 Morgan and Oudekerk, 13 (Table 14).

17 Independent innocence bureaus could be considered. See Lewis M. Steel, "Building a Justice System," *Raleigh (NC) News and Observer*, January 10, 2003, A17.

18 Kahneman, 250, 417.

1. HUMAN ERROR

1 Michael Risinger, "Unsafe Verdicts: The Need for Reformed Standards for the Trial and Review of Factual Innocence Claims," 41 *Houston Law Review* 1281, 1282–1283 (2004).

2 Risinger, 1283.

3 Lawyers in New York may speak to jurors after the conclusion of a trial.

4 A few defendants plead not guilty by reason of insanity.

5 Brian A. Reaves, "Felony Defendants in Large Urban Counties, 2009—Statistical Tables" (U.S. Bureau of Justice Statistics, December 2013), 24, www.bjs.gov.

6 Sarah K. S. Shannon, Christopher Uggen, Jason Schnittker, Melissa Thompson, Sara Wakefield, and Michael Massoglia, "The Growth, Scope, and Spatial Distribution of People with Felony Records in the United States, 1948–2010," 54 *Demography* 1795–1818 (2017), https://doi.org/10.1007/s13524-017-0611-1.

7 U.S. Census Bureau, "National Population by Characteristics: 2010–2019. Population Estimates by Age" (2019), www.census.gov.

8 Death Penalty Information Center, "Executed but Possibly Innocent" (2021), https://deathpenaltyinfo.org (data through July 16, 2021).

9 See Ronald J. Allen and Larry Laudan, "Why Do We Convict as Many Innocent People as We Do? Deadly Dilemmas," 41 *Texas Tech Law Review* 65, 75–80 (2008); Daniel Epps, "The Consequences of Error in Criminal Justice," 128 *Harvard Law Review* 1065 (2015); and Marvin Zalman, "The Anti-Blackstonians," 48 *Seton Hall Law Review* 1319 (2018).

10 Hans F. M. Crombag, "Adversarial or Inquisitorial: Do We Have a Choice?," in *Adversarial versus Inquisitorial Justice: Psychological Perspectives on Criminal Justice Systems* (Peter J. van Koppen and Steven D. Penrod, eds.) (New York: Kluwer, 2003), 21, 23, 24.

11 For example, prosecutors need only probable cause to bring charges against someone. American Bar Association, *Model Rules of Professional Conduct* (2020), 3.8(a).

12 *U.S. v. Garsson*, 291 F. 646, 649 (1923).

13 Some recent proposals have suggested reform. See Marvin Zalman and Ralph Grunewald, "Reinventing the Trial: The Innocence Revolution and Proposals to Modify the American Criminal Trial," 3 *Texas A&M Law Review* 189 (2015).

14 Innocence Project, "Exonerate the Innocent" (n.d.), https://innocenceproject.org (data through October 20, 2021).

15 Shane Frederick, "Cognitive Reflection and Decision-Making," 19(4) *Journal of Economic Perspectives* 25–42, 28 (2005), https://pubs.aeaweb.org/doi/pdfplus/10.1257/089533005775196732.

16 Frederick, 27.

17 Chris Guthrie, Jeffrey J. Rachlinski, and Andrew J. Wistrich, "Blinking on the Bench: How Judges Decide Cases," 93 *Cornell Law Review* 1, 10–11 (November 2007).

18 Frederick, 29.

19 Frederick, 37.

20 Daniel Kahneman, *Thinking, Fast and Slow* (New York: Farrar, Straus, 2011), 7.

21 Hugo Mercier and Dan Sperber, *The Enigma of Reason* (Cambridge, MA: Harvard University Press, 2017), 133, emphasis original.

22 Kahneman, 13–14.

23 Guthrie, Rachlinski, and Wistrich, 43.

24 Christopher Keleher, "The Repercussions of Anonymous Juries," 44 *University of San Francisco Law Review* 531, 533 (2010).

25 See Article III, section 2, and the Sixth Amendment of the U.S. Constitution; Keleher, 533.

26 Keleher, 532, note 1.

27 *State v. Chauvin*, "Order for Jury Sequestration and Anonymity," District Court, Fourth Judicial District, 27-CR-20-12646 (November 4, 2020).

28 D. Lynn Hazelwood and John C. Brigham, "The Effects of Juror Anonymity on Jury Verdicts," 22 *Law and Human Behavior* 695, 712 (1998).

29 Hazelwood and Brigham, 710.

30 Hazelwood and Brigham, 706.

31 Marco della Cava, "Anonymous Jury in Derek Chauvin Trial Part of a Growing Trend That Has Some Legal Experts Worried," *USA Today*, April 25, 2021, www.usatoday.com.

32 Associated Press, "Judge in Chauvin Trial to Release Names of Jurors on Nov. 1," October 25, 2021, https://apnews.com.

33 *McCleskey v. Kemp*, 481 U.S. 279 (1987).

34 *McCleskey*, 283.

35 *McCleskey*, 287.

36 *McCleskey*, 297.

37 National Registry of Exonerations, "Yutico Briley" (April 5, 2021) (data through July 1, 2021), www.law.umich.edu.

38 One of the cases in the registry concerns Barry Gibbs, who was convicted of murder in Brooklyn and served nineteen years in prison before his 1987 conviction was overturned. In 2006, the lead detective on the case, Louis J. Eppolito, and his detective partner were convicted in federal court for working with members of organized crime and helping to facilitate eight murders; they were sentenced to life. In the 1990s, Eppolito, whose father worked for the mafia in New York, appeared in the movie *Goodfellas* and had minor roles in a dozen other movies, as he befriended actor Robert De Niro. See Alan Feuer, "Detective, Actor, Author. And Defendant," *New York Times*, March 11, 2005, www.nytimes.com. Claiming that Eppolito framed Gibbs to protect an underworld friend, Gibbs's civil lawyers sued Eppolito and the city and state of New York City and obtained a settlement of almost $12 million. On the night Gibbs was arrested I was on call, working a twenty-four-hour shift in the district attorney's investigations bureau and went to a police precinct to interview Gibbs and conduct a lineup, in which an eyewit-

ness identified Gibbs. In the interview, Gibbs, after first claiming not to know the victim, said that he did know her and had smoked crack with her but claimed not to have killed her. Years later, after being contacted by Gibbs's civil lawyers, the eyewitness recanted and claimed that Eppolito had coerced him into identifying Gibbs. I did not observe Eppolito do anything improper. But given what came out later about him, one must keep an open mind. From the evidence I reviewed, my view is that the registry should not classify Gibbs as an innocent person. See A. G. Sulzberger, "City to Pay $9.9 Million in Man's Imprisonment," *New York Times*, June 3, 2010, www.nytimes.com.

39 National Registry of Exonerations, "Glossary" (n.d.), www.law.umich.edu.

40 Office of Justice Programs, *Statistical Briefing Book* (2019), www.ojjdp.gov. The number of estimated arrests from 1989 through 2019 was 408,416,360. The calculation of more than 423 million arrests includes an assumption of 10 million arrests in 2020 and 5 million arrests in the first six months of 2021, which would be lower than the annual number of arrests since 1989.

2. DEVALUATION OF FREEDOM

1 Jerome Frank and Barbara Frank, *Not Guilty* (Garden City, NY: Doubleday, 1957), 225.

2 Franklin Strier, "Making Jury Trials More Truthful," 30 *University of California, Davis, Law Review* 95, 101 (1996).

3 Strier, 182.

4 28 U.S.C., section 2254.

5 Stephen R. Reinhardt, "The Demise of Habeas Corpus and the Rise of Qualified Immunity: The Court's Ever Increasing Limitations on the Development and Enforcement of Constitutional Rights and Some Particularly Unfortunate Consequences," 113 *Michigan Law Review* 1219, 1241 (2015).

6 Alex Kozinski, in Eugene Volokh, "Judge Kozinski with Four Final Ideas on Improving the Criminal Justice System," *Washington Post*, July 21, 2015, www.washingtonpost.com.

7 *In re Davis*, 557 U.S. 952, 955 (2009) (Scalia dissenting).

8 Laura Collins and David McCormack, "First Weeks of Freedom after a Decade in Jail: Cleared Ryan Ferguson Shares His New Life Including a Cocktail with His Girlfriend," *Daily Mail*, November 24, 2013, www.dailymail.co.uk.

9 FBI Uniform Crime Reports, "Crime in the United States, 2017," https://ucr.fbi.gov.

10 Frances Robles, "As Doubts over Detective Grew, Prosecutors Also Made Missteps," *New York Times*, September 5, 2013, www.nytimes.com.

11 Michael Powell and Sharon Otterman, "Jailed Unjustly in the Death of a Rabbi, Man Nears Freedom," *New York Times*, March 20, 2013, www.nytimes.com.

12 Powell and Otterman.

13 Frances Robles, "No Wrongdoing Found Yet in Inquiry into Detective, Brooklyn Prosecutors Say," *New York Times*, November 7, 2013, www.nytimes.com.

14 Stephanie Clifford, "Brooklyn District Attorney Stands by 21 Convictions, So Far," *New York Times*, January 12, 2015, www.nytimes.com.

15 "David Ranta's Statement to Court, June 10, 1991" [at sentencing], *New York Times*, March 20, 2013, www.nytimes.com.

16 Michael Powell, "Just Freed, Cleared Man Has Heart Attack," *New York Times*, March 23, 2013, www.nytimes.com.

17 Frances Robles, "Man Framed by Detective Will Get $6.4 Million from New York City after Serving 23 Years for Murder," *New York Times*, February 20, 2014, www.nytimes.com.

18 *Dobbert v. Wainwright*, 468 U.S. 1231, 1233 (1984).

19 Kings County District Attorney, "Brooklyn District Attorney Publishes Report That Analyzes and Presents the Findings of His Conviction Review Unit" (July 9, 2020), www.brooklynda.org.

20 Innocence Project, "Exonerate the Innocent" (n.d.), www.innocenceproject.org.

21 Larry Celona and Dean Balsamini, "NYC Recorded 485 Murders in 2021," *New York Post*, January 1, 2022.

3. DEFENSE OF FALSITY

1 John H. Langbein, *The Origins of Adversary Criminal Trial* (Oxford: Oxford University Press, 2003), 265.

2 *Nix v. Whiteside*, 475 U.S. 157, 171 (1986).

3 Tom Stacy, "The Search for the Truth in Constitutional Criminal Procedure," 91 *Columbia Law Review* 1369, 1374–1381 (1991).

4 *Alford v. North Carolina*, 400 U.S. 25, 37 (1970).

5 Reality Check Team, "Death Penalty: How Many Countries Still Have It?," *BBC News*, December 11, 2020, www.bbc.com.

6 Justice Policy Institute, "Finding Direction: Expanding Criminal Justice Options by Considering Policies of Other Nations" (2011), www.justicepolicy.org.

7 National Registry of Exonerations, "Innocents Who Plead Guilty" (November 24, 2015), 1, www.law.umich.edu.

8 Hans F. M. Crombag, "Adversarial or Inquisitorial: Do We Have a Choice?," in *Adversarial versus Inquisitorial Justice: Psychological Perspectives on Criminal Justice Systems* (Peter J. van Koppen and Steven D. Penrod, eds.) (New York: Kluwer, 2003), 21, 24.

9 National Registry of Exonerations, "Innocents Who Plead Guilty," 3.

10 National Registry of Exonerations, "Exonerations by State" (July 2021), www.law.umich.edu.

11 Innocence Project, "Innocence Project and Members of Innocence Network Launch Guilty Plea Campaign" (2017), https://innocenceproject.org.

12 Robert P. Mosteller, "Why Defense Attorneys Cannot, but Do, Care about Innocence," 50 *Santa Clara Law Review* 1, 44–45 (2010).

13 Abbe Smith, "Defending Defending: The Case for Unmitigated Zeal on Behalf of People Who Do Terrible Things," 28 *Hofstra Law Review* 925, 944 (2000), https://scholarship.law.georgetown.edu.

14 Appointed by the president, who usually shares their political views and party membership, U.S. attorneys also confront political influence.

15 KARE 11, "New Research Shows Prosecutors Often Fight Winning Innocence Claims, Offer Deals to Keep Convictions," May 31, 2021, www.kare11.com.

16 See, for example, Federal Rules of Evidence, 404(b)(2). The prosecution may introduce evidence of prior crimes to prove a defendant's "motive, opportunity, intent, preparation, plan, knowledge, identity, absence of mistake, or lack of accident."

17 KARE 11, "After Another Man Confessed to the Crime, Hennepin County Offered Deal to Preserve Conviction," May 31, 2021, www.kare11.com.

18 Joel Hoekstra, "Truth Be Told," *Minnesota Monthly*, February 13, 2008, www.minnesotamonthly.com.

19 Kyle Potter, "Man's Request to Remove Conviction Denied," *MPRNEWS*, April 25, 2013, www.mprnews.org.

20 KARE 11, "After Another Man Confessed."

21 KARE 11, "After Another Man Confessed."

22 Langbein, 262, 261.

23 *Coffin v. U.S.*, 156 U.S. 432, 453 (1985).

24 Langbein, 262.

25 *In re Winship*, 397 U.S. 358 (1970).

26 Langbein, 265.

27 Langbein, 266.

28 *Frazier v. Cupp*, 394 U.S. 731, 739 (1969).

29 *Moran v. Burbine*, 475 U.S. 412, 430 (1986).

30 *Herrera v. Collins*, 506 U.S. 390, 393 (1993).

31 *Herrera*, 396, note 2.

32 Murderpedia, "Lionel Torres Herrera" (n.d.), https://murderpedia.org.

33 *McQuiggin v. Perkins*, 569 U.S. 383, 386 (2013).

34 *McQuiggin*, 401.

35 *Perkins v. McQuiggin*, 2013 U.S. Dist. LEXIS 125871.

36 *McQuiggin*, 392.

37 Langbein, 342.

38 Richard Vogler, *A World View of Criminal Justice* (New York: Routledge, 2016), 131.

39 Langbein, 343.

40 Langbein, 334.

41 *Upjohn Co. v. U.S.*, 449 U.S. 383, 389 (1981).

42 *In re Bieter Co.*, 16 F.3d 929, 935 (1994). In support of its decision, the court cited Supreme Court standard 503(b): "A client has a privilege to refuse to disclose and to prevent any other person from disclosing confidential communications made for the purpose of facilitating the rendition of professional legal services to the client, (1) between himself or his representative and his lawyer or his lawyer's representative, or (2) between his lawyer and his lawyer's representative, or (3) by him

or his lawyer to a lawyer representing another in a matter of common interest, or
(4) between representatives of the client or between the client and a representative
of the client, or (5) between lawyers representing the client.'"

43 *Swidler & Berlin v. U.S.*, 524 U.S. 399, 410 (1998).

44 American Bar Association, *Model Rules of Professional Conduct* (2020), 1.1–1.18
(Client-Lawyer Relationship) and 1.6 (Confidentiality of Information), www.
americanbar.org.

45 American Bar Association, *Modern Rules*, 1.6(b)(1).

46 In contrast, a Wisconsin Supreme Court rule mandates disclosure of client confidences if serious harm can be averted. "A lawyer shall reveal information relating
to the representation of a client to the extent the lawyer reasonably believes necessary to prevent the client from committing a criminal or fraudulent act that the
lawyer reasonably believes is likely to result in death or substantial bodily harm
or in substantial injury to the financial interest or property of another." Wisconsin
Supreme Court, Rule 20:1.6(b) (Confidentiality), www.wicourts.gov.

47 Hilary Stout, "G.M. Victim Compensation Program Is Largely Successful," *New
York Times*, February 2, 2015, www.nytimes.com.

48 Stout, "G.M. Victim."

49 Bill Vlasic, "G.M. 'Bullied' Manufacturer over Poorly Designed Part, Email Says,"
New York Times, November 21, 2014, www.nytimes.com.

50 Hilary Stout, "Class-Action Case Accuses G.M. of Neglect Beyond Ignition
Switch," *New York Times*, October 15, 2014, www.nytimes.com.

51 Rachel Abrams, "11 Years Later, Woman's Death Is Tied to G.M. Ignition Defect,"
New York Times, November 10, 2014, http://mobile.nytimes.com.

52 Rebecca Ruiz, "Woman Cleared in Death Linked to G.M.'s Faulty Ignition Switch,"
New York Times, November 24, 2014, www.nytimes.com.

53 Barry Meier and Hilary Stout, "Victims of G.M. Deadly Defect Fall through Legal
Cracks," *New York Times*, December 29, 2014, www.nytimes.com.

54 Meier and Stout.

55 Debra Cassens Weiss, "GM Lawyers Won't Face Michigan Ethics Probe," *ABA
Journal*, March 28, 2016, www.abajournal.com.

56 Michael W. Peregrine and William P. Schuman, "Reporting 'Up' Obligations,"
Harvard Law School Forum on Corporate Governance, April 28, 2016, https://corp-
gov.law.harvard.edu.

57 American Bar Association, *Model Rules*, 3.1 (2020) (Meritorious Claims and Contentions), www.americanbar.org.

58 American Bar Association, *Criminal Justice Standards for the Defense Function*,
4th ed. (2017), 4–7.7(b) (Examination of Witnesses in Court), www.americanbar.
org.

59 Smith, 948.

60 Smith, 948–949.

61 Smith, 953.

62 Smith, 953–954.

63 Smith, 955.

64 Smith, 954.

65 Smith, 955.

66 Jerome Frank and Barbara Frank, *Not Guilty* (Garden City, NY: Doubleday, 1957), 227.

67 Lloyd L. Weinreb, "Legal Ethics: The Adversary Process Is Not an End in Itself," 2 *Journal of the Institute for the Study of Legal Ethics* 59, 61 (1999), https://scholarly-commons.law.hofstra.edu.

4. EMERGENCE AND GLORY OF ADVERSARIAL COMBAT

1 Ellen E. Sward, "Values, Ideology, and the Evolution of the Adversary System," 64 *Indiana Law Journal* 301 (1989).

2 Richard Vogler, *A World View of Criminal Justice* (New York: Routledge, 2016), 24.

3 Vogler, 26.

4 Vogler, 28.

5 John H. Langbein, *The Origins of Adversary Criminal Trial* (Oxford: Oxford University Press, 2003), 340.

6 Vogler, 28.

7 Vogler, 29.

8 Langbein, 340.

9 Vogler, 29.

10 Vogler, 27.

11 Gerard E. Lynch, "Our Administrative System of Criminal Justice," 66 *Fordham Law Review* 2151 (1998), https://scholarship.law.columbia.edu.

12 Langbein, 45.

13 Vogler, 131.

14 Vogler, 132.

15 Langbein, 109.

16 Langbein, 148.

17 Langbein, 4.

18 Langbein, 4.

19 Langbein, 4–5.

20 Langbein, 69.

21 Vogler, 137.

22 Langbein, 253.

23 Vogler, 138.

24 Langbein, 106.

25 Vogler, 145.

26 Vogler, 138.

27 Vogler, 138.

28 Vogler, 138.

29 Sanjeev Anand, "The Origins, Early History and Evolution of the English Criminal Trial Jury," 43 *Alberta Law Review* 407, 408 (2014).

30 Anand, 409–414.
31 Roger D. Groot, "The Early-Thirteenth-Century Criminal Trial," in *Twelve Good Men and True: The Criminal Trial Jury in England, 1200–1800* (J. S. Cockburn and Thomas A. Green, eds.) (Princeton, NJ: Princeton University Press, 1988), 3.
32 Anand, 414–415.
33 Groot, 18.
34 Anand, 415.
35 Groot, 18.
36 Groot, 5.
37 Anand, 419–420.
38 Anand, 424.
39 Anand, 419.
40 Vogler, 142.
41 Vogler, 142.
42 Vogler, 145.
43 Vogler, 146.
44 Vogler, 146. See also Langbein, 309 (quoting 2 *The Trial at Large of Her Majesty Caroline Amelia Elizabeth, Queen of Great Britain; in the House of Lords, on Charges of Adulterous Intercourse* 3 [London, 1821] [2 vols.]).
45 Langbein, 309.
46 Vogler, 146.
47 George Mason University, "The Courvoisier Case" (n.d.), http://mason.gmu.edu.
48 British Library, "Broadside on the 'Life Trial Confession, and Execution of F.B. Courvoisier'" (1840), www.bl.uk.
49 Vogler, 147.
50 Vogler, 147 (citing the Indictable Offences Act 1848).
51 Johannes F. Nijboer, "The American Adversarial System in Criminal Cases: Between Ideology and Reality," 5 *Cardozo Journal of International & Comparative Law* 79, 96 (1997).
52 Nijboer, 96.
53 Monroe H. Freedman, "Our Constitutionalized Adversary System," 1 *Chapman Law Review* 57 (1998).
54 Freedman, "Our Constitutionalized Adversary System," 57–58.
55 See, for example, *Nix v. Whiteside*, 475 U.S. 157, 177, note 1 (Brennan concurring) (1986) and *U.S. v. Wade*, 388 U.S. 218, 258, note 7 (White dissenting and concurring) (1967).
56 *U.S. v. Ziegler*, 2021 U.S. App. LEXIS 17664, 17, note 5.
57 Monroe H. Freedman, "Professional Responsibility of the Criminal Defense Lawyer: The Three Hardest Questions," 64 *Michigan Law Review* 1469 (1966).
58 Freedman, "Professional Responsibility," 1470.
59 Freedman, "Professional Responsibility," 1469.
60 Freedman, "Professional Responsibility," 1482.

61 American Bar Association, *Criminal Justice Standards for the Defense Function*, Standard 4-1.4(b) (4th ed., 2017), www.americanbar.org.

62 Lloyd L. Weinreb, "Legal Ethics: The Adversary Process Is Not an End in Itself," 2 *Journal of the Institute for the Study of Legal Ethics* 63 (1999), https://scholarlycommons.law.hofstra.edu.

63 Weinreb, 64.

64 See generally Elizabeth Kimberly (Kyhm) Penfil, "In The Light of Reason and Experience: Should Federal Evidence Law Protect Confidential Communications between Same-Sex Partners?," 88 *Marquette Law Review* 815, 819–21 (2005) (providing a summary of privileged confidences).

65 See Federal Rules of Evidence, 502(a)—(g) (Attorney-Client Privilege and Work Product; Limitations on Waiver) (indicating privileges and limitations).

66 See U.S. Const. amend. V.

67 See *Taylor v. Kentucky*, 436 U.S. 478, 485 (1978), concluding "that one accused of a crime is entitled to have his guilt or innocence determined solely on the basis of the evidence introduced at trial, and not on grounds of official suspicion, indictment, continued custody, or other circumstances not adduced as proof at trial."

68 See *Carter v. Kentucky*, 450 U.S. 288, 305 (1981) (holding that upon a defendant's request a trial judge has a constitutional obligation to tell jurors that they may draw no adverse inference from the defendant's silence).

69 *Taylor*, 485–486.

70 Peter J. van Koppen and Steven D. Penrod, "Adversarial or Inquisitorial: Comparing Systems," in *Adversarial versus Inquisitorial Justice: Psychological Perspectives on Criminal Justice Systems* (Peter J. van Koppen and Steven D. Penrod, eds.) (New York: Kluwer, 2003), 5.

71 Gregory W. O'Reilly, "England Limits the Right to Silence and Moves towards an Inquisitorial System of Justice," 85 *Journal of Criminal Law & Criminology* 402, 451 (1994) (concluding that "curtailing the right to silence" will not deter crime, 451).

72 Anand, 427–428.

73 Weinreb, 59.

74 David Alan Sklansky, "Anti-inquisitorialism," 122 *Harvard Law Review* 1634, 1639 (2009).

75 Anand, 432.

5. ALONE WITH NO EVIDENCE

1 Brandon L. Garrett and Peter J. Neufeld, "Invalid Forensic Science Testimony and Wrongful Convictions," 95 *Virginia Law Review* 1, 4 (2009), www.virginialawreview.org.

2 Matthew R. Durose, "Census of Publicly Funded Forensic Crime Laboratories, 2005" (U.S. Bureau of Justice Statistics, July 2008), 4, http://bjs.ojp.usdoj.gov.

3 U.S. Department of Justice, Uniform Crime Reports, "Crime in the United States 2005," Table 1 (September 2006), www2.fbi.gov.

4 In limiting the use of DNA, Maryland and Montana, in 2021, prohibited the police, without judicial approval, from using genealogy databases to try to connect a suspect to a crime. See Virginia Hughes, "Two New Laws Restrict Police Use of DNA Search Method," *New York Times*, May 31, 2021, www.nytimes.com.

5 Spencer Hsu, "Federal Review Stalled after Finding Forensic Errors by FBI Lab Unit Spanned Two Decades," *Washington Post*, July 29, 2014, www.washingtonpost.com.

6 Hsu.

7 Hsu.

8 FBI Press Release, "FBI Testimony on Microscopic Hair Analysis Contained Errors in at Least 90 Percent of Cases in Ongoing Review" (April 20, 2015), www.fbi.gov.

9 Dee J. Hall, "Wisconsin, U.S. Used Flawed Hair Evidence to Convict Innocent People," *Capital Times*, April 30, 2017, http://host.madison.com.

10 Hall, "Wisconsin, U.S. Used Flawed Hair Evidence."

11 Dee J. Hall, "Wisconsin Man, Casualty of Flawed Hair Forensics, Latest to Be Exonerated," *Wisconsin Watch*, May 18, 2018, www.wisconsinwatch.org.

12 Hall, "Wisconsin Man."

13 Samuel R. Gross, Barbara O'Brien, Chen Hu, and Edward H. Kennedy, "Rate of False Conviction of Criminal Defendants Who Are Sentenced to Death," 111 *Proceedings of the National Academy of Sciences USA* 7230 (May 20, 2014), www.pnas.org.

14 Gross et al., 7231.

15 Gross et al., 7231.

16 Gross et al., 7235.

17 Office of Justice Programs, *Statistical Briefing Book* (2019), www.ojjdp.gov. The estimated number of arrests in 2012 was 12,196,960.

18 Gross et al., 7235.

19 Gross et al., 7231.

20 Gross et al., 7231.

21 *Kennedy v. Louisiana*, 554 U.S. 407, 437 (2008).

22 Marvin Zalman, "Qualitatively Estimating the Incidence of Wrongful Convictions," 48 *Criminal Law Bulletin* 221, 278 (2012).

23 Zalman, 242–243.

24 Marvin Zalman and Robert J. Norris, "Measuring Innocence: How to Think about the Rate of Wrongful Conviction," 24 *New Criminal Law Review* 601, 652 (2021).

25 D. Michael Risinger, "Innocents Convicted: An Empirically Justified Factual Wrongful Conviction Rate," 97 *Journal of Criminal Law and Criminology* 761, 799, 779 (2007), https://scholarlycommons.law.northwestern.edu.

26 Jon B. Gould and Richard A. Leo, "One-Hundred Years Later: Wrongful Convictions after a Century of Research," 100 *Journal of Criminal Law and Criminology* 825, 832 (2010), https://core.ac.uk.

27 Charles E. Loeffler, Jordan Hyatt, and Greg Ridgeway, "Measuring Self-Reported Wrongful Convictions among Prisoners," 35 *Journal of Quantitative Criminology* 259, 267 (2018).

28 Loeffler, Hyatt, and Ridgeway, 270.

29 Loeffler, Hyatt, and Ridgeway, 273.

30 Loeffler, Hyatt, and Ridgeway, 261.

31 Loeffler, Hyatt, and Ridgeway, 279.

32 National Registry of Exonerations, "Innocents Who Plead Guilty" (November 24, 2015), 1, www.law.umich.edu.

33 National Registry of Exonerations, 2.

34 National Registry of Exonerations, 2.

35 Laura M. Maruschak and Todd D. Minton, "Correctional Populations in the United States, 2017–2018" (U.S. Bureau of Justice Statistics, August 2020), 1, www.bjs.gov.

36 E. Ann Carson, "Prisoners in 2019" (U.S. Bureau of Justice Statistics, October 2020), 1, www.bjs.gov.

37 See, for example, Chrisje Brants, "Wrongful Convictions and Inquisitorial Process: The Case of the Netherlands," 80 *University of Cincinnati Law Review* 1069 (2013), and Fredericke Leuschner, Martin Rettenberger, and Axel Dessecker, "Imprisoned but Innocent: Wrongful Convictions and Imprisonments in Germany, 1990–2016," 66 *Crime & Delinquency* 687–711 (2020).

38 Brants, 1070.

39 Luca Lupária and Chiara Greco, "Unveiling Wrongful Convictions between the U.S. and Italy: Cross-Learning from Each Other's Mistakes," 1 *Wrongful Conviction Law Review* 101, 102 (2020).

40 Andrew Hammel, "How Many Innocent People Are in German Prisons?," *Hammel Translations*, August 25, 2019, https://hammeltranslations.com.

41 Leuschner, Rettenberger, and Dessecker.

42 Katrien Verhesschen and Cyrille Fijnaut, "Correcting Wrongful Convictions in France: Has the Act of 2014 Opened the Door to Revision?," 4 *Erasmus Law Review* 22 (2020).

43 Verhesschen and Fijnaut, 28–29.

44 Verhesschen and Fijnaut, 21.

45 James R. Acker, "Reliable Justice: Advancing the Twofold Aim of Establishing Guilt and Protecting the Innocent," 82 *Albany Law Review* 719, 746 (2019).

6. CONVICTIONS WITHOUT TRUTH

1 See Geraldine Szott Moohr, "Prosecutorial Power in an Adversarial System: Lessons from Current White Collar Cases and the Inquisitorial Model," 8 *Buffalo Criminal Law Review* 165, 193 (2004).

2 Peter J. van Koppen and Steven D. Penrod, "The John Wayne and Judge Dee Versions of Justice," in *Adversarial versus Inquisitorial Justice: Psychological Perspec-*

tives on Criminal Justice Systems (Peter J. van Koppen and Steven D. Penrod, eds.) (New York: Kluwer, 2003), 367.

3 John Thibaut and Laurens Walker, *Procedural Justice: A Psychological Analysis* (Hillsdale, NJ: Lawrence Erlbaum, 1975), 2. Thibaut and Walker believed that the adversarial system was superior to the inquisitorial, but their conclusion has been criticized. See Shari Seidman Diamond and Hans Zeisel, "Procedural Justice: A Psychological Analysis" (book review), 1977 *Duke Law Review* 1289, 1295–1296 (1975).

4 Thibaut and Walker, 3

5 *New Jersey v. Henderson*, 208 N.J. 208, 248–252 (2011). See also *State v. Anthony*, 237 N.J. 213, 233 (2019). "We modify the *Henderson* framework in this way: a defendant will be entitled to a pretrial hearing on the admissibility of identification evidence if *Delgado* and *Rule* 3:11 are not followed and no electronic or contemporaneous, verbatim written recording of the identification procedure is prepared." *Anthony*, 233. "In such cases, defendants will not need to offer proof of suggestive behavior tied to a system variable to get a pretrial hearing." *Anthony*, 233–234.

6 Hans F. M. Crombag, "Adversarial or Inquisitorial: Do We Have a Choice?," in van Koppen and Penrod, 21, 22.

7 National Academy of Sciences, *Identifying the Culprit: Assessing Eyewitness Identification* (2014), 21, www.nap.edu.

8 Robert P. Mosteller, "Why Defense Attorneys Cannot, but Do, Care about Innocence," 50 *Santa Clara Law Review* 1, 16–17 (2010).

9 Jon B. Gould, Julia Carrano, Richard A. Leo, and Katie Hail-Jares, "Predicting Erroneous Convictions," 99 *Iowa Law Review* 471, 503 (2014).

10 *Henderson*.

11 *State v. Cabagbag*, 127 Hawaii 302, 315 (2012).

12 *Commonwealth v. Bastaldo*, 472 Massachusetts 16, 24–25 (2015).

13 *People v. Boone*, 30 New York 3d 521, 535–536 (2017).

14 Task Force, "2019 Report of the United States Court of Appeals for the Third Circuit Task Force on Eyewitness Identifications," 92 *Temple Law Review* 1, 83 (2019).

15 President's Council of Advisors on Science and Technology, *Forensic Science in Criminal Courts: Ensuring Scientific Validity of Feature-Comparison Methods* (2016), 4, https://obamawhitehouse.archives.gov.

16 President's Council of Advisors, 47.

17 Federal Rules of Evidence, Rule 702 (Testimony by Expert Witnesses).

18 Federal Rules of Evidence, Rule 702.

19 *Kumho Tire v. Carmichael*, 526 U.S. 137, 153–154, 156 (1999).

20 See *Henderson*, 267, *Cabagbag*, *Bastaldo*, and *Boone*.

21 *Plessy v. Ferguson*, 163 U.S. 537, 541 (1896).

22 *Boone*, 535–536.

23 *Bastaldo*, 25.

24 *Bastaldo*, 26.
25 New Jersey Courts, *Model Criminal Jury Charges* (Identification: In-Court and Out-of-Court Identifications) (2020), sections 3, 8, 5, 9, https://njcourts.gov.
26 James R. Acker, "Reliable Justice: Advancing the Twofold Aim of Establishing Guilt and Protecting the Innocent," 82 *Albany Law Review* 719, 746 (2019).
27 *In re Davis*, 557 U.S. 952, 955 (2009).
28 *District Attorney v. Osborne*, 557 U.S. 52, 71 (2009).
29 *District Attorney*, 69, quoting *Medina v. California*, 505 U.S. 437, 446 (1992).
30 Margaret Raymond, "The Problem with Innocence," 49 *Cleveland State Law Review* 449, 463 (2001).
31 John H. Langbein, *The Origins of Adversary Criminal Trial* (Oxford: Oxford University Press, 2003), 343.
32 Lloyd L. Weinreb, "Legal Ethics: The Adversary Process Is Not an End in Itself," 2 *Journal of the Institute for the Study of Legal Ethics* 59, 61 (1999) (finding inquisitorial methods appropriate at some stages of the criminal legal process).
33 Jerome Frank, *Courts on Trial: Myth and Reality in American Justice* (Princeton, NJ: Princeton University Press, 1949), 371.
34 Frank, 371.

7. THE LOST DIALECTIC

1 Josef Pieper, *Guide to Thomas Aquinas* (Richard Winston and Clara Winston, trans.) (New York: Pantheon Books, 1962), 78 (discussing the intellectual approach of Thomas Aquinas and his ability to present an opponent's position better than the opponent, 77).
2 See *U.S. v. Gouveia*, 467 U.S. 180, 187 (1984).
3 Martin Guggenheim, "The People's Right to a Well-Funded Indigent Defender System," 36 *NYU Review of Law & Social Change* 395, 402 (2012).
4 Mary Sue Backus and Paul Marcus, "The Right to Counsel in Criminal Cases: A National Crisis," 57 *Hastings Law Journal* 1031, 1032 (2006).
5 Guggenheim, 404.
6 Guggenheim, 404.
7 Jacob Carpenter, "Facing a Felony, Would You Want a Private Investigator? Some Wisconsin Attorneys Don't Use Them," *Milwaukee Journal Sentinel*, April 22, 2017, www.jsonline.com.
8 Steven K. Smith and Carol J. DeFrances, "Indigent Defense" (Bureau of Justice Statistics, 1996), 1, http://bjs.ojp.usdoj.gov.
9 Bureau of Justice Statistics, "Two of Three Felony Defendants Represented by Publicly Financed Counsel" (November 29, 2000), www.bjs.gov.
10 New Jersey Courts, "Income Eligibility Guidelines for Indigent Defense Services" (2020), www.njcourts.gov.
11 Carol J. DeFrances, "State Funded Indigent Defense Services, 1999" (Bureau of Justice Statistics Special Report, 2001), 7, http://bjs.ojp.usdoj.gov.

12 Susan Kostal, "Solo and Small Firm Hourly Rates: Winners and Losers, by State and Practice Area," *Attorney at Work*, February 5, 2021, www.attorneyatwork.com, interpreting CLIO, "2020 Legal Trends Report," www.clio.com.

13 Samantha Stokes, "Will Billing Rates for Elite Firms Rise More in 2020?," *American Lawyer*, July 30, 2020, www.law.com.

14 ALM Staff, "The 2021 Am Law 100: Ranked by Profits per Equity Partner," *American Lawyer*, April 20, 2021, www.law.com.

15 Sara Randazzo, "Entry-Level Lawyers Are Now Making $200,000 a Year," *Wall Street Journal*, June 12, 2021, www.wsj.com.

16 *U.S. News & World Report*, "How Much Does a Lawyer Make?" (2019), https://money.usnews.com/careers/best-jobs/lawyer/salary.

17 Andrea Fuller, Josh Mitchell, and Sara Randazzo, "Law School Loses Luster as Debts Mount and Salaries Stagnate," *Wall Street Journal*, August 3, 2021, www.wsj.com.

18 Zippia, "Average Public Defender Salary," July 28, 2021, www.zippia.com.

19 Peter Wagner and Alexi Jones, "State of Phone Justice: Local Jails, State Prisons and Private Phone Providers" (Prison Policy Initiative, 2019), www.prisonpolicy.org.

20 See Federal Rules of Criminal Procedure, 17 (Subpoena). "A subpoena may order the witness to produce any books, papers, documents, data, or other objects the subpoena designates." Federal Rules, 17(c)(1).

21 See Federal Rules of Criminal Procedure, 41 (Search and Seizure).

22 See Gerard E. Lynch, "Our Administrative System of Criminal Justice," 66 *Fordham Law Review* 2117 (1998), https://ir.lawnet.fordham.edu.

23 See Susan Bandes, "Loyalty to One's Convictions: The Prosecutor and Tunnel Vision," 49 *Howard Law Journal* 475, 493 (2006) (finding that nonlegal factors contribute to premature prosecutorial decisions).

24 See *U.S. v. Gouveia*, 467 U.S. 180, 187 (1984) (concluding that the right to counsel does not apply prior to adversarial judicial proceedings).

25 Lynch, 2129.

26 *Gouveia*, 187. See also *Scott v. Illinois*, 440 U.S. 367, 374 (1979). "We therefore hold that the Sixth and Fourteenth Amendments to the United States Constitution require only that no indigent criminal defendant be sentenced to a term of imprisonment unless the State has afforded him the right to assistance of appointed counsel in his defense."

27 See *Gouveia*, 187 and *Kirby v. Illinois*, 406 U.S. 682, 688–699 (1972) (finding no right to counsel for identification procedures that occur prior to adversarial judicial proceedings).

28 See *Moran v. Burbine*, 475 U.S. 412, 429–430 (1986) (not finding in the Fifth and Sixth Amendments a right to counsel at a voluntary interrogation that occurs prior to judicial proceedings), and *Gouveia*, 180, 187–188 (summarizing the judicial history behind rejecting a constitutional right to counsel prior to an adversarial judicial proceeding).

29 Pieper, 82.

30 Joseph D. Grano, "The Adversarial-Accusatorial Label: A Constraint on the Search for Truth," 20 *Harvard Journal of Law & Public Policy* 513, 513 (1997).

31 David Alan Sklansky, "Anti-Inquisitorialism," 122 *Harvard Law Review* 1634, 1639 (2009).

32 Maximo Langer, "From Legal Transplants to Legal Translations: The Globalization of Plea Bargaining and the Americanization Thesis in Criminal Procedure," 45 *Harvard International Law Journal* 1, 9 (2004). See also William T. Pizzi, "The American 'Adversary System?,'" 100 *West Virginia Law Review* 847 (1998), https://scholar.law.colorado.edu. "There is no line that can be easily drawn between adversary and inquisitorial trial systems" (Pizzi, 847).

33 Sklansky, 1704.

34 Pizzi, 849 (seeing few distinctions between the adversarial and inquisitorial systems).

35 Amalia D. Kessler, "Our Inquisitorial Tradition: Equity Procedure, Due Process, and the Search for an Alternative to the Adversarial," 90 *Cornell Law Review* 1181, 1183 (2005).

36 Kessler, 1184.

37 Stephen C. Thaman, *Comparative Criminal Procedure* (Durham, NC: Carolina Academic Press, 2008), 3.

38 Langer, 62.

8. TRIALS WITHOUT FACTS

1 D. Michael Risinger, "Criminal Law: Innocents Convicted: An Empirically Justified Factual Wrongful Conviction Rate," 97 *Journal of Criminal Law & Criminology* 761, 762, note 2 (2007).

2 Tim Bakken, "Innocent Procedures for Innocent Persons: Beyond the Adversarial System," 41 *University of Michigan Journal of Law Reform* 553 (2008).

3 Bakken, 554.

4 Jerome Frank and Barbara Frank, *Not Guilty* (Garden City, NY: Doubleday, 1957), 202.

5 Jerome Frank, *Courts on Trial: Myth and Reality in American Justice* (Princeton, NJ: Princeton University Press, 1949), 22.

6 Frank, 4.

9. PROCEDURES OVER EVIDENCE

1 See Randall H. Warner, "All Mixed Up about Mixed Questions," 7 *Journal of Appellate Practice & Process* 101, 103–106 (2005).

2 Keith Findley, "Innocence Protections in the Appellate Process," 93 *Marquette Law Review* 591, 592 (2009).

3 Brandon L. Garrett, "Judging Innocence," 108 *Columbia Law review* 55, 74 (2008).

4 Garrett, 60.

5 Garrett, 61.

6 Findley, 609–610, and note 99.

7 John H. Langbein, *The Origins of Adversary Criminal Trial* (Oxford: Oxford University Press, 2003), 301.

8 Langbein, 302.

9 Langbein, 212.

10 Langbein, 304.

11 Langbein, 305.

12 Warner, 103.

13 Michael Risinger, "Unsafe Verdicts: The Need for Reformed Standards for the Trial and Review of Factual Innocence Claims," 41 *Houston Law Review* 1281, 1332 (2004).

14 Sara M. Moniuszko and Cara Kelly, "Harvey Weinstein Scandal: A Complete List of the 87 Accusers," *USA Today*, October 27, 2017, www.usatoday.com.

15 *Commonwealth v. Cosby*, Supreme Court of Pennsylvania [J-100-2020], June 30, 2021, 31, www.pacourts.us.

16 *Commonwealth v. Cosby*, 224 A.3d 372, 397 (2019).

17 *Commonwealth v. Cosby*, 224 A.3d at 397.

18 *Commonwealth v. Cosby*, 224 A.3d at 398, emphasis added.

19 *Commonwealth v. Cosby*, Supreme Court of Pennsylvania.

20 Tim Bakken, *The Cost of Loyalty: Dishonesty, Hubris, and Failure in the U.S. Military* (New York: Bloomsbury, 2020).

21 Hans F. M. Crombag, "Adversarial or Inquisitorial: Do We Have a Choice?," in *Adversarial versus Inquisitorial Justice: Psychological Perspectives on Criminal Justice Systems* (Peter J. van Koppen and Steven D. Penrod, eds.) (New York: Kluwer, 2003), 21, 22.

22 Associated Press, "West Point Cadet's Rape Conviction Reversal Outrages Victim Advocates," *The Guardian*, June 8, 2019, www.theguardian.com.

23 Barbara J. Shapiro, *A Culture of Fact: England, 1550–1720* (Ithaca, NY: Cornell University Press, 2000), 9.

24 U.S. Constitution, Article III.

25 U.S. Constitution, Amendment VII.

26 *Tibbs v. Florida*, 457 U.S. 31, 42 (1982).

27 *Miller v. Fenton*, 474 U.S. 104, 114 (1985) (holding that the voluntariness of a confession is not a question of fact but rather a "legal question meriting independent consideration in a federal habeas corpus proceeding," 115).

28 Albert Camus, *The Stranger* [trans. Stuart Gilbert] (New York: Knopf, 1946), 134.

29 *Jackson v. Virginia*, 443 U.S. 307, 319 (1979).

30 28 U.S.C., section 2254(d).

31 *Cervi v. McKeon*, 2012 U.S. Dist. LEXIS 85415.

32 *Davila v. Davis*, 137 S. Ct. 2058, 2066 (2017) (citations omitted).

33 National Registry of Exonerations, "Innocents Who Plead Guilty" (November 24, 2015), 1, www.law.umich.edu.

34 Ronald J. Allen and Michael S. Pardo, "The Myth of the Law-Fact Distinction," 97 *Northwestern University Law Review* 1769, 1770 (2003).

35 Allen and Pardo, 1770.

36 Jerome Frank, *Courts on Trial: Myth and Reality in American Justice* (Princeton, NJ: Princeton University Press, 1949), 105.

37 Geoffrey C. Hazard Jr., "Preclusion as to Issues of Law: The Legal System's Interests," 70 *Iowa Law Review* 81, 82 (1984) (finding distinctions between law and fact), https://core.ac.uk. "In deciding fact questions the court necessarily works through the medium of extrajudicial resources, for example, evidence from witnesses. That dependency on outside resources entails a possible discrepancy between what the court believes was the fact and what actually was the fact. By contrast, in the resolution of issues of law the court constructs a verbal formulation from materials of which the court has direct knowledge" (88).

10. NEUTRAL INVESTIGATIONS

1 *Watts v. Indiana*, 338 U. S. 49, 54 (1949).

2 See Monroe H. Freedman, "Our Constitutionalized Adversary System," 1 *Chapman Law Review* 57 (1998).

3 Ellen E. Sward, "Values, Ideology, and the Evolution of the Adversary System," 64 *Indiana Law Journal* 301, 302 (1989).

4 Sward, 355.

5 Franklin Strier, "Making Jury Trials More Truthful," 30 *University of California, Davis, Law Review* 95, 182 (1996).

6 Geraldine Szott Moohr, "Prosecutorial Power in an Adversarial System: Lessons from Current White Collar Cases and the Inquisitorial Model," 8 *Buffalo Criminal Law Review* 165, 219–221 (2004).

7 Peter J. van Koppen and Steven D. Penrod, "Adversarial or Inquisitorial: Comparing Systems," *Adversarial versus Inquisitorial Justice: Psychological Perspectives on Criminal Justice Systems* (Peter J. van Koppen and Steven D. Penrod, eds.) (New York: Kluwer, 2003), 4.

8 David Alan Sklansky, "Anti-inquisitorialism," 122 *Harvard Law Review* 1634, 1640 (2009).

9 Stephen C. Thaman, *Comparative Criminal Procedure* (Durham, NC: Carolina Academic Press, 2008), 35.

10 Michele Panzavolta, "Reforms and Counter-reforms in the Italian Struggle for an Accusatorial Criminal Law System," 30 *North Carolina Journal of International Law & Commercial Regulation* 577, 578 (2005).

11 Maximo Langer, "From Legal Transplants to Legal Translations: The Globalization of Plea Bargaining and the Americanization Thesis in Criminal Procedure," 45 *Harvard International Law Journal* 1, 27 (2004)

12 *Moran v. Burbine*, 475 U.S. 412, 429–430 (1986).

13 Thaman, 37.

14 Thaman, 37.

15 Thaman, 40.

16 Thaman, 40.

17 Richard Vogler, *A World View of Criminal Justice* (New York: Routledge, 2016), 19.

18 Vogler, 151–152.

19 *Miranda v. Arizona*, 384 U.S. 436 (1966), 445, 446.

20 Vogler, 148.

21 Vogler, 148.

22 Vogler, 148.

23 Vogler, 149.

24 See U.S. Constitution, Amendment V ("No person . . . shall be compelled in any criminal case to be a witness against himself"). In *Malloy v. Hogan*, 378 U.S. 1, 8 (1964), the Supreme Court held that the right to remain silent applies in almost all civil and criminal cases. In *Dickerson v. U.S.*, 530 U.S. 428, 431 (2000) (interpreting *Miranda v. Arizona*, 384 U.S. 436, 478–479 [1966]), the Court held that the Constitution (not a Court rule) requires rights warnings and a defendant's valid waiver before the defendant's subsequent statements may be admitted in court.

25 *Upjohn Co. v. U.S.*, 449 U.S. 383, 389 (1981).

26 *Swidler & Berlin v. U.S.*, 524 U.S. 399, 410–411 (1998).

27 See Roger C. Park, "Adversarial Influences on the Interrogation of Trial Witnesses," in van Koppen and Penrod, 131, 166.

28 *Moran v. Burbine*, 475 U.S. 412 (1986), 433–434.

29 *Gouveia*, 467 U.S. at 187.

30 *Kirby v. Illinois*, 406 U.S. 682 (1972), 688.

31 *Gouveia*, 467 U.S. at 187 (internal citations omitted).

32 Vogler, 154.

33 Vogler, 155.

34 See Lloyd L. Weinreb, "Legal Ethics: The Adversary Process Is Not an End in Itself," 2 *Journal of the Institute for the Study of Legal Ethics* 59 (1999).

35 *Watts*, 53.

36 *Watts*, 54.

11. A NEW PROCEDURE

1 John H. Langbein, *The Origins of Adversary Criminal Trial* (Oxford: Oxford University Press, 2003), 253.

2 Langbein, vii.

3 Lexis, "Search John Henry Wigmore" (2022), https://advance.lexis.com.

4 Langbein, 192.

5 Federal Rules of Criminal Procedure, 404.

6 Langbein, 218.

7 Langbein, 203.

8 Federal Rules of Evidence, 801–803.

9 Langbein, 233.

10 *North Carolina v. Alford*, 400 U.S. 25, 39 (1970). "The prohibitions against involuntary or unintelligent pleas should not be relaxed, but neither should an exercise

in arid logic render those constitutional guarantees counterproductive and put in jeopardy the very human values they were meant to preserve."

11 *Mitchell v. Wisconsin*, 139 S. Ct. 2525 (2019).

12 See *Mapp v. Ohio*, 367 U.S. 643 (1961).

13 Langbein, 277.

14 Langbein, 277.

15 See 18 U.S.C., section 1001.

16 Langbein, 277, 278, 279.

17 Langbein, 279.

18 Langbein, 278, note 125.

19 Langbein, 253 (quoting 2 Hawkins, PC 400).

20 Judicial College, "Crown Court Compendium: Part I: Jury and Trial Management and Summing Up" (2018), section 17–5 (3)(12), 17–21, www.judiciary.uk.

21 Evidence of Bad Character, Criminal Justice Act of 2003, Part 11, sections 98–113, www.legislation.gov.uk. See also Code for Crown Prosecutors, "Bad Character Evidence" (Crown Prosecution Service, September 10, 2021), www.cps.gov.uk.

22 Joshua Dressler, "Rethinking Heat of Passion: A Defense in Search of a Rationale," 73 *Journal of Criminal Law and Criminology* 421, 426 (1982).

23 National Justice Museum, "What Was the 'Bloody Code'?" (July 29, 2019), www.nationaljusticemuseum.org.

24 Langbein, 334.

25 Langbein, 230.

26 Langbein, 335–336.

27 Dressler, 426, 430. A man could also assert a heat-of-passion defense if he killed someone who had previously battered a man in a serious fashion.

28 American Law Institute, *Model Penal Code*, section 210.3(1)(b) (manslaughter).

29 Lizzie Seal, "A Brief History of Capital Punishment in Britain," *History Extra*, March 12, 2019, www.historyextra.com.

30 Seal.

31 Langbein, 336.

32 Langbein, 253.

33 Langbein, 271.

34 Brian A. Reaves, "Felony Defendants in Large Urban Counties, 2009—Statistical Tables" (U.S. Bureau of Justice Statistics, December 2013), 24, www.bjs.gov.

35 See John Grimlich, "Only 2% of Federal Criminal Defendants Go to Trial, and Most Who Do Are Found Guilty" (Pew Research Center, 2019), www.pewresearch.org, and U.S. Courts, "U.S. District Courts—Criminal Defendants Disposed of, by Type of Disposition and Offense, during the 12-Month Period Ending September 30, 2018," www.uscourts.gov.

36 Susan Bandes, "Loyalty to One's Convictions: The Prosecutor and Tunnel Vision," 49 *Howard Law* Journal 475, 493 (2006) (discussing the reasons for premature prosecutorial decisions).

37 Peter Joy, "The Relationship between Prosecutorial Misconduct and Wrongful Convictions: Shaping Remedies for a Broken System," 2006 *Wisconsin Law Review* 399, 427–429 (2006) (urging more transparency in prosecutors' discretionary decisions).

38 Ellen Yaroshefsky, "Wrongful Convictions: It Is Time to Take Prosecution Discipline Seriously," 8 *District of Columbia Law Review* 275, 298 (2004) (urging the creation of an independent commission to investigate alleged prosecutorial misconduct).

39 Judith A. Goldberg and David M. Siegel, "The Ethical Obligations of Prosecutors in Cases Involving Postconviction Claims of Innocence," 38 *California Western Law Review* 389, 410–412 (2002) (advocating a range of reforms, from better scientific methods to ethical obligations of prosecutors to seek truth).

40 Fred C. Zacharias, "The Role of Prosecutors in Serving Justice after Convictions," 58 *Vanderbilt Law Review* 171, 238 (2005) (urging prosecutors to assist defendants in their postconviction claims).

41 Mark Lee, "The Adversary System and DNA Evidence: Past, Present, and Future: The Impact of DNA Technology on the Prosecutor: Handling Motions for Post-Conviction Relief," 35 *New England Law Review* 663, 666–67 (2001) (urging prosecutors and defense lawyers to cooperate on DNA testing).

42 Mary Sue Backus and Paul Marcus, "The Right to Counsel in Criminal Cases: A National Crisis," 57 *Hastings Law Journal* 1031, 1127 (2006).

43 Michael Goldsmith, "Reforming the Civil Rights Act of 1871: The Problem of Police Perjury," 80 *Notre Dame Law Review* 1259, 1283–85 (2005) (arguing for a civil remedy for victims of "police perjury," 1270).

44 Brian Murray and Joseph C. Rosa, "He Lies, You Die: Criminal Trials, Truth, Perjury, and Fairness," 27 *New England Journal on Criminal and Civil Confinement* 1, 2 (2001) (arguing that the judicial standard for postconviction attacks on perjured testimony should be the same under Federal Rules of Criminal Procedure 33 and habeas corpus).

45 Valerie P. Hans, "The Jury's Role in Administering Justice in the United States: U.S. Jury Reform: The Active Jury and the Adversarial Ideal," 21 *St. Louis University Public Law Review* 85, 97 (2002).

46 Lloyd L. Weinreb, "Legal Ethics: The Adversary Process Is Not an End in Itself," 2 *Journal of the Institute for the Study of Legal Ethics* 59, 63 (1999).

47 Sharon Finegan, "Pro Se Criminal Trials and the Merging of Inquisitorial and Adversarial Systems of Justice," 58 *Catholic University Law Review* 445, 498–499 (2009).

48 Hans Sherrer, "The Complicity of Judges in the Generation of Wrongful Convictions," 30 *Northern Kentucky Law Review* 539, 583 (2003) (concluding that judges' political dispositions make them subject to outside influences).

49 Craig Bradley, "The Convergence of the Continental and the Common Law Model of Criminal Procedure," 7 *Criminal Law Review* 471, 483 (1996).

50 Rory K. Little, "Addressing the Evidentiary Sources of Wrongful Convictions: Categorical Exclusion of Evidence in Capital Statutes," 37 *Southwestern Law Review* 965, 969–970 (2008).

51 James R. Acker, "Reliable Justice: Advancing the Twofold Aim of Establishing Guilt and Protecting the Innocent," 82 *Albany Law Review* 719, 741–742 (2018).

52 Jacqueline McMurtrie, "The Role of the Social Sciences in Preventing Wrongful Convictions," 42 *American Criminal Law Review* 1271, 1278 (2005).

53 Richard A. Rosen, "Reflections on Innocence," 2006 *Wisconsin Law Review* 237, 257–59 (2006) (concluding that the interests of innocent victims and innocent defendants must be balanced in determining what procedures to reform and how to reform them, 289).

54 National Registry of Exonerations, "Yutico Briley" (April 5, 2021) (data through July 1, 2021), www.law.umich.edu.

55 Innocence Project, "DNA Exonerations in the United States" (2021), https://innocenceproject.org/dna-exonerations-in-the-united-states/. See also Emily West and Vanessa Meterko, "Innocence Project: DNA Exonerations, 1989–2014: Review of Data and Findings from the First 25 Years," 79 *Albany Law Review* 717, 723 (2014).

56 See Innocence Project, and West and Meterko, 717.

57 Andrew M. Siegel, "Moving Down the Wedge of Injustice: A Proposal for a Third Generation of Wrongful Convictions Scholarship and Advocacy," 42 *American Criminal Law Review* 1219, 1222 (2005).

58 Siegel, 1237.

59 North Carolina Innocence Inquiry Commission, "2020 Annual Report" (2021), 7–8, https://innocencecommission-nc.gov/.

60 North Carolina General Statutes, Article 92, section 15A-1469(h).

61 North Carolina Innocence Inquiry Commission.

62 North Carolina General Statutes, Article 92, section 15A-1467(a).

63 The data were compiled on October 1, 2021, according to the Commission.

64 Langbein, 333.

65 Weinreb, 63.

66 Gerard E. Lynch, "Our Administrative System of Criminal Justice," 66 *Fordham Law Review* 2151 (1998).

67 Lynch, 2129.

68 Lynch, 2147.

69 Jed S. Rakoff, *Why the Innocent Plead Guilty and the Guilty Go Free: And Other Paradoxes of Our Broken Legal System* (New York: Farrar, Straus and Giroux, 2021).

70 Darryl K. Brown, "How to Make Criminal Trials Disappear without Pretrial Discovery," 55 *American Criminal Law Review* 155, 158 (2018).

71 Geraldine Szott Moohr, "Prosecutorial Power in an Adversarial System: Lessons from Current White Collar Cases and the Inquisitorial Model," 8 *Buffalo Criminal Law Review* 165, 209 (2004).

72 Szott Moohr, 220.

73 Ellen E. Sward, "Values, Ideology, and the Evolution of the Adversary System," 64 *Indiana Law Journal* 301, 302 (1989).

74 David Alan Sklansky, "Anti-Inquisitorialism," 122 *Harvard Law Review* 1634, 1642 (2009).

75 "Robert Brooks and Charles Cuckin," in *Proceedings of the Old Bailey: London's Central Criminal Court, 1674 to 1913*, reference number t16851209-11, December 9, 1685, www.oldbaileyonline.org, emphasis added.

76 Ordinary's Account (Chaplain Stephen Roe), "Ohn Kello, James Whem, and James Collins," *Proceedings of the Old Bailey: London's Central Criminal Court, 1674 to 1913*, reference number OA17621013, October 13, 1762, www.oldbaileyonline.org, emphasis added.

77 Ordinary's Account (Chaplain Stephen Roe).

CONCLUSION

1 Daniel Kahneman, Olivier Sibony, and Cass R. Sunstein, *Noise: A Flaw in Human Judgment* (New York: Little, Brown Spark, 2021), 16.

 2 Kahneman, Sibony, and Sunstein, 16.

 3 *U.S. v. Booker*, 543 U.S. 220 (2005).

 4 Kahneman, Sibony, and Sunstein, 19–20.

 5 National Registry of Exonerations, "Yutico Briley" (April 5, 2021) (data through July 1, 2021), www.law.umich.edu.

 6 U.S. Department of Justice, *Statistical Briefing Book*, www.ojjdp.gov.

 7 Brian A. Reaves, "Felony Defendants in Large Urban Counties, 2009—Statistical Tables" (U.S. Bureau of Justice Statistics, December 2013), 24, www.bjs.gov.

 8 Dan Simon, *In Doubt: The Psychology of the Criminal Justice Process* (Cambridge, MA: Harvard University Press, 2012), 34.

 9 Hugo Mercier and Dan Sperber, *The Enigma of Reason* (Cambridge, MA: Harvard University Press, 2017), 31.

10 Mercier and Sperber, 31.

11 Mercier and Sperber, 329.

12 Simon, 37.

13 Simon, 38.

14 Daniel Kahneman, *Thinking, Fast and Slow* (New York: Farrar, Straus, 2011), 250.

15 Kahneman, Sibony, and Sunstein, 370.

16 Kahneman, Sibony, and Sunstein, 371.

17 Kahneman, Sibony, and Sunstein, 372.

18 Kahneman, Sibony, and Sunstein, 372.

19 Shane Frederick, "Cognitive Reflection and Decision-Making," 19(4) *Journal of Economic Perspectives* 25–42, 27 (2005).

20 Kahneman, Sibony, and Sunstein, 373.

21 Kahneman, Sibony, and Sunstein, 373, 374.

22 Carrie Leonetti, "The Innocence Checklist," 58 *American Criminal Law Review* 97, 145–149 (2021), www.law.georgetown.edu. The variables are "prosecutorial

disclosure; false evidence; coaching; witness hiding; deficient defense; forensic misconduct; police misconduct; reasonable doubt; alternate suspect; new science; presence of evidence casting doubt; diminished mental capacity; recantations; impeachment; incentives; changing science; biased or unvalidated scientific evidence; corroboration; maintenance of innocence; missing or inadequate corroboration; unreliable eyewitness identification; questionable confessions; inconstant theories; police corruption; snitch testimony; inconsistent witnesses; pretrial publicity."

23 Lewis M. Steel, "Building a Justice System," *Raleigh (NC) News and Observer*, January 10, 2003, A17.

24 Steel, A17.

25 John H. Langbein and Lloyd L. Weinreb, "Continental Criminal Procedure: 'Myth' and Reality," 87 *Yale Law Journal* 1549, 1563 (1978).

26 Marvin Zalman and Ralph Grunewald, "Reinventing the Trial: The Innocence Revolution and Proposals to Modify the American Criminal Trial," 3 *Texas A&M Law Review* 189, 258, note 442 (2015).

27 Robert P. Mosteller, "Why Defense Attorneys Cannot, but Do, Care about Innocence," 50 *Santa Clara Law Review* 1, 3 (2010).

28 Brooklyn District Attorney's Office, "426 Years: An Examination of 25 Wrongful Convictions in Brooklyn, NY" (2020), www.brooklynda.org.

29 Richard Vogler, *A World View of Criminal Justice* (New York: Routledge, 2016), 132.

30 Vogler, 132.

31 *Gideon v. Wainright*, 372. U.S. 375 (1963).

32 Vogler, 132.

33 Daniel Taylor, "Which States Use Criminal Grand Juries?," *FindLaw* (2013), https://blogs.findlaw.com.

34 Vogler, 133.

35 Maura Turcotte, Rachel Sherman, Rebecca Griesbach, and Ann Hinga Klein, "The Real Toll from Prison Covid Cases May Be Higher Than Reported," *New York Times*, July 7, 2021, www.nytimes.com.

36 Vogler, 134.

37 See Thomas G. Roth, "Book Review: Denial of Justice: Criminal Process in the United States," 6 *Fordham Urban Law Journal* 179 (1977).

38 Zalman and Grunewald, 189. One of the proposals was the plea of innocence. The other proponents were Keith Findley, Sam Gross, Michael Risinger, and Christopher Slobogen, law professors at Wisconsin, Michigan, Seton Hall, and Vanderbilt, respectively.

39 Zalman and Grunewald, 257–259.

40 Paul Cassell, "Freeing the Guilty without Protecting the Innocent: Some Skeptical Observations on Proposed 'Innocence' Procedures," 56 *New York Law School Law Review* 1063, 1095 (2011/2012).

41 Cassell, "Freeing the Guilty," 1095.

42 Samuel R. Gross, Barbara O'Brien, Chen Hu, and Edward H. Kennedy, "Rate of False Conviction of Criminal Defendants Who Are Sentenced to Death," 111 *Proceedings of the National Academy of Sciences USA* 7230 (May 20, 2014).

43 Paul Cassell, "Overstating America's Wrongful Conviction Rate? Reassessing the Conventional Wisdom about the Prevalence of Wrongful Convictions," 60 *Arizona Law Review* 815 (2018).

44 In *Herrera v. Collins*, 506 U.S. 390, 400 (1993).

45 *Herrera*, 419.

46 *Herrera*, 428 (Scalia concurring).

47 *Herrera*, 428 (Scalia concurring).

48 Southern Mysteries, "The Poet Murderess of Mississippi," Article and Podcast, Episode 78 (December 28, 2020), https://southernmysteries.com.

49 NEA Service, "Wife's Weakness for Writing Poetry Leads to Murder Confession," *Evening Journal*, January 10, 1930, www.newspapers.com.

50 NEA Service.

51 Southern Mysteries.

52 NEA Service.

53 NEA Service.

54 Southern Mysteries.

55 Though there have been proposals for third verdicts in the adversarial system, only Scotland and Italy provide a version of a third verdict. Since the seventeenth century, Scotland has provided a "not-proven" verdict. This verdict allows judges and juries to acquit defendants when they believe the evidence does not meet the beyond-reasonable-doubt standard and, at the same time, register suspicion that the defendants they acquitted committed a crime. See Hannah Phalen, "Overcoming the Opposition to a Third Verdict: A Call for Future Research on Alternative Acquittals," 50 *Arizona State Law Journal* 401, 403–404 (2018). In 1989, Italy transformed its legal system from inquisitorial to adversarial and included five types of acquittal verdicts (including "that the defendant is innocent of the crime, because evidence was insufficient to convict him"). Phalen, 405. Since 2000, several scholars in the United States have proposed new verdicts of acquittal. See Phalen, 405–411, and notes 6, 8, 32, and 35. For example, Professor Andrew D. Leipold proposed an additional hearing after a jury has found a defendant not guilty: "A defendant who has been acquitted of criminal charges, or who has had the charges against him dismissed, should have the statutory right to ask for a determination that he is factually innocent." Andrew D. Leipold, "The Problem of the Innocent, Acquitted Defendant," 94 *Northwestern University Law Review* 1297, 1300 (2000).

56 Monroe H. Freedman, "Professional Responsibility of the Criminal Defense Lawyer: The Three Hardest Questions," 64 *Michigan Law Review* 1469 (1966).

57 John H. Langbein, *The Origins of Adversary Criminal Trial* (Oxford: Oxford University Press, 2003), 33.

58 Langbein, 262.

59 *In re Winship*, 397 U.S. 358 (1970).

60 Simon, 195.
61 Langbein, 264.
62 Langbein, 263.
63 Langbein, 263–264.
64 Langbein, 264.
65 Langbein, 264.
66 New York State Unified Court System, "Criminal Jury Instructions and Model Colloquies 2d" (Final Instructions) (Reasonable Doubt), 13, www.nycourts.gov.
67 Simon, 85.
68 18 U.S.C., section 1861(2).
69 Langbein, 280.
70 Federal Rules of Civil Procedure 11(b)(2) and (3).
71 Langbein, 265–266.
72 *Salinas v. Texas*, 570 U.S. 178, 182 (2013).
73 *Salinas*, 182.
74 *Salinas*, 189.
75 See *State v. Parris*, 219 Connecticut 283, 292 (1991) (approving the admission at trial of pretrial statements of a sexual assault complainant and not requiring that they be made at a "natural" time, while upholding a prison sentence of twenty years, suspended after fifteen years); *People v. Brown*, 8 California 4th 746, 749–750 (1994) (holding that promptness is not a requirement for the admission of a sexual assault complainant's pretrial statement, while affirming a conviction and sentence of twenty-six years' imprisonment); and *Commonwealth v. King*, 445 Massachusetts 217, 237 (2005) (holding that the witness to whom a sexual assault complainant "first complains" may testify about the statement, regardless of when the statement was made).
76 See *State v. Parris* and *People v. Brown*.
77 *People v. Rosario*, 17 NY3d 501, 509 (2011). The court, in its decision, consolidated the cases of two defendants, Angel Rosario and Luis Parada. The facts here concern Parada's case.
78 *Rosario*, 518.
79 *People v. Parada*, 67 A.D.3d 581, 584 (dissent) (2009).
80 *Rosario*, 510–511.
81 New York State Unified Court System, "Criminal Jury Instructions and Model Colloquies 2d" (Final Instructions) (Prompt Outcry), www.nycourts.gov.
82 *Rosario*, 518 (concurrence by Judge Smith).
83 *Rosario*, 510.
84 *Rosario*, 515, emphasis added.
85 William M. Landes and Richard A. Posner, "Harmless Error," 30 *Journal of Legal Studies* 161 (2001). See also Daniel Epps, "Harmless Error and Substantial Rights," 131 *Harvard Law Review* 2117, 2119 (2008).
86 *Rosario*, 515.
87 *People v. Parada*, 67 A.D.3d 581, 582 (2009), emphasis added.
88 *Parada*, 582, emphasis added.

89 *Parada*, 582, emphasis added.

90 *Parada*, 583, emphasis added.

91 *Rosario*, 517.

92 *Parada*, 583.

93 *Parada*, 584.

94 Tim Bakken, "The Defendant's Plea of Innocent in Sexual Abuse Cases," in *Wrongful Allegations of Sexual and Child Abuse* (Ros Burnett, ed.) (Oxford: Oxford University Press, 2016), 271–282, 277.

95 *People v. Rice*, 75 N.Y.2d 929, 931 (1990).

96 Langbein, 284.

97 Langbein, 266–273.

98 Langbein, 279.

99 Gordon Van Kessel, "Quieting the Guilty and Acquitting the Innocent: A Close Look at a New Twist on the Right to Silence," 35 *Indiana Law Review* 925, 950–591 (2002).

100 Van Kessel, 951.

101 Van Kessel, 951.

102 Edwin M. Borchard, *Convicting the Innocent: Sixty-Five Actual Errors of Criminal Justice* (Garden City, NY: Garden City Publishing, 1932), 367–378.

103 Borchard, 370–371.

104 *Miranda v. Arizona*, 384 U.S. 436, 455, note 24 (1966).

105 *Murphy v. Waterfront Commission of New York Harbor*, 378 U.S. 52, 55 (1964).

106 Reaves, 24.

107 Office of Justice Programs, *Statistical Briefing Book* (2019), www.ojjdp.gov.

108 See *Murphy*, 77–78 (holding "the constitutional privilege against self-incrimination protects a state witness against incrimination under federal as well as state law and a federal witness against incrimination under state as well as federal law"). But see *U.S. v. Balsys*, 524 U.S. 666 (1998).

109 Langbein, 278.

110 Langbein, 284.

111 Langbein, 278.

112 See Stephen C. Thaman, "Miranda in Comparative Law," 45 *Saint Louis Law Journal* 581, 589 (2001).

113 Margaret Raymond, "The Problem with Innocence," 49 *Cleveland State Law Review* 449, 457 (2001).

114 Daniel S. Medwed, "Innocentrism," 2008 *University of Illinois Law Review* 1549, 1567–1568 (2008).

115 *Carter v. Kentucky*, 450 U.S. 288, 305 (1981).

116 Simon, 186.

117 Daniel Givelber and Amy Farrell, *Not Guilty: Are the Acquitted Innocent?* (New York: New York University Press, 2012), 3.

118 Givelber and Farrell, 33–39.

119 Zalman and Grunewald, 241.

INDEX

ABA. *See* American Bar Association
abuse, 115
accountability, 120–22
accused person: in defense, 132; lawyers
   helping, 56; oath taken by, 136–37;
   prosecution against, 165
Acker, James, 92
acquittal, 15, 78, 91–92
admissibility, 105; of identification, 211n5;
   risk and, 103–4; of testimony, 116
adversarial judicial proceeding, 95
adversarial system: capital punishment
   and, 141; combat ethos of, 2, 81; conviction reversed by, 69–70; defendant
   silenced by, 58; defense lawyer in, 1–2;
   distinction predating, 112; due process
   in, 15–16; error in, 9; exonerating facts
   in, 143; innocence in, 5, 13–14; innocent-
   person conviction in, 78, 194–95; innocent person in, 72, 186; inquisitorial
   system contrasted with, 65–66, 81–82,
   100, 125–30, 211n3; investigation in,
   108, 128; judge correcting, 134; Nijboer
   on, 62; oath in, 137; protection in, 127;
   public defenders in, 29; right to silence
   eroded by, 65; science reforming, 155–
   56; secrecy in, 48; self-incrimination
   in, 136; silence in, 180; Supreme Court
   glorifying, 125, 130–31; trials prioritized
   by, 120–21; truth and, 53, 93–94, 113,
   147–48, 156; Vogler on, 55
AEDPA. *See* Antiterrorism and Effective
   Death Penalty Act
affirmation, 178

Alford v. North Carolina, 38
Allen, Ronald, 121–22
America. *See* United States
American Bar Association (ABA), 47, 50, 63
Anand, Sanjeev, 58, 66
anonymity, 21–22
Antiterrorism and Effective Death Penalty
   Act (AEDPA), 27–28, 46, 120
appellate review: conviction affirmed by,
   110–11, 184–85; evidence in, 113, 118;
   facts in, 110, 115, 118, 121; innocent-
   person conviction and, 111; judge
   compared with, 116
argumentation, 27, 62
Aristotle, 95
arraignment, 34
arrest, 142, 201n40
Astin, Joseph, 30–31
attorney-client privilege, 47–48, 128
authority: of government, 94; of jurors,
   89–90; of military appellate courts, 117;
   of prosecution, 165

Baldus study, 24
behavior, 9, 139–40
Beranek, Richard, 68–72
beyond reasonable doubt, 142; burden of
   persuasion as, 193; error ameliorated
   by, 66; prosecution advantaged by, 174;
   Simon on, 175; truth and, 43; witness
   as, 173
bias, 9; in death penalty, 23–24; evaluation of, 159; of jurors, 190–91; Weinreb
   recognizing, 94

ABOUT THE AUTHOR

TIM BAKKEN is Professor of Law at West Point, the United States Military Academy. He has practiced law in New York City, including as a prosecutor in Brooklyn (Kings County). He has been a visiting professor at Ural State Law University in Russia and visiting scholar at the law schools of Columbia University, the Australian National University, the University of Sydney, and the University of Cambridge.